P9-CQY-970

Marriage AND THE family

Other books by Stephen A. Grunlan:

Christian Perspectives on Sociology (Stephen A. Grunlan and Milton Reimer, editors)

Cultural Anthropology: A Christian Perspective (Stephen A. Grunlan and Marvin K. Mayers)

Marriage AND THE Family

A CHRISTIAN PERSPECTIVE

STEPHEN A. GRUNLAN

ZondervanPublishingHouse

Grand Rapids, Michigan

A Division of HarperCollinsPublishers

SECOND EDITION

Marriage and the Family
Copyright © 1983, 1999 by Stephen A. Grunlan

Requests for information should be addressed to:

ZondervanPublishingHouse
Grand Rapids, Michigan 49530

Library of Congress Cataloging-in-Publication Data

Grunlan, Stephen A.
    Marriage and the family : a Christian perspective / Stephen A. Grunlan.
       p.   cm.
    Includes bibliographical references and indexes.
    ISBN: 0-310-20156-X
    1. Marriage—Religious aspects—Christianity.   2. Family—Religious life.   I. Title.
BV835.G78   1999
248.4—dc21
                            99-27098
                            CIP

This edition printed on acid-free paper.

Interior design by Sherri L Hoffman

Printed in the United States of America

01 02 03 04 05 06 /❖ DC/ 10 9 8 7 6 5 4 3 2

TO MY CHILDREN:

Stephen Arthur, Jr.
Jaime Christopher
Rebecca Sue

Contents

FIGURES

TABLES

Preface

When I taught marriage and the family classes at Christian colleges, the task of finding a suitable textbook became more difficult each year. A sociological treatment of marriage and the family from a Christian perspective was not available. Texts being produced by secular publishers have, in my opinion, moved further from presenting data and more toward editorializing. Many of the positions propagated in these texts, again, in my opinion, are not consistent with a biblical worldview.

I recognize that there are scholars in the evangelical community more qualified than I am to produce a text with a Christian perspective. However, since there was no text available when I wrote the first edition and I have no knowledge of a forthcoming text, I felt the need to revise this work. I have been encouraged to do so by several colleagues teaching in Christian colleges. As a Christian, a husband, and a father, as well as a professor, I believe that students need to develop a Christian perspective on marriage and the family. It is my prayer that this book will help fill this need.

Sincere Christians do not always understand biblical truth in the same way, so I recognize that there can be honest disagreement on some of the issues in this book. It has not been my purpose to provide the "right" answers, but rather to help readers think through the issues and come to their own conclusions.

The Study of the Family

The Sociological Study of Marriage and the Family

So God created man in his own image, in the image of God he created him; male and female he created them. God blessed them and said to them, "Be fruitful and increase...."

GENESIS 1:27–28

With their wedding date still a few months off, George broke his engagement to Carol because he felt she was too "immature" to develop a meaningful relationship. Two weeks later Carol met Carl, who is thirty-two—twelve years her senior—and has been married twice before. His last wife divorced him while he was in a state mental hospital for observation of aggressive tendencies (wife beating). Carol's parents are evangelical Christians and are against her marrying Carl, to whom she became engaged six weeks after they met. Carol has been raised in a Christian home, whereas Carl, although baptized as an infant, has not involved himself with a church since he was a child. Carol's parents want her to go to college and are also concerned that Carl is a high-school dropout. Are Carol's parents' concerns warranted?

Fred and Alice have been married for three years and find that they are arguing more and more. Communication seems to have completely broken down. As Alice describes it, they seem to talk *at* each other rather than *to* each other. They both feel that they love each other, and they both want their marriage to work. Are there any techniques or procedures that could improve their communication with each other?

Ralph and Edith have been married for twenty-three years and have two children, the youngest of whom will be leaving for college in a couple of months. Their other child is married. Ralph suffered a mild heart attack last year, and his doctor has restricted his activities so that he had to turn down a job offer with another firm that would have meant a major advance in his career. Edith had three years of college before they were married, and now that their youngest child is leaving for college, she wants to start attending classes at a local branch of the state university to work toward a teaching degree. Ralph is upset by this because he feels he earns enough money to support the family and because his aged mother, who was just widowed, needs a place to live. Ralph would like to bring her to his home and have Edith stay home and care for her. This has led to serious tension in their relationship. Are the tensions being experienced by Ralph and Edith typical for couples in midlife? Can these types of tensions be avoided or reduced?

As we will see, sociology is a research science rather than a helping or service discipline. However, sociological research in the area of marriage and the family investigates issues such as those raised in these three case studies. The research findings can be of great assistance to social workers, therapists, ministers, and others who work with individuals facing marriage and family problems. In this book we will examine sociological research that applies directly to these case studies as well as research related to a variety of other issues.

Since each of us is a member of a family, and since over 90 percent of all adults will marry at least once (U.S. Bureau of Census 1990:2), marriage and family is a reality that is part of life for each of us. However, marriage and family are not just personal realities but also social realities, and therefore they are subject matter for study by sociologists. Before looking at the sociological study of marriage and the family, we should have a brief introduction to the discipline of sociology.

THE DISCIPLINE OF SOCIOLOGY

While there is not a universally accepted division of the academic disciplines, many scholars divide them into two broad categories—the humanities and the sciences (see table 1.1). The humanities, sometimes referred to as the liberal arts, include such subjects as literature, languages, philosophy, music, and the visual arts. The sciences are usually broken down into two subcategories—the natural sciences and the social sciences. The natural sciences include such disciplines as biology, chemistry, and physics. The social sciences include disciplines such as history, economics, geography, political science, anthropology, psychology, and sociology.[1] As an academic discipline, sociology is one of the social sciences.

---

[1]Some academicians would further divide the social sciences into the social studies—including history, economics, geography, and political science—and the behavioral sciences, including anthropology, psychology, and sociology.

The Sociological Study of Marriage and the Family

	HUMANITIES	SCIENCES	
		Natural	*Social*
TABLE 1.1	Literature	Biology	History
	Languages	Chemistry	Economics
The Academic	Philosophy	Physics	Geography
Disciplines	Arts	etc.	Political Science
	etc.		Anthropology
			Psychology
			Sociology

If we examine sociology textbooks, we will find that various writers have defined sociology as "a systematic approach to . . . studying and understanding society, human social behavior, and social groups" (Farley 1998:2); "the systematic study of social life and behavior" (Johnson 1996:9); "the scientific study of social interaction and organization" (Vander Zanden 1996:2); and "the scientific study of human social life" (Horton and Hunt 1980:482). While these definitions vary in their wording, they each contain two common ideas: first, that sociology uses the scientific method; and second, that the object of its study is human social life. We will examine the second of these ideas before discussing the use of the scientific method by sociologists.

As we have seen, sociology is the study of human social life. Since it is concerned with the behavior of human beings in social contexts, a foundational question for the discipline concerns the essence of human nature. Our view of human nature is critical to our understanding of social issues such as abortion, capital punishment, assisted suicide, and genetic engineering.

Secular sociologists are generally committed to the view that humans are the product of a random/chance-evolutionary process. From an evolutionary perspective, human nature is not innate to a person but is acquired by a person. As James Vander Zanden puts it, "We are not born human, but become human only in the course of socialization" (1996:68). Broom, Selznick, and Darroch have written, "Socialization transforms the human animal into a human being" (1981:84).

In contrast to many secular sociologists, evangelical sociologists generally see human nature as God-given. Responding to the contention that infants become human by the process of socialization,[2] Milton Reimer argues:

---

[2]Socialization is the process by which people learn the roles, knowledge, skills, beliefs, and values of their culture.

The Christian, however, is compelled to begin with a biblical view of human nature. God created humans in His own image, and the reflection of God's image continues in all people regardless of age, sex, skin color or moral condition. The child does not *become* human when it begins to assimilate the cultural patterns of environment. Rather, the child *is* human by virtue of God's creative act (Gen. 1:26–27). (1982:21)

What is the essence of the image of God in humanity? A number of theologians suggest that the image of God refers to our ability to relate to God. This ability involves self-consciousness, reason or rationality, and responsibility. These same characteristics that enable us to relate to God allow us to relate to each other. It is our ability to be self-conscious, to reason, and to be responsible that is foundational to human cultures and societies.

Evangelicals also recognize that the image of God was affected by the Fall. The Reformed theologian Emil Brunner says that a direct consequence of the Fall was a distortion in humanity's sense of direction. He argues that God set the direction for humankind but people sought to become gods themselves and set their own direction (1952:125–28). It is the desire of people to be their own gods and to set their own direction that is the basis for secular humanism.

Fortunately, God has not left us to our own ways. While there was nothing we could do about the power of sin over our lives, God provided a way of reconciliation and renewal. As the apostle Paul writes:

Therefore, if anyone is in Christ, he is a new creation; the old has gone, the new has come! All this is from God, who reconciled us to himself through Christ and gave us the ministry of reconciliation: that God was reconciling the world to himself in Christ, not counting men's sins against them.... God made him who had no sin to be sin for us, so that in him we might become the righteousness of God. (2 Cor. 5:17–19, 21)

To understand human social life, we need to have a proper understanding of human nature. Any approach to sociology that ignores the biblical account of the origin of humans and its implications, as well as the effects of the Fall and the potential of redemption, will always come short of the full truth. An understanding of the scriptural view of human nature is essential for a valid sociology (Grunlan 1982:411–12).

The Sociological Study of Marriage and the Family

SOCIOLOGY AS A SCIENCE

It was pointed out that most definitions of sociology have two common ideas—first, that sociology uses the scientific method; and second, that the object of its study is human social life. We have already discussed the essence of human nature and now we will turn to sociology as a science.

Some people may have a difficult time thinking of disciplines such as sociology as sciences. Many believe that only the natural sciences are true science. However, the scientific nature of a discipline is not determined by the subject matter or the setting of the study but by the methodology used to study the subject matter. The scientific method embodies the following qualities:

1. The procedures are public.
2. The definitions are precise.
3. The data collecting is objective.
4. The findings must be replicable.
5. The approach is systematic and cumulative.
6. The purposes are explanation, understanding, and prediction. (Berelson and Steiner 1964:16–17; Hess et al. 1996:29–30)

Besides embodying the above qualities, the scientific method follows specific steps in doing research:

1. The problem is defined.
2. The literature on previous research in the area of the problem is reviewed.
3. A hypothesis is formulated.
4. A research design is planned.
5. The data are collected.
6. The data are analyzed.
7. Conclusions are drawn.

To the extent that sociology embodies the qualities of the scientific method and follows the research steps of the scientific method, it is a science. As Milton Reimer states, "As a science, sociology is committed to the use of the scientific methodology, and most scientists will do so scrupulously" (1979:7).

Some Christians are leery of sociology because what they have read or heard of sociological research appears to run contrary to a biblical view of humanity and society. However, it is important for us to distinguish between the data and the interpretations of that data. It is my conviction that there are no conflicts between the facts of science and the words of Scripture. Rather, the conflicts arise between the *interpretations* of the facts of science and the words of Scripture. We need to remember that neither the scientist nor the theologian is infallible, and either or both may misinterpret the data.

We should approach both the facts of science, including sociology, and the words of Scripture with the knowledge that all truth is God's truth. As Malcolm Jeeves has put it, "As a Christian, it is my belief that what God has chosen to give to man down the ages through his special messengers will not ultimately conflict with what he has encouraged us to discover as we exercise his gifts of mind and hand in exploring the created order, including, of course, man himself, his experience and his behaviors" (1976:18). We recognize that the Christian sociologist has the truth of God's Word and the indwelling of the Holy Spirit to guide the analysis of the data.

SOCIOLOGICAL CONCEPTS

Sociology, like any other discipline, has basic concepts and vocabulary that it uses in the study of its subject matter. A brief definition of a few of these basic concepts will provide us with a foundation for the following discussions on marriage and the family.[3]

Status and Role

Who are you? What do you do? Our answers to these questions are really sociological in nature. We generally define ourselves in terms of relationships: I am a minister; I am a professor; I am Sandy's husband; I am Jaime and Becky's father; I teach at Grossmont College. It is difficult to define ourselves apart from our statuses and roles.

A *status* may be defined as a position or place in a social system with its attendant rights and duties. A *role* is defined as the behavior that is expected from the holder of a particular status. The positions of both professor and student are statuses. We would expect a certain general behav-

---

[3]For those readers who have had an introductory sociology course, this discussion will be a review. For those readers who have not previously studied sociology, it will serve as an introduction to a few basic sociological concepts.

The Sociological Study of Marriage and the Family

ior of the professor for a particular class, whether the professor is Dr. Jones or Dr. Smith. We would expect lectures, discussions, examinations, and so on. We would expect a certain general behavior of any given student in the class, whether the student is Mary Brown or Roger Carlson. We would expect regular attendance, note taking, studying, and so on. The reason we can expect and predict the behavior of the person holding a particular status is that roles are generally governed by a set of "rules" called *norms.* For example, it is a norm in North American culture to greet another person with a handshake. When a person meets another, he or she extends the right hand and expects the other to do likewise and shake hands.

Ralph Linton (1936) noted that statuses are generally acquired in one of two ways. Some statuses are assigned to an individual, often on the basis of characteristics of birth, such as sex, age, race, ethnic group, and social class. These are called *ascribed statuses.* The day I was born I was assigned the statuses of son, grandson, nephew, and American—among others. Ascribed statuses are assigned to the individual by society; other statuses, which are acquired by choice and effort, are called *achieved statuses.* I am also a husband, a father, and a professor. These statuses were acquired by choice and effort. Both ascribed and achieved statuses are present in the family structure.

As you read this book, you will discover that the concepts of status and role are not only foundational to the study of sociology in general but also to the study of marriage and the family. Every member of a family has several statuses—mother, wife, and aunt, or father, husband, and uncle, for example. Each of these statuses has a role. My role as a husband differs from my role as a father, which differs from my role as an uncle. However, it is important for us to realize that these roles are not static; rather, they are constantly changing. In later chapters we will explore changing family roles.

Groups

Horton and Hunt (1980:174) see the concept of groups as one of the more important concepts in sociology. Sociologists use the term *group* in a more specific sense than it is generally used. In everyday speech we might speak of a group of people at a bus stop. Sociologists would refer to people waiting at a bus stop as an *aggregation* or a *collectivity.* They generally define a *group* as two or more persons who share some organized patterns of recurrent interaction and share a consciousness of common membership.

The Study of the Family

Sociologists distinguish between two basic types of groups—primary and secondary. A *primary group* is a small, intimate, and informal group. The members are intimately involved in each others' lives. Primary groups—such as a close set of friends, a small Bible study or prayer group, or the family—share intimate human companionship. A *secondary group* is generally impersonal and utilitarian. Secondary groups, such as a class, a club, or business associates, tend to be more formal than primary groups. Secondary groups are more concerned with the group product, whereas primary groups are more concerned with relationships.

Since families, both immediate and extended, are groups, the insights from research on groups is often applicable to the study of the family. Talcott Parsons and Robert Bales (1955) studied the family as a primary group. They had observed that groups generally work on two problems simultaneously. The first is the group's goal or product, which they call the *instrumental* problem. The second is the maintenance and smooth functioning of the group, which they call the *socioemotional* problem. In their study of families in the early 1950s, they discovered that the husband generally was concerned with the instrumental aspects of the family, and the wife with the socioemotional aspects of the family. Winston Johnson points out that while this was a classic study in primary groups, "the effect of the work was to reinforce stereotypical roles for the husband and wife" (1982:158). While husband-wife roles are changing, the family continues to be the classic example of the primary group.

Johnson explains the value of studying the family as a group when he writes:

> The family is the small group in which most of us are familiar. Understanding its dynamics and the functions and roles of its members can help build the church up as well as the family unit itself. The family is an important interface or link between us as individuals and the society at large. In it primary values are taught and reinforced. The right use of this basic and naturally occurring group can strengthen both the individual and the groups to which a person belongs. (1982:159–60)

Social Institutions

Another basic sociological concept used in the study of human social life is social institutions. As with the term *group,* the term *institution,* as used by sociologists, differs from common usage. In everyday speech, the term refers to the building where certain activities take place, such as a school or a hospital, or to a large organization, such as Bell Telephone or the United States Army. However, in sociological usage, *institution* refers to an organized system of social relationships that embody common values and procedures (norms) to meet certain basic needs of a society.

Sociologists are generally agreed that all complex societies have five major social institutions, although they argue about whether all five exist in preliterate societies. The first institution, and one that is found in all societies—preliterate and complex—is the *family,* the social institution on which we will focus in this book. The second social institution is *religion*—the way a society or members of a society organize their beliefs (doctrines) and practices (rituals) for the worship and manipulation[4] of the supernatural. Religion is another institution that is found in all societies, preliterate and complex. The third institution is *education*—the way a society organizes itself for the socialization of its members. The fourth institution is *economics*—the way a society organizes itself for the production, distribution, and consumption of goods and services. The fifth institution is *government*—the way a society organizes itself for communal decision making and the maintenance of social control. While these last three institutions are clearly present in all complex societies, in some preliterate societies their functions appear to be carried out by the family and religion. Even in complex societies, we need to recognize that there is much overlap among the institutions. As we examine the family in this book, the effects on it of religion, education, economics, and government will be explored.

THE SOCIOLOGICAL STUDY OF THE FAMILY

In their study of marriage and the family, sociologists tend to use five basic perspectives. While various sociologists emphasize one or the other of these perspectives in their research and writing, all five are needed to fully study marriage and the family. All five perspectives will be used in this book.

1. Structural Functionalism

This perspective focuses on the structure of a social system and how the parts function within the whole. Every family is a system. It is made up

---

[4]*Manipulation* is another word that differs in its sociological and common usages. Sociologically, in this context, it refers to attempting to have the supernatural act in behalf of humans.

of parts that work together to make a unified whole. The concepts of status and role, as well as the concept of groups, are useful in studying the family as a system.

This perspective also looks at the functions of the family in society at large. Whether it is an intact nuclear family, a single-parent family, a stepfamily, a blended family, or a cohabiting family, there are at least four basic functions that these families perform.

The first function is *economic.* The family is an economic unit. Earlier in our history, the family was a producing unit. Many Americans lived and worked on family farms. Others worked in family businesses from blacksmith shops to bakeries, from general stores to grain elevators, from doctor's offices to law offices. Much of the production in our country took place in family businesses.

Today, however, most Americans are employed outside the family. Even people in such professions as doctors, dentists, lawyers, and accountants, who until recently were self-employed, now, for the most part, work for clinics and large firms. And the American family has changed from a producing unit to a consuming unit. Even as a consuming unit, the family has a major impact on society and the economy. Consumer spending drives the American economy.

While the members of the family generally do not get paid for labor in the home, it has economic value. When the husband builds a shelf, fixes a leaky faucet, changes the oil in the car, or cleans the house, that has economic value. When the wife paints a room, sews clothing, or cooks meals, that has economic value. When a child cuts the lawn, washes the dishes, or watches younger siblings, that has economic value. If family members were compensated for household work, it would be equal to the total wages paid by every corporation in America (Strong, DeVault, and Sayad 1998:18). We will look more at this function in Chapter 8.

The second function of the family is *reproduction and socialization.* Society needs to replace itself and rear its young. This is a primary function of the family. Reproduction includes, but goes beyond, the sex drive. It is psychological as well as physical. It is also a function that modern technology has affected and changed. With modern contraception techniques on one hand, and artificial insemination, in vitro fertilization, and surrogate motherhood on the other hand, families have more control over the reproductive process. We will look more at this process in Chapters 4 and 10.

The Sociological Study of Marriage and the Family

When a child is born, it is a helpless being that needs to be taught everything necessary to survive. Children need to learn to walk and talk, to feed and dress themselves. They need to learn the values, norms, and beliefs of society and a thousand other things. While schools, churches, day care, Scouts, and other agencies play an important role in the socialization process, the primary responsibility is with the family. We look further at socialization in Chapter 11.

The third function of the family is *companionship*. Sociologists recognize that "companionship is a primary human need" (Strong et al. 1998:14). Humans have emotional and interpersonal needs that can only be met in intimate social settings. Research has consistently shown that married adults are healthier and have lower mortality rates than widowed, divorced, separated, and never-married adults (Ross, Mirowsky, and Goldsteen 1991). The family provides companionship for the husband and wife and a source of love and nurturance for children. We will learn more about this function in Chapters 9 and 11.

The fourth function of the family is *status conferring*. Virtually all of our ascribed statuses are assigned to us at birth. I was in the delivery room with my wife when our third child was born. As the doctor delivered the baby, the umbilical cord was between the legs. The doctor said, "Let's see what we have here," as he moved the umbilical cord. Then he announced, "It's a girl." At that moment it was as if someone entered the delivery room with a wheelbarrow full of statuses and dumped them on our baby. When the doctor announced, "It's a girl," she became a daughter, a granddaughter, a sister, and a niece. At birth she also became a United States citizen, a resident of the state of Illinois, and a member of the middle class. All of these statuses came from her family. We will see more of this function in the next chapter.

2. Symbolic Interaction

This theory for studying marriage and the family, also known as the *interactionist perspective*, begins by studying the interaction that takes place between individuals. Sociologists using this approach emphasize symbolic interaction. They point out that humans interact through symbols such as words and gestures. These symbols have shared meanings. That is, the members of a society share the meaning of words and gestures. For example, in the United States the word *hammer* denotes a tool for driving nails. When I ask my son to hand me a hammer, he is able to get the correct tool because we share the same meaning of the word or symbol.

This approach also looks at the interaction and the person's interpretation of the interaction. For example, if my son ignores me and does not hand me the hammer, I need to interpret his response. If I interpret his ignoring me as his not hearing me, I will repeat the request. However, if I interpret his ignoring me as unwillingness to do what I requested, I may become angry. This perspective, which deals with meaning and understanding in social interaction, will be most evident in the second and third parts of this book.

3. Conflict Theory

While the structural functionalism perspective focuses on how the parts of a social system function together, the conflict perspective focuses on conflict between the parts. To conflict theorists, the most important force shaping social systems is conflicting self-interest among groups and individuals in society.

The source of conflicting self-interest, according to this theory, is competition over scarce resources. The major scarce resources are money and power. Social research shows that these two issues are leading sources of conflict in the home. We will apply insights from this perspective in the third and fourth sections of this book.

4. Social Exchange Theory

This perspective studies social interaction in terms of exchange. Relationships are seen as having benefits and costs, and people want to maximize benefits and minimize costs. Interaction and relationships are an exchange in that we give up some things to gain others.

Suppose you were introduced to a married couple, and the wife was young and attractive, while the husband was older, overweight, and balding. What would you assume about the husband? That he was rich. Why? You assume that the woman has exchanged youth and attractiveness for wealth.

While many of us tend to think of rewards and costs in tangible terms such as money and beauty, in close relationships they are often emotional. Emotions such as love, loneliness, fear, and self-esteem can be more valuable than money, looks, or status. Social exchange theory provides insight into the mate-selection process as well as family relationships and interaction, as we will see in Chapters 3 and 9.

5. **Family Development Theory**

This perspective, also known as the *life-cycle approach,* studies the family from marriage through a series of sequential stages. Sociologists see families moving through eight stages: (1) beginning family, (2) childbearing, (3) preschool children, (4) school-age children, (5) adolescents, (6) launching, (7) middle years, and (8) aging families.

The developmental or life-cycle approach lets us study the family over time. The stages allow us to focus on the changing roles, tasks, and challenges as a family develops. By analyzing statistics from thousands of families, sociologists are able to develop a general profile of each stage. While sociologists use these findings for descriptions and predictions, their research is of great value to those who work with families. This approach is the focus of the fourth section of this book.

BASIC CONCEPTS IN STUDYING MARRIAGE AND THE FAMILY

In their study of marriage and the family, sociologists have developed some basic concepts. As we have already seen, scientific language needs to be precise. When I refer to "my family," am I referring to my wife and children, my parents and siblings, my grandparents and aunts and uncles—or to all of them? Specific terms are used to differentiate these various family groups. The unit consisting of a husband and wife and their dependent children is called a *nuclear family.* My wife, my three children, and I make up a nuclear family. Two or more related nuclear families are called an *extended family.* My nuclear family and my wife's parents and brother, combined, form an extended family.

Married adults are members of two families, the one they were born into and the one that was created by marriage. The family into which we are born is called our *family of orientation* or sometimes the *family of origin.* The family in which we are a spouse and parent is called the *family of procreation.* Our family of orientation and family of procreation together are part of our extended family.

Two additional terms we often encounter in the study of marriage and the family are *conjugal* and *consanguineal.* The *conjugal* relationship refers to the husband-wife relationship. The *consanguineal* relationship refers to relationships by blood, such as parent-child and sibling-sibling. In a *consanguineal* family, the emphasis is on the blood relationships.

METHODS OF STUDYING MARRIAGE AND THE FAMILY

Observation

Sociologists use various methodologies to study marriage and the family. One of these is observation. While each of us is continually observing events, scientific observation differs from casual observation. Scientific observation strives for accuracy and avoids jumping to conclusions. It is also precise. A sociologist would not report, "I saw several couples spend considerably more time than individuals spent while grocery shopping." Rather, a sociologist would state, "Fourteen couples and thirty-six individuals were observed shopping for groceries. The average time spent at this task was thirty-six minutes per couple and twenty-two minutes per individual." Scientific observation is also systematic. If we were observing people shopping for groceries, we might discover that the time of day or day of the week affected their behavior. A systematic approach would, therefore, involve observing on various days at various times.

Surveys

A more frequently used method of studying marriage and family is the survey. There are two basic survey methods—questionnaires and interviews. A questionnaire is a self-administered instrument; that is, individuals fill it out themselves. In an interview, a researcher asks the questions and records the responses. Surveys are useful for obtaining information on people's attitudes and beliefs on various issues, such as premarital sex, abortion, marriage, and childbearing. Surveys are also useful for gathering data about what has taken place or is taking place in the lives of people and families. For example, one of my sociology classes interviewed a sample of students at the college, asking, among other questions, their birth order and grade-point average. When the data was tabulated, it was found that the mean grade-point average dropped with birth order. This finding was consistent with research on birth-order effect (Zajonc and Markus 1975; Steelman and Mercy 1980; Pfouts 1980). Some implications of the birth-order research will be discussed in Chapter 10.

Statistical Studies

Another frequently used research method in studying marriage and the family is statistical studies. A significant amount of information of interest to researchers has already been collected by the government. All births and deaths as well as marriages and divorces are recorded. The census collects data on household composition, marital status, and other information of interest to researchers. The *Statistical Abstract of the United States*, published annually, summarizes statistics collected by many government agencies.

An example of a statistical study using census data is the relationship between married-couple families and single-parent families. From 1970 to 1990, married couples with children under eighteen fell from 50 percent to 37 percent of all families. However, between 1990 and 1997, they declined only 1 percent. Meanwhile, the number of single-parent families doubled from 6 percent to 12 percent from 1970 to 1990. However, they increased less than 2 percent between 1990 and 1997. The remainder of the families are couples who have never had children and "empty-nesters."

Part of the reason for the decline in the percentage of married-couple-with-children families is the increase in the number of married-couple-without-children families. This has resulted from young couples delaying having children, couples choosing not to have children, and, with increased life-expectancy, more couples in the empty-nest stage of family life.

At this point, a word of warning about the use of statistics is important. Statistics are nothing more than organized measured facts. These "facts" may be used in misleading ways. I recently heard a preacher speaking on the decay of the American family. To dramatize his point, he said that in the preceding year there was one divorce for each marriage in California. While those "facts" are approximately true, the statement is highly misleading. California is gaining population. Couples married in other states are moving into California. If they divorce, it shows up on California's statistics, not the state where they were married. Also, the preacher's statement compares the marriages taking place in one year with the divorces from marriages over the past fifty years or more. As Horton and Hunt warn us, "Citizens who hope to be intelligently aware of the world they live in must have some understanding of statistical interpretation, lest they be duped by every clever propagandist in sight" (1980:25).

Experiments

Another research method is the experiment. Although for both ethical and practical reasons this method has its limitations when dealing with human subjects, it is used occasionally in marriage and family research.

One example is an experiment that studied gender-role socialization. A six-month-old infant was dressed as a boy and presented individually to a group of mothers. The infant was then dressed as a girl and presented to a group of mothers. The mothers smiled more at the infant when it was dressed as a girl. They also handed the infant a toy appropriate to the sex of its dress (Shepard 1981:240–41).

Observation, surveys, statistical studies, and experiments are all used by sociologists in their research of marriage and the family. We will be examining findings from all of these research methods as we look at marriage and the family.

TOWARD A CHRISTIAN PERSPECTIVE

Why should we study marriage and the family? Does not the Bible teach us everything we need to know about the subject? While everything in the Bible is true, not all truth is in the Bible. God has revealed much about himself and his creation in the Scriptures, but he has also left much for us to discover. As Koteskey puts it, "Since the world created by God was created by a rational being, it is real, it is good, and it is orderly, having patterns and regularities. These patterns are discoverable by humans since humans are made in the image of God, and they can be discovered by examining the world" (1980:17).

Koteskey goes on to argue:

Christians need to develop Christian perspectives on science and make positive contributions. Since all truth is unity ... we need not fear truth discovered by anyone, because all truth should dovetail. Too often we reject truth discovered by the non-Christian because we believe that it is not the whole truth or that there are non-Christian elements in the system. (1980:14)

We need to take the truth found in God's Word and the truth found in God's world and integrate them in both doctrine and practice. Applying this idea to husband-wife roles, DeJong and Wilson point out that

The Bible gives fundamental principles regarding the sexes and their behavior, not a full list of specific, timeless role obligations for each. And so, as with many other matters, the Christian community must take the basic principles revealed in the Bible and attempt to apply them to life in a complex, changing society. (1979:31)

The Sociological Study of Marriage and the Family

We should recognize that the cultures of the biblical periods were vastly different from modern Western cultures. The study of marriage and the family from a sociological perspective can provide Christians with insights that will aid them in applying biblical principles across time and cultures. As I have previously written:

> As we study the Scriptures, we discover God's purpose and plan for marriage and the family. These purposes and plans are played out in human cultures. It is important for us to recognize that the biblical guidelines for marriage and the family may take different forms in different cultures. It is only as we become familiar with both the Scriptures and culture that we can apply the biblical teachings in a manner consistent with both Scripture and culture. (Grunlan and Mayers 1988:159)

The family is the basic social unit in every society. It was the first social unit established by God (Gen. 2:18–24). The Bible gives the basis for marriage and discusses the functions and requirements of marriage and the family. As the sociological study of marriage and the family are examined in this text, the teachings of Scripture on the topic at hand will also be examined. With this approach, an attempt will be made to aid you in developing a Christian perspective on marriage and the family.

DISCUSSION QUESTIONS

1. Why is an understanding of the essence of human nature important for a valid sociology?

2. Do you believe sociology has as much right to be called a science as do such disciplines as biology and chemistry? Why?

3. What is your reaction to the author's contention that there are no conflicts between the facts of science and the words of Scripture? Why?

4. Can you find biblical support for the four functions of the family discussed in this chapter?

5. Which of the five methods discussed in this chapter for studying marriage and the family do you believe are most useful? Why?

6. In what ways might a sociological study of marriage and the family contribute to your development of a Christian perspective on marriage and the family?

SUGGESTED READING

Jack Balswick and Judith Balswick, *The Family* (Grand Rapids: Baker, 1991). An overview of marriage and the family from a Christian perspective. While this book is based on social science research, it is more application-oriented as it deals with mate selection, communication, parenting, and other aspects of the family.

Gary R. Collins, *Family Shock* (Wheaton, Ill.: Tyndale House, 1995). Written by a noted Christian psychologist, this book deals with many of the critical issues facing marriages and families today. The author draws on both current social research and the Word of God as he not only discusses the issues but also offers solutions.

John E. Farley, *Sociology*, 4th ed. (Upper Saddle River, N.J.: Prentice Hall, 1998). An introductory sociology text that gives a balanced overview of the field of sociology. If the reader is not familiar with sociology, this work will provide a good introduction to the discipline.

Stephen A. Grunlan and Milton K. Reimer, eds., *Christian Perspectives on Sociology* (Grand Rapids: Zondervan, 1982). Although out of print, this work is available in many Christian college libraries. It is a collection of essays on sociology as a discipline, its methods, and the major subtopics. It provides a Christian perspective on the discipline.

Cross-Cultural and Intercultural Perspectives

The nuclear family is a universal human social grouping. Either as the sole prevailing form of the family or as a basic unit from which more complex familial forms are compounded, it exists as a distinct and strongly functional group in every known society.

GEORGE PETER MURDOCK, *SOCIAL STRUCTURE*

The Nayar are a Hindu warrior subcaste living in southern India. At puberty a Nayar woman is ritually married to a young man chosen by her family. A few days later they are ritually divorced and have no further rights or obligations toward each other. Gough (1959) reports that in this matrilineal society men live with a matrilineal kinswoman; that is, the man lives with his sister or another female he is related to through his mother. Women, following their ritual marriage and divorce, engage in sexual relations with a "visiting husband," a man who arrives after supper and leaves before breakfast. A woman may have a series of these "visiting husbands." There is no legal or social bond between the woman and a "visiting husband." If a woman becomes pregnant, one of the "visiting husbands," not necessarily the genitor, publicly announces that he is the father and provides a small gift for the midwife. This action is to "legitimize" the child, and the "father" has no further obligations. The child will be cared for and socialized by its mother and her brother or another matrilineal male relative.

In the Israeli kibbutz, little emphasis is placed on marriage and the family. According to Spiro (1968), there are no formal ceremonies on the kibbutz. If a couple wish to be partners, they merely apply to the community's housing committee for a common room. If children are born, they are raised, not with their parents, but in a separate children's residence. The kibbutz cares for all the children's education and health needs.

In the traditional Chinese family, a man's first loyalty is to his parents, not to his wife. Levy (1949) argues that in the traditional Chinese family, except for sex, the nuclear family is indistinguishable from the extended family and does not function as a distinct unit. He says that the economic and socialization functions are carried out by the extended family. Levy does not believe that the nuclear family is the basic unit in the traditional Chinese family.

The three cases just presented have all been used in attempts to challenge Murdock's assertion that the nuclear family is a universal social unit (the quotation at the beginning of the chapter). Murdock defined the nuclear family as "a married man and woman with their offspring" (1949). He argued that the universality of the family is based on its functions:

> In the nuclear family or its constituent relationships we thus see assembled four functions fundamental to human social life—the sexual, the economic, the reproductive, and the educational. Without provision for the first and third society would become extinct; for the second life itself would cease; for the fourth culture would come to an end. The immense social utility of the nuclear family and the basic reason for its universality thus begin to emerge in strong relief. (1949:10)

Some social scientists have argued that the Nayar, the kibbutz, and the traditional Chinese family do not meet Murdock's definition or functions of the nuclear family. However, most social scientists today support Murdock's position on the universality of the nuclear family (e.g., Belkin and Goodman 1980; Stephens 1963; Zelditch 1964). The reason for this support of Murdock's position is that the cases cited do not make as strong an argument as might first appear. In the cases of the Nayar and the Israeli kibbutz, these are not independent cultures but rather minor subcultures within a larger society. They are tolerated deviations more than norms. Also, the practices of the Nayar have been coming more in line with the larger society for some time (Menchar 1965). As for the case of the kibbutz, even Spiro concedes that the case is not very strong. In fact, the children raised in dormitories, when asked where their home is, usually answer that it is their parents' room. This is because, in spite of living in dormitories, the children spend considerable time with their parents in their room. Also, while the kibbutz provides for the children's health and education needs, ultimate responsibility still lies with the parents.

As for Levy's Chinese example, Zelditch (1964) points out that this case rests more on Levy's interpretation of the traditional Chinese family. Other researchers have not understood the traditional Chinese family in the same way. Yang (1971) points out that much familial behavior is often largely ceremonial and that closer ties exist between the husband and wife than may at first be apparent.

Murdock's assertion that the nuclear family is universal and is the basis or foundation for other familial arrangements seems to be consistent with a biblical understanding of the family. Throughout the Scriptures we find the husband and wife and their children as a unique social unit. In Genesis 2:24 God said, "A man will leave his father and mother and be united to his wife." God has set the nuclear family apart as a distinct unit.

TYPES OF FAMILY SYSTEMS

Monogamy

While the nuclear family is a universal social unit, it is generally not found standing alone, but rather as the basic unit in a larger familial network. There are two major types of family systems. The first is *monogamy*, which refers to a family system in which each person has only one spouse. This type of family arrangement is common to North America and most of Western Europe. The norm in these societies is a family unit consisting of a husband and a wife.

Polygamy

The second major type of family system is *polygamy*, which refers to a family system where there are multiple spouses. Polygamy takes various forms. The most common form is *polygyny*. In this type a man has more than one wife. The Old Testament Hebrews practiced polygyny. While God's law regulated polygyny (Ex. 21:1–11; Lev. 18:18; Deut. 21:15–17), it never forbade the practice. One form of polygyny involves a man marrying a woman and her sisters. This is referred to as *sororal polygyny.* Jacob, in the Old Testament, practiced sororal polygyny when he married Leah and her sister Rachel (Gen. 29:1–30). Hundreds of years later, under the Mosaic Law, the Hebrews were forbidden to practice sororal polygyny.

A polygynous family actually consists of a series of nuclear families. The husband and his first wife and their children make up one nuclear family, and so on. In other words, the husband is in a series of nuclear families, with the husband and each wife and their children being distinct units. In many polygynous societies each wife and her offspring have a separate hut or dwelling. Thus, the nuclear family is still the basic unit even in polygynous societies.

When polygyny is discussed, many Westerners view it as a sexual arrangement. If we are honest, what we usually think of is an Arab sheik with an insatiable sexual appetite and his harem. The fact is, the basis for polygyny is not generally sexual. Among the Baganda, a tribal society in central Africa, the basis of polygyny is economic. As Queen and Haberstein point out, "Each wife becomes a source of income and constitutes an economic investment" (1971:67). The Baganda are a farming and herding society, and additional wives and children allow a man to farm more land and herd more cattle. A strong evidence of the economic basis for polygyny is the finding that in those areas of Africa that have had a subsistence economy, when wage labor is introduced, the rate of polygyny is dramatically reduced (Grunlan and Mayers 1979:37–38).

Another basis for polygyny is political. Often alliances between rulers are sealed by the marriage of one ruler or his son to the sister or daughter of another ruler. A ruler who has made several alliances could end up with several wives. Alliance marriages were practiced during the Old Testament period. In 1 Kings 3:1 we read, "Solomon made an alliance with Pharaoh king of Egypt and married his daughter." Among many African tribes, political alliance by marriage is still being practiced. For example, many wives are acquired by Sudanese chiefs by the making of political alliances. In many tribal societies, marriage alliances are used not only by chiefs but also by regular families for the achievement of some mutual end.

A second form of polygamy, which is quite rare, is *polyandry.* In this type a woman has more than one husband. The Todas, a pastoral tribe living in southern India, provide a classic example of polyandry. The Todas practiced female infanticide that resulted in a male population larger than the female population. Typically, the oldest son in a family would take a wife, and she would become the wife of all his brothers as well. Technically this arrangement is referred to as *fraternal polyandry.* When the wife becomes pregnant, one of the brothers, usually the oldest, is chosen to "give the bow." He crafts a ceremonial bow and arrow and presents these to the wife before the relatives. He is then recognized as the "legal" father of the unborn child and any other children the wife should bear. However, if she bears more than two or three children, another brother will often "give the bow" and become the "father" of all the children born thereafter. Since early in this century, infanticide has been outlawed, and the male-female ratio has been becoming more equal. This has led to more than one brother taking a wife, resulting in a form of group marriage. With the equalization of the sex ratio, the society has moved toward monogamy (Queen and Haberstein 1971). Polyandry has also been reported in parts of Tibet (Grunlan and Mayers 1988) and among the Kalapalo Indians of Brazil (Basso 1973).

Polygamy and the Bible

We have already seen that the Old Testament never condemned polygyny, which was practiced by the Hebrews, but only regulated it. Some have suggested that the law of levirate marriage, which requires a man to marry a deceased brother's wife (Deut. 25:5–10), may have required polygyny in some instances (Grunlan and Mayers 1979:273). Writing in *Moody Monthly,* Graham Walker points out that "despite King David's several wives and many concubines, he remained in fellowship with God" (1982:6).

When we turn to the New Testament, we find no references to the issue of polygyny. Some have suggested that 1 Timothy 3:2, 12 and Titus 1:6 are referring to polygyny when they say that elders and deacons should be "the husband of but one wife." However, it is most unlikely that Paul is addressing the issue of polygyny because it was not practiced by the Jews, Greeks, or Romans of Paul's day. What Paul is addressing in these passages is the nature of the marriage relationship and possibly issues such as divorce and remarriage, keeping of mistresses, and frequenting temple prostitutes. These passages are emphasizing the quality of marriage and family life (Grunlan and Mayers 1988:268–69).

While the Scriptures do not condemn polygyny, it is my personal conviction that God's intention in creation was for a one-man-and-one-woman relationship (Gen. 2:24). As a result of sin and the Fall, many of God's perfect intentions of creation were corrupted. With sin came death and a struggle for life. Polygyny is a functional marital arrangement for pastoral, nomadic peoples with high male mortality. While God permitted polygyny as an accommodation to societal problems, it was not his perfect plan. In polygynous societies, when people are converted to Christ, if they are in a polygynous relationship, it may be best to maintain it; but for unmarried converts, the biblical idea of one man and one woman should be taught.

RESIDENCE PATTERNS

Families are typed not only by their marriage arrangements but also by their living arrangements. The residence pattern we are most familiar with is called *neolocal residence.* In this type, a nuclear family lives by itself rather than with either set of parents or other relatives. While some American couples live with one or the other's parents or with relatives, the ideal in our culture is for a nuclear family to have its own place.

In its strict sociological definition, an *extended family* refers to two or more related nuclear families sharing a household (Grunlan and Mayers 1988:154; Strong, DeVault, and Sayad 1998:72). In the *patrilocal extended family* a newly married couple takes up residence as part of the groom's parents' household. The Old Testament Hebrews practiced patrilocal residence. When Isaac married Rebekah, they lived in Abraham's household (Gen. 24). This arrangement is also illustrated by the Tiv of Nigeria, among whom the household compound

> consists of an open central area surrounded by huts and granaries arranged in a circle or oval. The compound group is headed by the senior man, the oldest male in the group, who functions as the group's leader. He usually has several wives, each of whom generally has a separate hut in the compound. Also included in the group compound are . . . his married sons along with their wives and children. (Grunlan and Mayers 1988:154)

The residence pattern of a couple residing with the bride's parents is called a *matrilocal extended family.* The Navahos of the American Southwest practice matrilocal residence:

> The homestead group, however, is clearly functional and easily defined. . . . Most often the group consists of an older woman, her daugh-

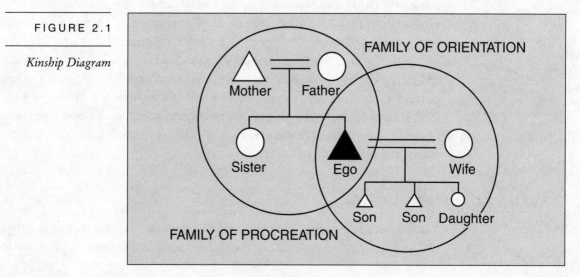

FIGURE 2.1

Kinship Diagram

ters, and perhaps younger sisters. In addition, the group will include the husbands of the married women.... The dominant woman may not be the eldest; an old grandmother or aunt may have a dowager position, although no longer able to contribute much labor to the group's maintenance. Essentially, then, this homestead group is a number of nuclear units related to each other by connection to the family of one of the spouses. (Downs 1977:346)

Another residence pattern, called *avanculocal extended family,* involves the newly married couple's joining the household of the groom's uncle, his mother's brother. This residence pattern is practiced by the Trobriand Islanders of the South Pacific. A young man inherits land from his mother in this matrilineal society. However, because of the practice of avanculocal residence, his mother is living in the household of her husband's uncle. His mother's brother is farming the family land, so he and his wife go to live with his uncle.

KINSHIP

In its broadest sense, the family reaches beyond the nuclear family to a whole network of relationships. We refer to this larger network as a kinship system. *Kinship* is a network of biological, marital, and social ties making up a familial social system. The basis of this system is the connecting bonds between individuals. These bonds are called *kinship ties.*

Kinship Ties

There are three types of kinship ties. The first type, called *affinal ties,* refers to kinship relationships based on marital bonds. I am affinally related to my wife. I am also affinally related to her parents and brother. In North America, except for our spouses, we refer to those with whom we are affinally tied as "in-laws" or as "related by marriage."

The second type of kinship ties are those based on biological or "blood" relationships. These are referred to as *consanguine ties.* My sons and daughter are consanguinely related to me. Affinal ties are made by contract, whereas consanguine ties are made by birth. Our affinal ties are achieved, but our consanguine ties are ascribed.

The third type of ties are called *fictive ties.* These are a sociolegal "fiction" whereby a person is legally, ceremonially, or religiously tied into a kinship network. A familiar fictive tie in our culture is adoption. When a child is legally adopted, he or she has all the rights, privileges, and responsibilities of a natural-born child.

Diagraming

In order to study kinship systems, social scientists have developed a system for diagraming them. While primarily used by anthropologists, this diagraming system is being used more and more by sociologists. Many marriage and family counselors also use the system to diagram a client's kinship network.

In the diagraming system males are represented by triangles and females by circles. Affinal ties are noted by parallel lines and consanguine ties by a single line. In diagraming, a reference point is needed—that is, the person from whose perspective the diagram is being viewed. A woman may be one man's wife, another's sister, and still another's mother. The reference person is referred to as *ego,* and his or her symbol is darkened to indicate this. My families of orientation and procreation are diagramed in figure 2.1.

RULES OF DESCENT

My mother is getting on in years, so the last time both my sister and I were at home she asked us to pick out which particular family heirlooms, some with sentimental value and some with monetary value, we would like to have so she could list them in her will. This was a wise and somewhat normal approach to the problem of inheritance in the American culture. However, in other cultures this may have been totally unnecessary because cultural norms would have called for all property to go to me as the son, or for all of it to go to my sister as the daughter. These types of norms are called *rules of descent.* Rules of descent are cultural norms that govern the determination of family line and inheritance. There are two basic types of rules of descent.

Unilinear Descent

The first type of descent is called *unilinear descent.* In this type, kinship is traced through either only the paternal line or only the maternal line. When kinship is traced through the paternal line, it is called *patrilineal descent.* Figure 2.2 illustrates a patrilineal kinship group. When kinship is figured through the maternal line, it is called *matrilineal descent,* and the family line is traced through the female descendants. One is a member of the kin group by virtue of consanguine ties to the females of the lineage. Figure 2.3 illustrates a matrilineal kinship group.

FIGURE 2.2

Patrilineal
Kinship Group

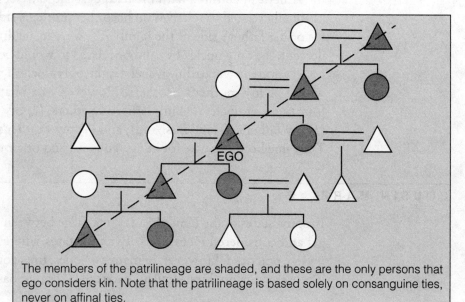

The members of the patrilineage are shaded, and these are the only persons that ego considers kin. Note that the patrilineage is based solely on consanguine ties, never on affinal ties.

Grunlan and Mayers 1988:169

FIGURE 2.3

Matrilineal
Kinship Group

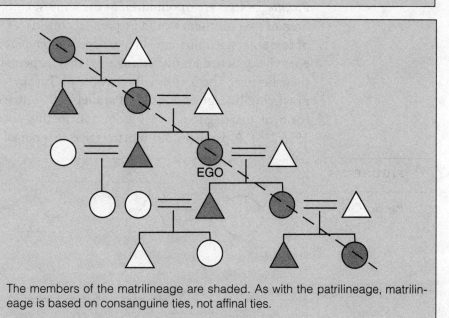

The members of the matrilineage are shaded. As with the patrilineage, matrilineage is based on consanguine ties, not affinal ties.

Source: Grunlan and Mayers 1988:171

Bilateral Descent

The second type of descent is *bilateral descent.* This is the system used in the American culture. With bilateral descent, one sees himself or herself as equally related to relatives on his or her mother's side of the family and his or her father's side of the family. If I were in a culture with patrilineal descent, the only uncles I would be related to would be my father's brothers. If I were in a matrilineal society, the only uncles I would be related to would be my mother's brothers. However, in a bilateral system I have four types of uncles: (1) my father's brothers, (2) my mother's brothers, (3) my father's sisters' husbands, and (4) my mother's sisters' husbands. The same becomes true for aunts, cousins, and other relatives.

COUSIN MARRIAGE

In some states in the United States, marriage between first cousins is illegal and considered incestuous. Even in states where it is legal, it is not widely practiced. However, in many societies, first-cousin marriage is the ideal relationship. First-cousin marriage takes two basic forms.

Parallel-Cousin Marriage

Parallel cousins are the children of the same-sex siblings. That is, the children of two brothers would be parallel cousins, as would be the children of two sisters. Parallel-cousin marriage is often practiced in unilinear societies that practice lineage *endogamy;* that is, persons must marry within their lineage. The Yoruk tribespeople of Turkey are a patrilineal group practicing lineage endogamy. Parallel-cousin marriage is the preferred form of marriage and very common in this society (Plog and Bates 1976:214). A parallel-cousin marriage is diagramed in figure 2.4.

FIGURE 2.4

Parallel-Cousin Marriage

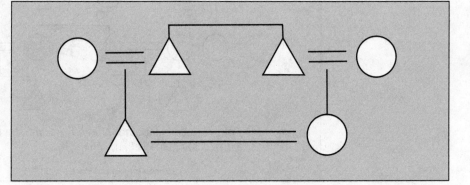

Cross-Cultural and Intercultural Perspectives

Cross-Cousin Marriage

Cross-cousins are the children of opposite-sex siblings. That is, the child of a woman would be the cross-cousin of the woman's brother's child. Cross-cousin marriage, like parallel-cousin marriage, is practiced primarily in unilinear societies. Societies in which cross-cousin marriage is practiced are lineage *exogamous;* that is, persons are required to marry outside their lineage. Many African tribal groups as well as some South Pacific societies practice cross-cousin marriage. See figure 2.5 for a diagram of a cross-cousin marriage.

FIGURE 2.5

*Cross-Cousin
Marriage*

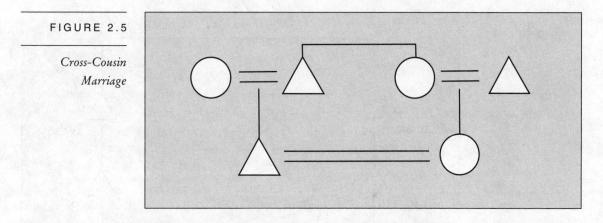

OLD TESTAMENT HEBREW KINSHIP SYSTEM

The Old Testament gives us rich insights into the Hebrew kinship system. Many of the concepts we have been looking at are illustrated by the Hebrews. Let us examine the kinship system of the Hebrews during a particular period of Old Testament history.

At the time of the patriarchs (Abraham, Isaac, and Jacob), the Hebrews practiced polygyny, including, in the case of Jacob, sororal polygyny. Their kinship system was patrilineal in descent, patrilocal in residence, and clan-endogamous in marriage. Parallel-cousin marriage was a preferred arrangement at this time. The ideal mate for a man was his father's brother's daughter or granddaughter (see figure 2.6). During this period they also practiced levirate marriage as illustrated by the case of Judah's sons Er and Onan (Gen. 38:6–10). It is also interesting to note that levirate marriage may still have been in existence in Jesus' day, since the Sadducees raised a question about it to Jesus (Matt. 22:24–28).

The Study of the Family

A knowledge of various kinship systems and marriage forms is a tremendous aid in understanding the Bible in general and the Old Testament in particular. The Hebrews were a product of their culture and time. Studying the kinship systems of the Egyptians and other Near Eastern societies of that period sheds rich light on the Scriptures. A knowledge of various kinship systems is also an invaluable aid to those involved in cross-cultural ministry.

FIGURE 2.6

*Parallel-Cousin
Marriage Among
the Patriarchs*

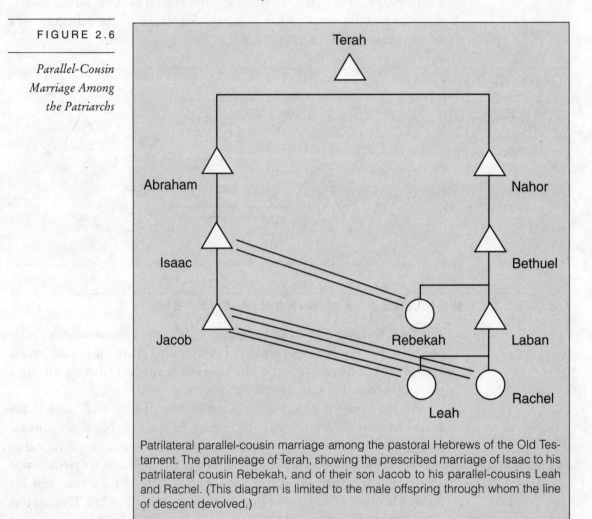

Patrilateral parallel-cousin marriage among the pastoral Hebrews of the Old Testament. The patrilineage of Terah, showing the prescribed marriage of Isaac to his patrilateral cousin Rebekah, and of their son Jacob to his parallel-cousins Leah and Rachel. (This diagram is limited to the male offspring through whom the line of descent devolved.)

Source: Hoebel 1972:407

INTERCULTURAL PERSPECTIVE

Until the 1960s the study of marriage and the family in America was primarily the study of the white, middle-class family. When ethnic families were studied, it was from the perspective of the white family. Studies that were done on ethnic families focused on their problems. However, in recent years more research has been done on ethnic families, looking at their structure, strengths, and values, as well as their problems. We live in a multicultural society, and we need to understand each other. As Strong, DeVault, and Sayad point out:

> In America's pluralistic society, it is important that students and researchers alike reexamine diversity among our different ethnic groups as possible sources of strength rather than pathology.... For instance, cultures may vary widely in how the best interests of the child are defined.... Differences may not necessarily be problems but solutions to problems; they may be signs of adaptation rather than weakness. (1998:62)

Keeping this perspective in mind, we will examine the families of four major ethnic groups found in America: African-American families, Hispanic families, Native-American families, and Asian-American families.

African-American Families

According to the U.S. Census Bureau, in 1996 there were 33.5 million African Americans in the United States, making up to almost 13 percent of the population (1996a). The Census Bureau also reports that 46 percent of African-American households are married-couple households, 48 percent are female-headed households, and 6 percent are male-headed households (see table 2.1).

TABLE 2.1

Percentage of Married-Couple Households, Female-Householder, and Male-Householder by Race

	WHITE	AFRICAN-AMERICAN
Married-Couple Household	82%	46%
Female Householder	14%	48%
Male Householder	4%	6%
Source: U.S. Bureau of Census 1996b:61		

While African Americans have high divorce rates and high rates of birth among unmarried women, these seem to be more associated with socioeconomic status than with race. When socioeconomic status is controlled for, their divorce rates are similar to white families (Raschke 1987). African-American family life cannot be understood apart from socioeconomic status and the impact of poverty.

There are several unique features found in African-American families (Strong, DeVault, and Sayad 1998:64). One is that due to economic need they have had to be dual-earner families throughout their history in the United States. This has resulted in employed women playing an important economic role in African-American families. It has also resulted in more equal family roles as well as in more female-headed households. Second, the extended family is a major source of economic and emotional support. Third, they have a strong emphasis on intergenerational relationships. Grandmothers often have an active role in raising their grandchildren. Fourth, African-American families place a high value on children. Fifth, they are more likely to live in multifamily households.

Hispanic Families

In 1996 there were almost 28 million Hispanics in the United States, according to the census figures (1996a). The majority of Hispanics are of Mexican descent, with Puerto Ricans making up the next largest group. The third largest group of Hispanics are Cubans. The rest come from various Central and South American countries.

Coming from different backgrounds, Hispanic families have a great deal of diversity. While over 60 percent of Mexican and Cuban families are in married-couple households, only about half of Puerto Rican households consist of married couples (U.S. Bureau of the Census 1996b). Almost half of all Cuban families have an annual income over $35,000, while only 15 percent of Puerto Rican families exceed that income.

While there is diversity in Hispanic families, there are also some common elements. Even though most Hispanics reside in nuclear families, the extended family usually lives close by, often in the same neighborhood. The importance of children can be seen in the fact that over one-third of Hispanic families have five or more children. Hispanic culture has a tradition of male dominance; however, in the daily operation of the home, the power resides with women.

Native-American Families

According to the U.S. Bureau of the Census (1996a), there are about 2.3 million Native Americans in the United States, approximately half of them living on reservations. Most of those who have left the reservation are living in urban areas.

Like the Hispanics, Native-American families are diverse. This results from at least two factors. First, almost half of those who are married have non-Native-American spouses. Second, different tribes have different kinship rules. Some tribes are matrilineal, and some are patrilineal. Some practice matrilocal residence, some patrilocal, and some neolocal. Some tribes practice clan exogamy—that is, one must marry outside his or her clan. This wide variety of kinship rules results in diversity.

With all the diversity, there is still one common factor among Native-American families: the significance of the extended family. Among Native Americans, the extended family is often based on clan membership rather than affinal or consanguine kinship ties. Whatever the basis of the extended family, it plays an important part in Native-American family life.

Asian-American Families

In 1996 there were some 10 million persons of Asian descent in the United States (U.S. Bureau of the Census 1996a). Like Hispanics, Asian Americans come from a variety of backgrounds (see table 2.2). However, the greatest diversity in Asian-American families is based on whether they are immigrant families, first-generation families, or long-time resident families.

Traditional Asian families emphasize the family over the individual. They are male-led and have great respect for their elders. There is parental control over children and an emphasis on a strong work ethic and

TABLE 2.2		
1990 Population of Largest Asian-American Groups	Chinese Americans	1,645,000
	Filipino Americans	1,407,000
	Japanese Americans	848,000
	Asian Indian Americans	815,000
	Korean Americans	799,000
	Vietnamese Americans	615,000
	Source: U.S. Bureau of the Census 1991:3	

motivation for achievement. They place a high value on education. Asian Americans are generally better educated and have higher incomes than other groups.

As we look at marriage and family in the United States from an intercultural perspective, we need to keep in mind that three factors shape these families. One is the cultural background of each group. A second factor is socioeconomic status. Those groups with higher socioeconomic status tend to have a higher percentage of married-couple households and stable families. As we will see in Chapter 8, economics has a tremendous impact on family life. The third factor is life opportunities. Different racial and ethnic groups have faced different levels of prejudice and acceptance in this country. Also the circumstances under which they arrived in the United States have differed widely. All of these factors influence family life.

DISCUSSION QUESTIONS

1. Why do you think the nuclear family is the basis for kinship systems in every culture?

2. In your opinion, why did God permit the Old Testament Hebrews to practice polygyny? What is your opinion about present-day tribal societies that practice polygyny?

3. Why do you think a relationship that one culture sees as an ideal marriage another culture views as incestuous?

4. What was the advantage of practicing parallel-cousin marriage for the Old Testament Hebrews?

5. Why do you think African Americans, Hispanics, and Asian Americans put a greater emphasis on the extended family?

6. What factors, in your opinion, are responsible for the educational and economic achievement of Asian Americans?

Cross-Cultural and Intercultural Perspectives

SUGGESTED READING

Mary Kay DeGenova, *Families in Cultural Context: Strengths and Challenges in Diversity* (Mountain View, Calif.: Mayfield, 1997). In this secular work, the author looks at the family systems of eleven different ethnic groups. She analyzes the strengths and weaknesses of these family systems.

Stephen A. Grunlan and Marvin K. Mayers, *Cultural Anthropology: A Christian Perspective,* 2d ed. (Grand Rapids: Zondervan, 1988). An introduction to cultural anthropology that helps the reader gain a cross-cultural perspective. The book contains chapters on marriage and kinship that expand on the discussions in this book.

Lee N. June, ed., *The Black Family* (Grand Rapids: Zondervan, 1991). Sixteen black leaders present their perspectives on the issues facing black families in America. They look at the historical perspective as well as the current situation. They also look at the future of the black family.

Clarence Walker, *Breaking Strongholds in the African-American Family* (Grand Rapids: Zondervan, 1996). A guidebook for helping African-American families engage in spiritual warfare to protect themselves.

Pairing and Singlehood

Dating and Courtship

Remember how our love began?
Years ago, I offered you my arm
   that September night we first went out.
You reached for it
   as we leaped a puddle together.
Then you walked just close enough
   to show you liked it.
I glimpsed your face under the streetlight,
   excitement splashing gently on it....
No commitment—just beginnings.

HAROLD MYRA, "AN ODE TO MARRIAGE"

When I was in graduate school, my wife became a friend of the wife of a graduate student from India. One day they were discussing how they had met their husbands. The Indian woman explained how their marriage had been arranged by their parents. My wife described how we had met and dated. The woman from India, who was high caste and a college graduate, shared with my wife that she found the American dating system degrading. She thought it was awful to have to go out and "try out" different men to find one to marry.

In many cultures marriages are arranged as was the marriage of the couple from India. In other cultures the kinship system determines whom one will marry. For example, among some African tribes a person is expected to marry his or her father's brother's child, and among other African tribes young people are expected to marry their mother's brother's child. In North American culture, where mate selection is freer and more open, the dating process is generally used to get to know persons of the opposite sex more personally.

How does dating differ from courtship? While a clear line cannot be drawn between the two processes since they obviously overlap, generally *dating* is concerned with the particular event and with getting to know another person, whereas *courtship* is concerned with mate selection and preparation for marriage. Dating and courtship often differ more in terms of intent than behavior.

SOCIAL FACTORS IN DEVELOPMENT OF DATING

Dating, at least as most of us have experienced it, is a modern practice. It is generally accepted that dating did not become widespread in the United States until after World War I (Orthner 1981:61; Yorburg 1993:126). Before this time dating was quite formal, limited to circumscribed activities, and generally chaperoned. Orthner (1981:62–63) suggests four social factors that led to the development of modern dating: industrialization, urbanization, increased free time, and the automobile.

Industrialization

The Industrial Revolution had a profound effect on society and social relationships, including marriage and the family. Before the Industrial Revolution most men worked in or around the home. With the advent of industrialization and factories, work moved away from the home. Fathers were absent for most of the day and were not as involved in the lives of their children. During World War I many women joined the labor force and began to strive for greater independence. In 1920 women received the vote—a major step in their emancipation.

Social changes brought about by industrialization tended to weaken traditional family ties and the family's control over its members. Attitudes developed that were conducive to dating. Individual values became more important than family values. The next three social factors may be seen as results or extensions of industrialization.

Urbanization

Industrialization with its factories required large numbers of workers in a concentrated area, and large urban areas developed around industrial centers. Urbanization brought many young people together and exposed them to a large group of potential mates. Urban centers provided a sense of anonymity unknown in small rural communities. A couple could get together in the city without everyone knowing about it. The coeducational school systems in urban areas also fostered contact between the sexes.

Increased Free Time

With the enactment of child-labor laws and compulsory education, the amount of free time increased for many young people. The development of modern machinery and appliances for farm work and household chores also allowed young persons more free time.

The Automobile

Perhaps nothing has shaped modern dating more than the automobile. It provided both the mobility to engage in a variety of recreational activities and a place of privacy. In fact, many dating activities, such as drive-in theaters and carhop restaurants, began to center around the automobile. While most dates involved attending a concert, movie, dance, or party, they frequently ended in a parked automobile on a "lover's lane."

ATTRACTION

Why do we find some people more attractive than others? How important is physical appearance to attractiveness? Why are some physically less attractive persons socially attractive? Do men and women find the same features in others attractive, or are there sex differences? These are some of the questions and issues social scientists are attempting to study.

Physical Attractiveness

Usually, the first thing that attracts or repels us about another person is his or her physical appearance. While "beauty is in the eye of the beholder," there are certain social norms by which physical attractiveness is judged. If this were not so, we would not have beauty contests, fashion models, movie stars, and centerfolds. Our culture generally prefers slender to fat, tall to short, hair to bald, and muscular to skinny. If you took photographs of five different men who varied in physical appearance and asked people to rank them by physical attractiveness, you would not get unanimous agreement, but you would very likely get a high level of agreement. An illustration of how social norms affect our perception of physical attractiveness is men's hair styles. When I was a teenager in the 1950s, the most popular hair style was the crew cut (the hair cropped short all over the head), and a man with hair over his ears was considered effeminate. By the 1970s, long hair was in style, and the crew cut was considered odd. However, in the 1990s short hair came back in style, and many young men wore crew cuts again.

American culture places a heavy emphasis on physical attractiveness. Social research indicates that, all other things being equal, we attribute higher social status to more attractive persons and lower social status to less attractive persons (Vander Zanden 1987:48–49). Several studies have demonstrated that physical attractiveness affects how we react to people. A study done in a traffic court found that attractive defendants were treated more leniently than unattractive defendants (Piehl 1977). Another study, using simulated court cases, found that under identical circumstances, attractive defendants received more favorable treatment than unattractive defendants (Stephan and Tully 1977). Even professionals can be biased toward physically attractive people. A study found that clinicians were more likely to find an unattractive person mentally disturbed than an attractive person exhibiting the same behavior (Jones, Hansson, and Phillips 1978).

We tend to attribute favorable characteristics to attractive persons. Physically attractive persons are seen as more romantic and sexual. They are perceived as being more exciting dates. Physically attractive people are also seen as possessing more socially desirable traits than less attractive persons (Baron and Byrne 1994:284). It is easy to see why physical attractiveness is such an important aspect of interpersonal attraction.

What should be our attitude as Christians toward physical attractiveness in general and these research findings in particular? In the Old Testament, Samuel fell prey to attributing socially desirable characteristics to a physically attractive person. God sent Samuel to Bethlehem to the home of Jesse to anoint a king to replace Saul. When Samuel saw Jesse's oldest son, Eliab, who was tall and good-looking, he thought, "Surely the LORD's anointed stands here" (1 Sam. 16:6). God's reply was, "Do not consider his appearance or his height, for I have rejected him. The LORD does not look at the things man looks at. Man looks at the outward appearance, but the LORD looks at the heart" (1 Sam. 16:7). The same principle is found in the New Testament. Peter advises Christian wives, "Your beauty should not come from outward adornment, such as braided hair and the wearing of gold jewelry and fine clothes. Instead, it should be that of your inner self, the unfading beauty of a gentle and quiet spirit" (1 Peter 3:3–4).

The Bible teaches us that we should be careful not to be fooled by outward appearances, but be concerned with inner qualities. While we should attempt to be well-groomed and dress attractively, our emphasis should be on developing the "fruit of the Spirit" (Gal. 5:22–23). Also, we need to be careful not to judge people by their appearance, but rather by their personhood (James 2:1–12). We need to take care that we do not allow the world's emphasis on physical appearance to overshadow the Bible's emphasis on inner qualities.

LOVE

Attraction for some people often leads to love. And love, at least in North American culture, is seen as the basis for marriage. One of Frank Sinatra's hit songs years ago had the line, "Love and marriage go together like a horse and carriage; you can't have one without the other." Love is an important aspect of dating, courtship, and marriage.

While most of us have experienced love, we have a hard time defining it. For one thing, there are several different types of love. Even if we eliminate the trite types of love, such as love for a car or a type of food, there are still several significant types of love. These include the following:

1. Neighborly love. This is care, concern, and respect for other human beings; it is the type of love the Bible refers to when it says, "Love your neighbor" and "Love your enemies."
2. Friendship love. Sometimes referred to as "brotherly/sisterly love," this is the love between close friends, such as David and Jonathan in the Bible.
3. Familial love. This is the love between a parent and child, between siblings, and between other close family members.
4. Heterosexual love. This is the love between a man and a woman; it is the type of love on which marriage is usually based.

Theories of Love

In their study of love as a behavioral and social phenomenon, sociologists and psychologists have developed a number of theories. Two of the more widely accepted theories are the Triangular Theory and the Wheel Theory.

Triangular Theory of Love

Robert J. Sternberg and Michael Barnes (1988) see love as made up of three components: intimacy, passion, and commitment. The *intimacy* component consists of feelings of closeness, connectedness, and bonding. It involves warmth, caring, and sharing. The sharing is personal and intimate communication. It also includes the giving and receiving of emotional support. The *passion* component involves physical and sexual attraction and the feelings of romance. The *commitment* component consists of two aspects. The first is the decision to love someone. According to this theory, love is more than a feeling; it is also a choice. The second aspect is the decision to maintain the love. This is the commitment.

According to Sternberg and Barnes, all three components of love do not develop simultaneously. Usually the first to appear is passion. But for love to grow, the relationship must move on to intimacy, with its sharing and support. Finally, the decision of commitment is made. When all three components are present, you have what Sternberg and Barnes call "consummate love."

Wheel Theory

One of the most widely cited theories of love is Ira Reiss's Wheel Theory (1980, 1986). His theory consists of four interconnected processes: rapport, self-revelation, mutual dependency, and intimacy and need fulfillment. The processes are cyclical, with one running into the next. Reiss pictures the relationship between the processes as a wheel (see figure 3.1).

The love relationship develops and deepens as one moves clockwise through the processes or stages of the wheel. One "falls out of love" by moving counterclockwise through the stages. We will examine the individual stages briefly and then discuss the whole wheel.

FIGURE 3.1

Reiss's Wheel Theory of Love

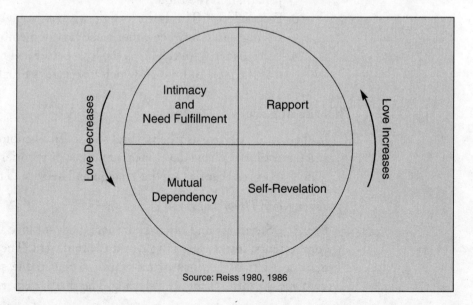

Source: Reiss 1980, 1986

The first stage is *rapport.* In this stage a couple meet and become acquainted. They begin to discover if they have mutual interests and if they are comfortable with each other. If they find they share some things in common and are able to communicate easily with each other, rapport begins to build. Reiss argues that a couple must first develop rapport before they can move on to the next stage.

The second stage, *self-revelation,* grows out of the first. As a couple becomes comfortable with each other, their communication will move from more superficial matters to more personal issues. As each reveals intimate information about himself or herself to the other, a feeling of closeness develops. Reiss believes that a couple must have intimate communication and understanding for real love to develop.

Self-revelation leads to *mutual dependency,* the next state. As a couple gets to know each other more intimately, they begin to desire each other. They enjoy being together, and each one begins to develop a lifestyle that involves the other. A mutual dependency begins to form. According to Reiss, it is at this stage that the relationship becomes serious and the love bond begins to form.

The final stage is *intimacy and need fulfillment.* This stage centers around some of our deepest needs—acceptance, trust, support, and love. These needs can be met only in an intimate relationship. Because these needs are so pervasive, most people look for a permanent relationship in which these needs can continue to be met. This is one reason why people marry. It also helps explain why some marriages break up. If a person's needs are not being met in the relationship, dependency weakens, and the person begins to withdraw.

Looking at Reiss's Wheel Theory, we can see that he understands love as developing from a social relationship. At each stage a couple may move backward or forward. If a couple moves forward through the stages, the result will be a paired dependency bond or love. Some people may commit themselves to marriage before moving through all the stages. While they might complete the process after marriage, the probability is that the process will begin to reverse and the marriage will dissolve. A good marriage requires intimacy and mutual need fulfillment. We will look further at the bases for marriage in the next chapter.

Authentic Love Versus Infatuation

Not all romantic attraction is authentic love. It may be only infatuation. We may define *infatuation* as an immature emotional response to a person

Pairing and Singlehood

of the opposite sex based on superficial or idealized characteristics rather than the whole person. Saxton says, "Infatuation tends to focus on a single aspect of the other, whereas love focuses on the whole person. An infatuated person tends to relate to the other as an *object* to be manipulated, controlled, or used, whereas a person in love tends to identify with the other. Further, this identification tends to be persistent and enduring in love, while infatuation tends to be relatively short-lived" (1980:205).

Saxton goes on to contrast love and infatuation as follows:

Infatuation is self-centered, whereas love is other-centered; that is, infatuation tends to be characterized by preoccupation with oneself and

TABLE 3.1	INFATUATION	AUTHENTIC LOVE
The Difference Between Infatuation and Authentic Love	1. Infatuation is born at first sight and will conquer all.	1. Authentic love is a developing relationship and deepens with realistically shared experiences.
	2. Infatuation demands exclusive attention and devotion and is jealous of outsiders.	2. Authentic love is built on self-acceptance and is shared unselfishly with others.
	3. Infatuation is characterized by exploitation and direct need gratification.	3. Authentic love seeks to aid and strengthen the loved one without striving for recompense.
	4. Infatuation is built on physical attraction and sexual gratification. Sex often dominates the relationship.	4. Authentic love includes sexual satisfaction, but not to the exclusion of sharing in other areas of life.
	5. Infatuation is static and egocentric. Change is sought in the partner in order to satisfy one's own needs and desires.	5. Authentic love is a growing and developing reality. Love expands to include the growth and creativity of the loved one.
	6. Infatuation is romanticized. The couple does not face reality or is frightened by it.	6. Authentic love enhances reality and makes the partners more complete and adequate persons.
	7. Infatuation is irresponsible and fails to consider the future consequences of today's action.	7. Authentic love is responsible and gladly accepts the consequences of mutual involvement.

Adapted from Kelley 1969:212–13

with one's own feelings. The person often feels awkward, constrained, self-conscious, unfulfilled, fragmented, and insecure and may withdraw from sensory experience and contact with others, becoming less and less aware of incoming stimuli (daydreaming, staying away from friends, being unable to eat). On the other hand, a person in love is oriented toward the well-being of the other and tends to be *less* self-conscious or concerned with feelings of difficulty or inadequacy, feeling relatively *more* self-assured, secure, and adequate. The person in love is active and open to sensory experience and feels healthy and keenly alive, delighting in all aspects of the environment—food, friends, sights, and sounds. A person in love is moved to put dreams into action. (1980:205)

How can we tell if we are in love with someone or only infatuated? A number of distinctions between love and infatuation are presented in table 3.1. Perhaps the most important distinction is that love takes time to develop. Contrary to the statements found in some novels and poetry, there is no such thing as "love at first sight" or "falling in love." Authentic love involves the total person, and it takes time to get to know another person. In terms of Reiss's Wheel Theory, infatuation develops at the rapport state, whereas authentic love develops as one moves through all the stages. In the next chapter we will see that short acquaintanceships before marriage produce a higher divorce rate. In all likelihood many couples who married after short acquaintanceships thought they were in love but were only infatuated with each other. Before a step as serious as marriage is considered, two people need to be certain their relationship is based on authentic love—not just infatuation.

Biblical Love

The Bible has much to say about love. Not only does it talk about God's love for us and our love for God, but it also discusses neighborly love, friendship love, familial love, and heterosexual love. When the Bible speaks of heterosexual love, it generally speaks of it in connection with marriage. The Song of Solomon speaks of the love between a man and a woman and presents the ideal of heterosexual love.

In the New Testament, when Paul tells husbands to love their wives (Eph. 5:25, 28; Col. 3:19), he uses the Greek word *agape*. When most of us think about love, we think of an emotion. *Agape* love is not an emotion; it is an act of the will. In the Bible, love is never described in terms of feelings, but in terms of action. Feelings are the by-products of love,

Pairing and Singlehood

not the essence of love. Someone has paraphrased 1 Corinthians 13:4–8 to show how a person in love will act:

I will be patient with you;
I will be kind to you;
I will not envy you;
I will not boast or proudly elevate myself above you;
I will not be rude to you;
I will not exploit you for my own selfish ends;
I will not be easily angered with you;
I will keep no record of wrongs;
I will not delight when you are harmed or when I hear evil
   concerning you;
I will rejoice with truth;
I will always protect you;
I will always trust you;
I will always hope in you;
I will persevere with you;
I will never fail you.

Source unknown

COURTSHIP: THE MATE SELECTION PROCESS

Yes, I chose you.
Out of all the lovely girls I knew,
I chose you.
How marvelous are the women of planet Earth,
   hair flaring in the wind
   rich browns and golds
   a thousand delicious shapes
   girls who laugh saucily
   girls who read Browning
   girls who play sitars
   girls who fix carburetors
Of all those fascinating possibilities,
I chose you.

From "An Ode to Marriage"
Harold Myra (1979b:61)

Dating and Courtship

While dating is the process of meeting and interacting with persons of the opposite sex, courtship is the process of selecting a specific person and moving toward marriage. Even though there may not be a definite point at which a couple moves from dating to courtship, the two processes can be distinguished by their purpose.

Field of Eligibles

As we consider the mate selection process, think of your own situation. If you are single, is every unmarried person of the opposite sex a potential mate? If you are married, did you consider every unmarried person of the opposite sex before making your selection? Of course not. Most of us did, or will do, our mate selection from a limited group of individuals. Sociologists refer to this group from whom we select our mate as the *field of eligibles.* How is our field of eligibles determined? There are several factors involved.

Exogamy

Every society has a culturally defined group within which one may not select a mate. The rule of *exogamy* requires a person to select a mate outside this group. In some societies this may include members of one's clan or extended kin group. For example, among many West African tribes a person may marry cousins of their mother's side of the family but not marry cousins of their father's side.

In the culture of the United States, the rule of exogamy requires people to marry outside of their close family and sex. All states forbid homosexual marriages as well as marriages between siblings, parents and children, grandparents and grandchildren, and children and their aunts and uncles. Many states forbid marriage between first cousins and half-siblings. Some states forbid marriage between stepparents and stepchildren, and some states forbid marriage between a man and his father's former wife or son's former wife. The mating or marrying of a close relative is called *incest.* This will be discussed further in other chapters.

Endogamy

Endogamy requires or encourages mate selection within a culturally defined group. For example, in evangelical circles we practice a rule of endogamy that requires us to select our mate from within the body of

Pairing and Singlehood

FIGURE 3.2

*The Field of
Eligibles*

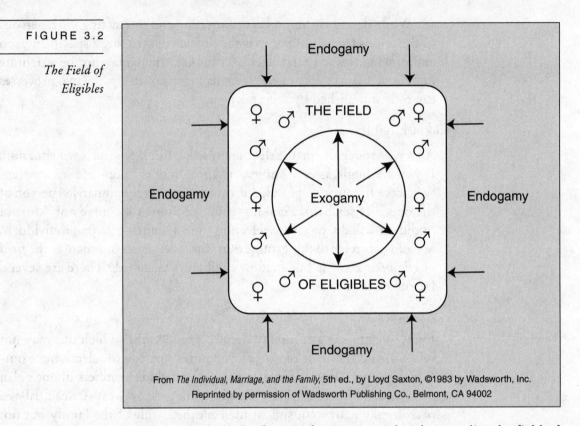

THE FIELD

Endogamy

Endogamy

Exogamy

Endogamy

OF ELIGIBLES

Endogamy

From *The Individual, Marriage, and the Family,* 5th ed., by Lloyd Saxton, ©1983 by Wadsworth, Inc.
Reprinted by permission of Wadsworth Publishing Co., Belmont, CA 94002

believers. Between the forces of exogamy and endogamy lies the field of eligibles (see figure 3.2).

Closely related to endogamy is the concept of *homogamy*. Homogamy is the marriage of two persons who are socially alike, whereas *heterogamy* is the marriage of two persons who are socially different. Most marriages are homogamous—that is, most people marry someone of the same race, social class, and religion, close to the same age. In general, homogamous marriages have greater potential for success than do heterogamous marriages, as we shall see later in this chapter.

Propinquity

One of the major factors in mate selection is *propinquity*, the geographical closeness of the other person. If you are living in Chicago, the eligible persons of the opposite sex in New York, Los Angeles, or Atlanta are very unlikely to be selected by you.

Green (1978:113) reports on several studies that demonstrate the effect of propinquity on mate selection. One study found that over half the couples surveyed lived within sixteen blocks of each other during courtship. Another study found that 43 percent of the couples lived within twenty blocks of each other and that 21 percent lived within five blocks of each other.

Propinquity is a factor in mate selection at Christian colleges, which bring together hundreds of single young people of marriageable age who share a common faith and many common values. With this propinquity, it is not surprising that many young people find their life partners at college. In fact, this is so common that many Bible colleges are jokingly called "bridal colleges."

Theories of Mate Selection

Even with the field of eligibles narrowed by endogamy, exogamy, and propinquity, why do we select the particular person that we do? Behavioral scientists have suggested several theories to explain mate selection. We will examine two that are the subject of current research.

Complementary-Needs Theory

We have all heard the phrase "Opposites attract." To a certain extent that may be true in mate selection. While most marriages are homogamous on social factors such as age, race, religion, and social class, the complementary-needs theory suggests that people will select a mate whose psychological needs or personality complements theirs.

The complementary-needs theory was initiated by Robert Winch, who states:

> The basic hypothesis of the theory of complementary needs in mate selection is that in mate selection each individual seeks within his or her field of eligibles for that person who gives the greatest promise of providing him or her with maximum need gratification. It is not assumed that this process is totally or even largely conscious.
>
> It follows from the general motivation theory that both the person to whom one is attracted, and the one being attracted, will be registering in behavior their own need patterns. Many secondary hypotheses follow from the first—that the need pattern of B, the second person or the one to whom the first is attracted, will be complementary rather than similar to the need pattern of A, the first person. (Winch, Ktsanses, and Ktsanses 1954:242)

Winch illustrates the theory with the following hypothetical anecdote:

Let us assume that there is a chap by the name of Jonathan, and that Jonathan's most distinguished characteristic is a need to be dominant in interpersonal relationships. We shall assume further that among his acquaintances are two girls, Jean and Jennifer. Jennifer is like Jonathan in being dominant and in being intolerant of differences in viewpoint, whereas Jean does not have strong convictions and is used to being governed by the judgments and wishes of others. If we are informed that Jonathan is about to marry one of these women, and if on the basis of the information cited above we are asked to guess which one, probably we should agree that Jean would be the more likely choice for Jonathan to make.... Thus Jonathan should see Jean as a "truly feminine, tractable, agreeable young lady who knows when and how to help a man," whereas to Jean, Jonathan might well appear as a "vigorous and decisive tower of strength." I should expect further that Jonathan would be repelled by Jennifer and would see her as bossy, unfeminine, and probably shrewish. (1958:97)

Some common examples of complementary needs include:

1. Dominance-Deference. In this type one person has the need to influence and control another, while the other needs to have someone lead and make decisions.
2. Nurturance-Succorance. In this type one person needs to give sympathy to or help another, while the other needs to be helped, loved, and supported.
3. Achievement-Vicarious. In this type one person needs to accomplish goals and achieve success, while the other obtains enjoyment and satisfaction from the other's accomplishments.

While some complementary needs might support a good relationship, other complementary needs are unhealthy (McLeod 1995). A more obvious example of unhealthy complementary needs is sadist-masochist—one person has a need to hurt another and the other has the need to be hurt. In this situation two unhealthy needs feed on each other. Some instances of spouse abuse fit this pattern. Another unhealthy set of complementary needs is the parent-child pattern—one person needs to "mother" or "father," and the other needs to be "babied."

Stimulus-Value-Role Theory

Developed by Bernard Murstein (1976), this theory hypothesizes that mate selection proceeds through a series of stages. The first stage is the

Dating and Courtship

stimulus stage. A person is drawn to another by the other's physical attractiveness and social attributes. Murstein describes this stage in terms of the exchange theory. One is attracted to another whom he or she perceives as being of equal attraction. For example, a physically attractive woman may be attracted to a less handsome man who has a higher social status, such as a medical doctor or lawyer.

The second stage is that of *value comparison.* Murstein suggests that if there has been mutual stimulus attraction, the couple will engage in value comparison. If the couple discovers they have similar values, they will move on to the third stage—the role stage.

In the third stage, the couple explore *role compatibility.* Murstein sees these three stages as filters. Generally, only persons passing through all three filters would be considered potential mates. The stages are diagramed in figure 3.3.

FIGURE 3.3

*Stimulus-Value-Role
Theory*

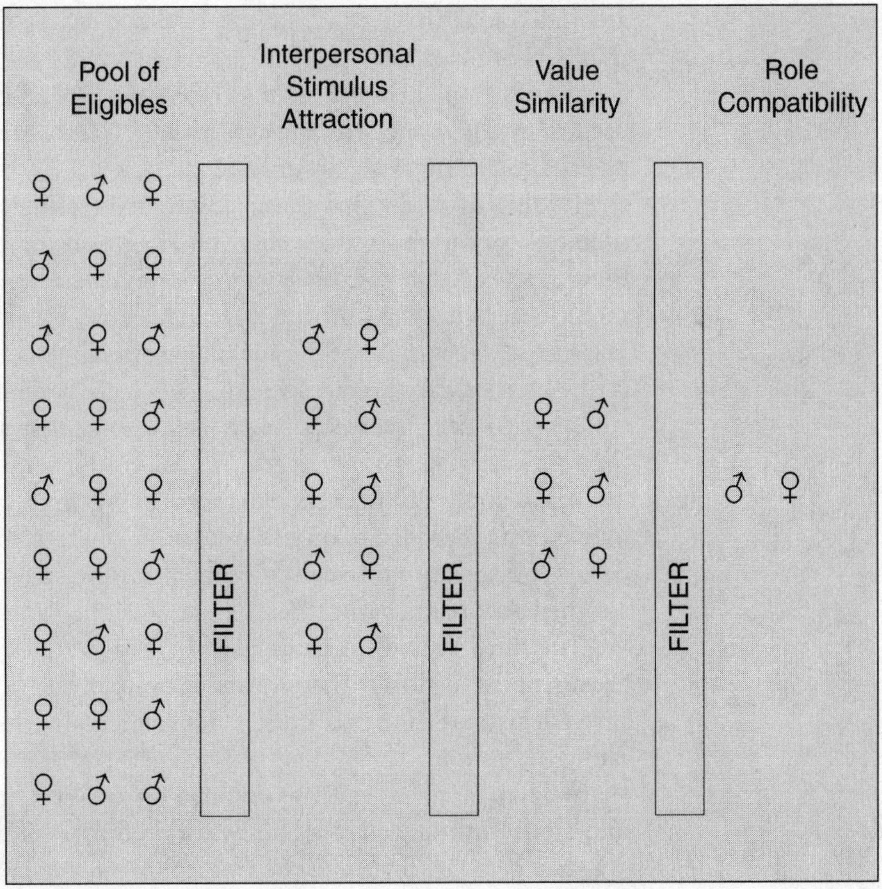

Both of the these theories attempt to explain the mate-selection process. While each helps us better understand the process, neither of them gives a full explanation of mate selection. This is an ongoing area of sociological research.

PREDICTORS OF MARITAL SUCCESS

Is it possible to know the chances for success of a marriage before a couple marries? Can we predict the possibility for success or failure of the marriage based on characteristics of the couple? These questions are of interest not only to sociologists but also to pastors, marriage counselors, and individuals preparing to marry.

Life insurance companies, basing their projections on a person's age, sex, occupation, lifestyle, place of residence, and other factors, can predict the chance or probability of a person living for thirty more years. For any individual, the prediction may be more or less accurate, but for large numbers of people the predictions are accurate enough for the insurance companies to make a profit. If personal and social characteristics can be used to predict life expectancies with a high level of probability, can they be used to predict marital success?

Dozens of studies have been conducted relating various personal and social factors to marital success. The first and most commonly used in these studies is divorce. The assumption is that a nondivorced marriage is more successful than one that ends in divorce. While this may be a crude measure of success, it has the advantage of being objective; either a couple is divorced or they are not. Sociologists usually determine if couples are still married after five years, since they know most divorces take place in the first four years of marriage.

The second type of measure is some sort of marital index. Each couple is given a standard list of questions to answer about their marriage. A standard scoring key and scaling convention are used, and the couple is assigned a score indicating their degree of marital adjustment or "success."

The third type of measure used in these studies is the least common because it is the most subjective and is more susceptible to bias. This measure consists of the researcher, a marriage counselor, or other observer rating the couple.

William Stephens (1970) examined many of the studies done up to the mid-sixties and suggested a number of predictors of marital success. Lynn White (1990) has reviewed the research from the 1980s and found many of the same predictors. Based on these and other studies, we are able to list a number of predictors of marital success.

Age at Marriage

The predictor on the basis of age has the strongest research support, showing that age is positively correlated with marital success. The younger a couple is at marriage, the lower their probability of success; the older a couple is at marriage, the greater the probability of success.

Research studies show that when both parties are teenagers, the divorce rate is more than double that of marriages begun by couples after age twenty (Norton and Moorman 1987; Kurdek 1993). The fact is, teenage marriages have 50 percent less chance of surviving. The probability of marital success becomes much greater in the mid-twenties.

Length of Acquaintanceship

According to Stephens (1970:192), the research unanimously demonstrates a correlation between length of acquaintanceship and marital success. The longer a couple has known each other, the greater the probability of a successful marriage. Cox argues that the problem with a short relationship is that the couple does not have enough time to really get to know each other and that the relationship is based on intense physical contact (1981:135). Stephens (1970:192) suggests that marriages that begin after acquaintanceships of less than a year have a low probability of success.

Premarital Pregnancy

All of the data available indicates that marriages begun with the bride pregnant have a higher divorce rate than those not involving pregnancy (Teachman 1983; Teti and Lamb 1989). Also, research shows that the earlier in a marriage a child is born, the greater the probability of divorce (Belkin and Goodman 1980:436). Obviously, when the bride is pregnant, a child is born early in the marriage.

It should be apparent from the data that marriage may not be the best solution to a premarital pregnancy. Although from a biblical perspective premarital sex is wrong, to attempt to correct one mistake with a second mistake may not be the solution. While I believe both the father-to-be and the mother-to-be should be responsible, marriage may not be the most responsible course of action. If the couple is not ready to marry, perhaps they should share the maternity costs and place the infant with an evangelical adoption agency.

Religious Involvement

Sociologists generally measure religious involvement by measurable factors such as church membership, frequency of attendance, level of stewardship, and hours volunteered in religious service. The research shows a correlation between religious involvement and marital success (Glenn and Supancic 1984). The more a couple is involved in religious activity, the greater the probability of marital success. Also, marriages performed by clergy have a lower divorce rate than those performed by a justice of the peace or other civil official.

Similarity of Faith

When we examine religious experience, there is another factor to consider—interfaith marriages. Interfaith marriage usually refers to marriages between members of America's three major religious groups—Protestant, Catholic, and Jewish. Most studies have found a higher divorce rate among interfaith marriages (Kephart 1981:491; Eshleman 1981:273; Stephens 1970:193). These last two indicators demonstrate the wisdom of the biblical injunction not to be unequally yoked. Although this injunction has specific reference to believer with unbeliever, it certainly has implications for interfaith marriages as well.

Social Class

Generally speaking, the higher the social class, the lower the divorce rate when social class is measured by income or occupation (Martin and Bumpass 1989; Strong, De Vault, and Sayad 1998:492). According to Saxton (1980:388), income is an even more powerful predictor of marital success than occupation.

What about marrying someone of a different social class? Research on social-class heterogamy and marital success indicates that it results in greater marital conflict and divorce (Stephens 1970:193; Eshleman 1981:268–69). Apparently, rich-girl-marries-poor-boy-and-they-live-happily-ever-after usually happens only in fairy tales. Actually, it is not difficult to understand why marriages between persons of different social classes are generally not successful. Each social class develops a worldview and a value system. When two people bring different perspectives and values, not to mention lifestyles and tastes, to a relationship as intimate as marriage, there is a strong potential for conflict and misunderstanding.

Level of Education

The research results are unanimous in finding that as years of education increase, divorce rates decrease (Stephens 1970:193; Saxton 1980:387). The 1970 census also shows that divorce rates decrease as education increases. The divorce rate is higher for those with only a high-school education than it is for college graduates (White 1990).

Divorced Parents

Children of divorced parents have higher divorce rates than young people from intact homes (Raschke 1987). The effect of parental divorce on the marital success of their children appears to be greater for men than for women (Stephens 1970:193).

NEGATIVE REASONS FOR MARRIAGE

Individuals have many reasons for marrying, some of them positive and others negative. If a couple marry for negative or poor reasons, the marriage will have less chance for success. H. Norman Wright suggests several negative reasons for marriage (Wright 1977a:20–21).

Pregnancy

Wright points out that in one out of every four weddings the wife is pregnant. He goes on to say that many of these weddings would not have taken place if the bride had not been pregnant (Wright 1977a:20). We have already seen the statistics on marital success when the bride is pregnant, and they are not very encouraging. Frequently a couple is pushed into marriage by well-meaning friends and family in order to "legitimize" the child and protect the family's reputation. If a couple is older and had intended to get married before the pregnancy occurred, it might be feasible for the couple to marry because there already was a commitment to marriage. However, a pregnancy, in and of itself, is a negative reason for marrying. In fact, marriage may well only make a bad situation worse.

Rebound

It is not uncommon for a person who has just had an engagement broken or a marriage ended by death or divorce to quickly marry someone else. The person had an emotional attachment to one person, and when that person is no longer available, the emotions are transferred to another person.

The problem is that the emotions associated with the first person eventually dissipate, leaving one with no emotional attachment to the second person.

Widowhood, divorce, or a broken engagement result in a loss. The most common emotional reaction to a major loss is grief. It is generally agreed that it takes at least a year to work through the grief of a major loss (Collins 1972:146; Grunlan and Lambrides 1983:116). We have already seen that a year is the minimum period of acquaintanceship for marital success. Therefore, a good rule of thumb would be to consider any marriage occurring less than two years after a death, divorce, or broken engagement a rebound marriage.

Rebellion

Rebellion is often a motive for marriage. Young people rebel against their parents' wishes as a means of demonstrating their independence. In fact, parental opposition often pushes a couple closer together. This is called the Romeo and Juliet effect. A group of researchers administered a questionnaire to dating couples that measured the intensity of their love for each other as well as the amount of parental opposition they experienced. The findings indicated that those couples with the greatest parental opposition were the most intensely in love (Driscoll, Davis, and Lipetz 1972:1–10; Katz and Liu 1988).

Escape

Some people marry to escape an unhappy or stressful home life or some other intolerable situation (Katz and Liu 1988). Cox, writing about escape as a basis for marriage, says, "Rather than dealing with a current relationship, many persons run away, hoping a new person or a new environment will be better. A marriage so conceived is often the first of a series of failures" (1981:134).

Loneliness

While marrying for companionship is a positive reason for marriage, marrying to avoid loneliness is a negative one. Cox points out that "if overcoming loneliness is one's only motivation for marriage, chances are high that this reason alone will not sustain a long-lasting relationship" (1981:134). A lonely person will frequently place unreasonable demands on his or her partner, putting a strain on the relationship. Many problems can develop from this type of relationship.

Physical Appearance

There is nothing wrong with finding the one we are considering marrying attractive. The truth is that physical appearance most likely influences everyone to some extent. While physical attraction is a legitimate aspect of a romantic relationship, it should not be the sole basis for a marriage.

One danger of physical attractiveness is what is called the halo effect. Belkin and Goodman (1980:109–10) report on a number of studies that indicate attractive persons have more positive characteristics attributed to them than less attractive persons. Attractive persons are perceived to be more intelligent, more honest, more kind, and to generally have more socially desirable characteristics than less attractive persons. The danger is that we may attribute characteristics to a physically attractive person that they do not possess.

Some people desire a physically attractive partner to enhance their own prestige. An attractive partner adds to one's value socially. Belkin and Goodman (1980:110) report on a study that found college women who were seen with an attractive man were rated more positively by their peers than they were when seen with an unattractive man. Whether one chooses an attractive mate for one's own gratification or as a status symbol, it is a negative reason for marriage. The Scriptures seem to indicate that as Christians we should be more concerned with inner beauty than with outer beauty (1 Peter 3:3–4).

Social Pressure

Friends, family, and society all extend the same message: "It is normal to get married; there is something wrong with you if you do not marry." Since over 90 percent of all adult Americans will marry, it is easy to see how marriage has become a cultural expectation. An unmarried adult past thirty years of age will often find himself or herself the object of well-meaning friends' pity or attempts at matchmaking. This can be irritating and insulting to many single persons who have chosen either not to marry or to delay marriage.

Another social pressure to marry is a desire for adult status. Single persons are often not perceived as adults in the same way their married peers are. For example, we speak of a single *girl* and a married *woman* or a play*boy* and a married *man*.

Guilt

Guilt is a powerful motivator, albeit a very negative one. A person may marry another person because of guilt—over shared physical intimacies, over leading the other person on as far as they have, or any number of other reasons. It should be apparent that guilt does not lead to a stable marriage relationship.

Pity

It is easy to confuse pity with love. Pity felt for a person because of a handicap, illness, or a poor lot in life is not a sound foundation on which to build a marriage relationship.

Romance

Every marriage should be romantic. I feel sorry for couples who have let the romance go out of their marriages. However, a marriage needs more than romance to survive. Sitting up all night with a sick child is not very romantic, especially by the third or fourth night. Caring for your mate when he or she has the flu is not romantic. Changing dirty diapers is not at all romantic. There are many aspects to marriage that are not romantic and that require more than infatuation to get through. Romantic love is based on feelings; however, genuine love is based on commitment. It is commitment, not romance, that will carry a couple through the difficult times.

POSITIVE REASONS FOR MARRIAGE

While there are negative reasons for marrying, there are also positive reasons. God has created us as male and female and has established marriage as the framework within which most of us will spend our adult lives. While a person can live a fulfilled and meaningful life without a partner, we are so created that most of us will find our fulfillment and meaning with another person. Golanty and Harris (1982:84) present several positive reasons for marriage that are consistent with a biblical understanding of marriage. We will briefly examine each of these reasons.

Conformity

While in its "popular" usage most persons do not like to be considered conformist, sociologically, all behavior is either conformist or deviant. That is, one either conforms to social norms or deviates from them. The

Scripture teaches that Christians should conform to social norms unless the norms violate scriptural teachings (Rom. 13:1–7; 1 Cor. 9:19–23; 11:2–16). In our culture it is the norm for a couple desiring to live together to become legally married. A couple wishing to live together should conform to both biblical and social standards by marrying.

Legitimation of Sex

As a couple moves through courtship, there will naturally be a desire for physical union symbolic of their deepening relationship. This physical desire is a normal part of human sexuality. We must remember that it was God who created us male and female. Marriage is the setting for physical union between a man and a woman (1 Cor. 7:3–5, 9; Heb. 13:4).

Love

Earlier we distinguished between mature and immature love. It was pointed out above that romantic love, based on feelings, is a negative reason to marry. However, mature love, based on commitment and self-giving, is a positive reason for marrying.

Companionship

According to Golanty and Harris (1982:84), companionship may be the most important reason for marriage. Companionship leads to security and stability and meets some of our deepest needs. Marriage is a means of having regular companionship. The writer of Ecclesiastes put it so well when he wrote:

> Two are better than one,
>   because they have a good return for their work:
> If one falls down,
>   his friend can help him up.
> But pity the man who falls
>   and has no one to help him up!
> Also, if two lie down together, they will keep warm.
>
> Ecclesiastes 4:9–11

Sharing and Communication

We all need someone to share ourselves with. We need someone to share our success and failure, someone to share our dreams and fears. Experiences are more meaningful when we have someone to share them with.

We also need people to communicate with. God created us as social beings with the ability and need to communicate. Communication is a key to a good marriage. In fact, when communication breaks down, then a marriage begins to break down.

Marriage meets many of our needs, and there are many positive reasons for marrying. Taken by itself, any one of the above reasons might not provide a strong foundation for marriage; but taken together, these reasons provide such a foundation for marriage.

BASES FOR MARRIAGE

On the basis of the sociological research and statistics we have examined, it is possible to suggest some criteria for a successful marriage. Personal maturity and a healthy outlook are foundational to a good relationship. Common backgrounds and common interests also increase the probability of a stable marriage. A courtship of sufficient length to get to know one another well, along with family support, also portends a successful marriage.

From a Christian perspective, the primary basis for a marriage is a shared faith (2 Cor. 6:14–16; 1 Cor. 7:39). The Scriptures also call for a lifetime commitment (Gen. 2:24; Matt. 19:4–6; 1 Cor. 7:39). A Christian marriage is a couple's commitment both to each other and to God.

DISCUSSION QUESTIONS

1. How important do you believe physical attraction is for obtaining a date? Why?

2. Why do you think favorable characteristics are attributed to attractive people?

3. While the Bible doesn't discuss dating directly, what biblical principles do you believe Christian young people should apply to the dating process?

4. What is your field of eligibles? How did you delineate the field?

5. How much consideration should a person give to the predictors of marital success in this chapter? Why?

6. What do you see as the biblical requirements for mate selection?

SUGGESTED READING

Alice Fryling and Robert Fryling, *A Handbook for Engaged Couples,* 2d ed. (Downers Grove, Ill.: InterVarsity, 1996). This is a workbook for engaged couples to encourage communication on the issues they will face in marriage. The authors bring a biblical perspective to the discussion.

John Holzman, *Dating with Integrity* (Waco, Tex.: Word, 1990). The book deals with sex, honesty, relationships, and other issues faced in dating from a Christian perspective. Each chapter ends with discussion questions.

Joyce Huggett, *Dating, Sex and Friendship* (Downers Grove, Ill.: InterVarsity, 1985). The author combines a biblical perspective with practical counsel in dealing with the issues surrounding dating, premarital sex, and opposite-sex friendships.

Les Parrott and Leslie Parrott, *Saving Your Marriage Before It Starts* (Grand Rapids: Zondervan, 1995). Written for engaged couples by a husband-wife team of counselors, this book helps couples to identify and overcome stumbling blocks to a healthy marriage. Men's and women's workbooks are available.

Premarital Intimacy

Engagement was the worst period in our relationship. We experienced frustration when we maintained our moral standards and guilt when we violated them.

A BIBLE COLLEGE COUPLE

In the last chapter we looked at dating and courtship. Both of these processes generally involve physical intimacy between the couple. This physical intimacy may involve activities from holding hands to a good-night kiss, from making out to petting, from tongue kissing to sexual intercourse.

Each of us draws the line at various places on what is acceptable physical intimacy at different stages of a relationship. This is an issue with which Christians have struggled in the past and will continue to struggle. When I was a teenager, in many conservative Christian groups it was considered improper for a couple to kiss before they were engaged. Today many Christians would not oppose a good-night kiss after a date.

When Christians turn to the Bible for guidance in this area, they find basically a single principle—a prohibition against sexual intercourse before marriage (e.g., 1 Cor. 6:9–20; 7:1–9; Gal. 5:19–21; Eph. 5:3). But what of holding hands, kissing, and petting? Because dating was unknown in the biblical cultures and courtship in biblical times was vastly different from modern practices, these are never discussed. For the most part, a couple had little or no physical contact before their wedding. Marriages were often arranged by the couple's families, with the young people having limited choice. Since the Scriptures do not directly address issues such as holding hands and good-night kisses, Christians have sought to draw up guidelines based on what they believed were biblical principles. After examining some current practices and statistics, we will discuss the issue of Christian standards for dating and courtship.

Pairing and Singlehood

DEGREES OF PREMARITAL INTIMACY

As pointed out above, physical intimacy can range from holding hands to sexual intercourse. For purposes of discussion and research, scholars, as well as the general public, have attempted to define and label various degrees of physical intimacy. There is not a standard division of sexual activity agreed upon among social researchers; however, most would recognize the following four categories.

Touching

Touching involves a number of activities, including holding hands, hugging, walking arm-in-arm, walking with arms around each other, and nonsexual caressing. These acts are engaged in not to sexually stimulate the other person, but to communicate caring and affection.

While touching can be a prelude to further physical intimacy, it can also be an end in itself. It is a way to be close to another person. It is a means of communicating on a nonverbal level. Touching provides security and a sense of belonging. It is also a way of giving and receiving nonsexual pleasure.

Kissing

Kissing is generally recognized as a romantic act that symbolizes both attraction and affection (Tucker, Marvin, and Vivian 1991). Research also indicates that kissing is widely seen as an acceptable premarital sexual activity (Jurich and Polson 1985). Because both the lips and the mouth are highly sensitive to touch, kissing is an erotic act. Kissing is generally arousing and often excites the whole body.

While kissing is often seen as a more innocent form of intimacy, in some ways it may be the most intimate of all sexual activities. It is interesting that we seal wedding vows with a kiss. One research study found that most people could not imagine engaging in sexual intercourse without kissing (Blumstein and Schwartz 1983). This same study found that the amount of kissing a couple engaged in was correlated to the level of closeness the couples felt.

Sexual Stimulation

Sexual stimulation involves activities such as caressing and fondling the breasts and caressing the genitals. These activities are also known as *petting* (Kinsey et al. 1953; King, Balswick, and Robinson 1977). Sexual stimulation may be an end in itself, it may result in mutual masturbation, or it may result in intercourse.

Another form of sexual stimulation is oral sex. The stimulation of the female's vulva by the man's tongue and mouth is called *cunnilingus.* The stimulation of the male's penis by the woman's tongue and mouth is called *fellatio.* Oral sex has become an accepted sexual activity. Research studies have found that more than half of all adults have engaged in oral sex (Delamater and MacCorquodale 1979; Michael et al. 1994; Petersen et al. 1983). Another study found that oral sex is widely practiced among university students. Some feel less guilt engaging in oral sex than in intercourse because they are not "going all the way" (Newcomer and Udry 1985).

Sexual Intercourse

Sexual intercourse, also known as *coitus,* involves the insertion of the penis into the vagina and the stimulation of the genitals. The goal of sexual intercourse is orgasm.

The definitions above clearly show that premarital intimacy involves everything from holding hands, to caressing the breasts and genitals, to sexual intercourse. While there is a vast difference between holding hands and caressing genitals, it may be useful for us to view these activities as various stages of a single process. As Cox says, "In the broadest sense, intimate physical contact of any kind between male and female is sexual behavior" (1981:119).

EXTENT OF PREMARITAL INTIMACY

While any physical contact between males and females may be construed as sexual behavior, the types of behaviors that are generally of concern to both sociologists and the public are sexual stimulation and coitus. To what extent are these activities taking place among the unmarried? Sociologists have questioned teenagers and college students about their practices, and we will examine the findings. First, it should be pointed out that the findings are self-reports that may or may not be true. Some individuals may attempt to "cover up" their behavior, and others may tend to exaggerate or "brag." Many researchers assume that these two groups will tend to cancel each other out. However, as Kephart warns us, "The available figures refer only to *reported* behavior; hence, all statistics on the subject should be regarded as approximations" (1981:288).

Pairing and Singlehood

A Roper survey in 1994 questioned high school students, grades 9 to 12, about the type of sexual activities in which they had engaged. The results of the survey are summarized in table 4.1.

The Alan Guttmacher Institute conducted a study titled "Sex and America's Teenagers" (Ingrassia 1994). Their findings reveal that the median age for first intercourse for boys was 16.6 years and for girls it was 17.4 years. That means that half of all teenagers had sex before that age. The results of the study are summarized in table 4.2. Another study found that college students generally expect to have sexual intercourse during their college years (Robinson et al. 1991).

TABLE 4.1

Sexual Activities Engaged in by High School Students

SEXUAL ACTIVITY	PERCENTAGE ENGAGING IN THE ACTIVITY
Kissing	90%
Touching above the waist	72%
Touching below the waist	54%
Sexual intercourse	36%
Oral sex	26%
Mutual masturbation	15%

Source: Ingrassia 1994:64

TABLE 4.2

Percent of Teenagers Who Have Had Intercourse

AGE	PERCENTAGE HAVING INTERCOURSE
12	9%
13	16%
14	23%
15	30%
16	42%
17	59%
18	71%
19	82%

FACTORS IN THE RISE OF PREMARITAL INTIMACY

We need to realize that premarital sex has long been a social issue. In the Old Testament, premarital sex was prohibited, and various degrees of punishment, including the death penalty, were prescribed for violators (Ex. 22:16–17; Lev. 19:20–22; Deut. 22:13–29). In the New Testament, Joseph thought Mary had engaged in premarital sexual intercourse, and he was going to break their engagement until he learned the nature of her pregnancy (Matt. 1:18–25). The apostle Paul also addressed the issues of premarital sex and chastity (e.g., 1 Cor. 6:12–20; 7:1–9).

While premarital sex has long been a social issue, the incidence of coitus before marriage was quite low in American society before World War I (Kephart 1981:275). Since that time, the proportion of the population engaging in premarital sex has steadily increased. What is responsible for this rise in premarital sex?

Changing Attitudes

Many factors have probably contributed to the rise in premarital sex. It would be difficult to determine which factor is dominant or antecedent to the others since the factors obviously interact and feed back into each other. Research shows that attitudes toward premarital sexual activity have become more permissive in recent years (Wade and Cirese 1991:485).

In a national survey on attitudes toward premarital sex (Kephart 1981), respondents were asked if they thought premarital sexual relations were (1) always wrong, (2) almost always wrong, (3) wrong only sometimes, (4) not wrong at all. The subjects responded as shown in table 4.3.

It is interesting to note that more people thought premarital sex was never wrong than thought it was always wrong. Also over 70 percent felt premarital sex was all right—at least under certain circumstances. Research reveals that "most people now regard premarital sex favorably if the couple is in love" (Wade and Cirese 1991:485).

TABLE 4.3

Attitudes Toward Premarital Sex

Always wrong	29.3%
Almost always wrong	11.7%
Wrong only sometimes	20.3%
Not wrong at all	38.7%

Source: Kephart 1981:284–85

What is interesting is that, while people have more permissive views in general, when it comes to their partners, their views are more conservative. Research has found that when respondents could indicate the level of sexual experience they would prefer in a person they were dating or a person they were going to marry, they preferred chastity. Respondents were able to choose whether they would prefer a date or marital partner to have been chaste, to have had moderate sexual experience, or to have had extensive sexual experience. Both male and female respondents preferred chastity. They also preferred moderate sexual experience over extensive sexual experience (Sprecher et al. 1997).

Media

A large debate exists over whether the media shape our attitudes or reflect our attitudes. The truth is that probably they do both. However, a number of social scientists believe that the media have played a role in changing sexual attitudes and behavior (e.g., Wolf and Kielwasser 1991; McMahon 1989).

We need only to observe current movies and television programming to discover that the treatment of sex outside of marriage is quite permissive. As Kephart states, "Whether the theme is that of adultery or premarital coitus, the persons involved are likely to be portrayed in a sympathetic light, while the activity itself is seen as a more-or-less natural manifestation of man's inexorable nature" (1981:287).

One researcher who has studied the sexual attitudes and behaviors of college students comes to this conclusion:

The direct sources of students' sexual ideas were located almost entirely in mass consumer culture: the late-adolescent/young adult exemplars displayed in movies, popular music, advertising, and on TV; Dr. Ruth and sex manuals; *Playboy, Penthouse, Cosmopolitan, Playgirl,* etc.; Harlequins and other pulp romances (female only); the occasional piece of real literature; sex education and popular psychology as it is filtered through these sources ... classic soft-core and hardcore pornographic movies, books, and ... video cassettes. (Moffat in Strong et al. 1998:206)

Contraception and Abortion

One factor that often receives the blame for the rise in premarital coitus is modern contraceptives and particularly "the pill." While modern contraceptives and their ready availability have more than likely affected premarital sexual behavior, their effect may not be as great as is often thought. While teen birth rates rose rapidly from 1980 to 1991, they have dropped slightly since then. However, in 1996 there were almost 60 live births per 1,000 females 15 to 19 years of age. This is the highest teen birth rate among industrialized countries. And the birth rate does not include abortions. Teenagers had 300,000 abortions in one year (U.S. Bureau of the Census 1995). So the actual number of pregnancies is much higher.

If modern contraceptives are so convenient and readily available, how does one explain the large increase in premarital pregnancies? Scanzoni and Scanzoni (1981) suggest that it results from what they call the "nice girl dilemma." They point out that even in our modern, permissive society, virtue is still valued. A "nice girl" is not promiscuous; she does not "sleep around." However, a "nice girl" may be swept away by the passion of a moment. This slip would be seen as an exception to her normal virtue. But if a woman uses contraceptives, it is an acknowledgment that she is going to engage in sexual intercourse. Therefore she loses her excuse of being swept away by passion.

Extended Adolescence

A factor that may be as responsible for the increase in premarital sex as any of the others is extended adolescence. *Adolescence* may be defined as the period between puberty and adulthood. Before the Industrial Revolution, adolescence as we know it today was virtually nonexistent. Puberty came later and responsible adulthood came earlier, so that the two events tended to be simultaneous. In the twentieth century, puberty has come increasingly earlier and responsible adulthood increasingly later, creating the period of time called adolescence.

Data from several northern European countries and the United States show that the average age of *menarche* (first menstrual flow) for females was 17 in 1830 and that it had dropped to 12.8 years by the mid-1970s (Dworetzky 1981:497–98). Males reach puberty (able to produce mature sperm), on the average, between 13 and 14 years of age. This means that the average adolescent is sexually mature by 13 or 14. However, the legal age for marriage without parental consent in most states is 18. But marriages usually take place later, at about 22 for females and 24 for males, according to current census data. Thus the average adolescent is sexually mature eight to ten years before marriage.

Before the Industrial Revolution, young people married about the time they reached puberty. According to the Talmud (the collection of Jewish law and tradition), people were expected to be married before they were 18; and in Roman society, a female who was not married by 19 was considered an "old maid." During the Renaissance in Europe, parents considered it a disgrace if their daughters were not married by 17. In eighteenth-century England the legal age for marriage was 14 for males and 12 for females (Koteskey 1981:25).

Koteskey argues that extended adolescence is a major cause for increased premarital sexual activity: "There is a period of five or more years during which it is impossible for young men and women to get married. While other factors ... no doubt play a part in the rising incidence of both masturbation and premarital intercourse, it seems to me that postponing marriage for legal and economic reasons is a major cause" (1981:27).

LIVING TOGETHER

When premarital sex is discussed, we often tend to think of it as isolated acts. However, much premarital coitus takes place in an arrangement where a couple live together. This arrangement is called *cohabitation.* Duvall defines cohabitation as "sharing a bed with someone of the opposite sex to whom one is not married for four or more nights a week for three or four months" (1977:120).

To what extent is cohabitation taking place? In 1960 about 400,000 couples were living together. In 1994 almost 4 million unmarried couples were living together (Strong, DeVault, and Sayad 1998:193; Lamanna and Riedmann 1997:160). That is almost a tenfold increase in thirty-four years.

Although a significant number of persons are living together without the benefit of marriage, they are not all doing so for the same reasons or with the same intent. Scanzoni and Scanzoni (1981) suggest that there are three basic categories of cohabitation: trial marriage, common-law marriage, and ad hoc arrangements.

Trial Marriage

Some people believe that with the high rate of divorce, it might be better for couples to live together for a while to discover if they are really compatible and want to make the arrangement permanent. As someone has said, "You would not buy a car without a test drive, so why take a spouse without a test period?" The idea of a trial marriage is not new. It was brought up by Maurice of Saxony in the eighteenth century. Again in 1926, Judge Ben B. Lindsey proposed the idea. Bertrand Russell suggested it for college students in 1929, and Margaret Mead reintroduced the idea in 1966.

Researchers have conducted a number of studies to determine whether couples who cohabit before marriage have better or worse marriages, or greater or lesser risk of divorce than couples who did not. One longitudinal study based on a national sample of married couples found that couples who had cohabited before marriage had more marital disagreements and a higher probability of divorce (Booth and Johnson 1988). Other studies have found that couples who cohabit before marriage have lower levels of happiness and higher divorce rates (De Maris and Leslie 1984; Bennet, Blanc, and Bloom 1988; Thomas and Colella 1992).

Common-Law Marriage

In thirteen American states, Washington, D.C., and the Virgin Islands, a couple may live together without license or ceremony, blood tests or witnesses; and if they consent to be considered husband and wife, the state will recognize their status (Kephart 1981:312–13). This arrangement is known as common-law marriage. The amount of time the couple must live together varies from state to state, but in the thirteen states that recognize common-law marriage, after a prescribed period of time a couple living together can receive legal status.

It needs to be pointed out that common-law marriage is an after-the-fact legality. As Scanzoni and Scanzoni remind us, "Whether or not a union has been a valid marriage according to common-law is something that is determined *after* the union has been entered" (1981:216). In order for common-law marriage to be recognized, a couple must have been cohabiting for a specific period of time.

It also needs to be understood that where common-law marriage does take place, it is as binding as a licensed marriage and can be broken only by divorce or death. If a couple live together in a common-law state and pass themselves off as husband and wife, after a period of time they may, in fact, be considered legally married.

Ad Hoc Arrangements

According to the *Merriam-Webster Dictionary*, the Latin expression *ad hoc* means "concerned with a particular purpose." Couples may cohabit for a variety of reasons. There are couples who live together and are engaging in neither a "trial marriage" nor a "common-law marriage."

Pairing and Singlehood

Some couples want to live together for a variety of reasons but are not interested in marriage or being considered married.

CONSEQUENCES OF PREMARITAL INTIMACY

Frank Cox, a secular sociologist, writes, "As American mores have relaxed, the differentiations between premarital and marital sex activities have lessened. However, there are still a number of problems that are clearly related to premarital sex" (1981:123). Cox goes on to suggest at least four problems. We will briefly examine each of these.

Sexually Transmitted Diseases

More Americans are infected with *sexually transmitted diseases (STDs)* than at any time in our history. The fact is, the spread of STDs has reached epidemic proportions in the United States. The Center for Disease Control estimates that over 12 million people are infected with an STD each year. The Center for Disease Control also estimates that one million Americans (1 out of every 270 people) is infected with the *human immunodeficiency virus (HIV)*. Over 550,000 Americans have developed or died from *acquired immune deficiency syndrome (AIDS)*, which results from HIV.

Sexually transmitted diseases can be more than just painful and embarrassing; they can have serious effects. Untreated or improperly treated, they can result in sterility; damage to reproductive organs; brain damage; and, in some cases, death. For a description of the various venereal diseases, their causes, consequences, and treatments, see the appendix.

Unwanted Pregnancies

As we saw earlier in this chapter, even with the advent of modern birth control techniques and the availability of abortion on demand, the rate of illegitimate births continues to rise. There are well over a million pregnancies a year among 15–19-year-old females. While many of these pregnancies will be terminated by abortion, many more will give birth.

While as Christians we recognize that premarital intercourse goes against the teachings of Scripture and that sin has its consequences, it is important for us not to be judgmental (Matt. 7:1–2) but rather to support and help the unmarried pregnant woman to find forgiveness and the best solution to her problem (Gal. 6:1–2). We must recognize that premarital sexual relations are always wrong because God's Word teaches us that sexual intimacy is reserved for marriage (Heb. 13:4). Even so, while we cannot overlook sin, we must always reach out and minister to the sinner. The person who has sinned is often aware of his or her failure and certainly does not need our words of condemnation but needs God's message of forgiveness and restoration when there is repentance.

Early Commitment and Isolation

When a young couple move into heavy petting and coitus, they often begin isolating themselves from their peers. They tend to want to be alone and have privacy. Because of this tendency, they narrow their social relationships and hence their social development.

Because sex is a powerful force and is related to emotions, there is also a tendency for two people involved in heavy petting and premarital coitus to make an early commitment to each other. If they marry, they may discover that their relationship was based primarily on sex.

Particularly during the teen years, young people need to interact with a number of persons and have a variety of social experiences. There is a need to have a wide range of relationships with persons of the opposite sex as well as same-sex peers, rather than the exclusive relationships that tend to develop when engaged in premarital sex.

Quality of Marital Sex

Premarital sexual experience may affect the quality of marital sex. Cox presents an interesting argument when he hypothesizes that "early sexual experiences largely set the attitudes that an individual will hold toward sexual intercourse throughout his or her life. If one's early sexual experiences occur premaritally, the chances are that the quality of such experiences will be under less than optimum conditions. As a result, large numbers of our youth may begin their adult sexual life with negative attitudes toward the sexual act" (1981:126).

Research also indicates that females who engage in premarital sex are more likely to engage in extramarital sex. Because of the nature of premarital sex, it lays the seeds for both guilt and mistrust. There is no evidence that premarital sex enhances marital sex, but there is good reason to believe that premarital sex may adversely affect the quality of marital sex.

Guilt

In addition to the four consequences to premarital sex presented by Cox, a fifth consequence is guilt. While research indicates that many persons experience guilt from premarital intercourse, this problem is particularly acute for the Christian. As we have seen, the Scriptures teach that pre-marital coitus is a sin. Many Christians would extend the prohibition to heavy petting. When a Christian practices sin and violates his or her conscience and the teachings of God's Word, guilt will result. The Holy Spirit will bring conviction into the life of the believer. If a person does not respond to that guilt with confession and repentance, he or she may be able to suppress it. However, suppressing the guilt does not make it go away. The guilt is only pushed below the surface of consciousness to produce other symptoms, such as anxiety and/or depression (Minirth and Meier 1978:101–3; Grunlan and Lambrides 1983:146).

This discussion has not been intended to "scare" young people out of engaging in premarital sex, but rather to present some of the possible consequences. It is my firm belief that the Christian's motive for obeying God and his Word is not fear but love (John 15:10–14; 1 John 2:5–6). However, we must also understand that the Bible teaches that there are consequences of sin (Gal. 6:7–8).

CHRISTIANS AND PREMARITAL SEX

How Far?

A standard question asked by young people in general and Christians in particular is "How far can we go?" Which expressions of physical intimacy are acceptable before marriage, and which ones are restricted to married couples? As we discussed earlier, there was little if any physical contact between couples before marriage in Bible times; therefore, the Scriptures do not deal with kissing and petting but only with sexual intercourse. In modern Western culture physical contact between couples before marriage is permitted, the only question being that of extent. Differing degrees of physical intimacy at various stages of a relationship are presented in figure 4.1.

While levels 1 to 8 in figure 4.1 show a progression from permissive to conservative degrees of physical intimacy, level 9 portrays the situation faced by many Christian young people. Early in their dating they have gone as far as they believe is right, and they spend the next stages of their relationship frustrated because they maintain their standards, or guilty because they violate them (see quote at beginning of the chapter). While Christian couples may differ in how far they feel it is okay to go, most experience this syndrome.

FIGURE 4.1

Degrees of Sexual Behavior

STAGES					
Levels	Friendship	Dating	Going Steady	Engaged	Married
1	L T	h H k K fk B		SO SI	
2	L T	h H k K fk B	SO SI		
3	L T	h H k K fk	B SO	SI	
4	L T	h H k K	fk B	SO SI	
5	L T	h H k	K fk	B SO	SI
6	L T	h H k	K	fk B	SO SI
7	L T	h H	k K	fk	B SO SI
8	L T	h H	k	K	fk B SO SI
9	L T	h H k K fk			B SO SI

Key:
  L —Look
  T —Touch
  h —Holding Hands Lightly
  H —Constant Holding Hands
  k —Light Kiss
  K —Strong Kiss
  fk —French Kiss
  B —Fondling of Breasts
SO —Sexual Organs
SI —Sexual Intercourse

Source: Wright and Inmon 1978

Level 5 in figure 4.1 illustrates what the literature calls "technical virginity" (Scanzoni and Scanzoni 1981:118). Since the Scriptures only prohibit sexual intercourse before marriage (e.g., Acts 15:28–29; 1 Cor. 6:9–10; Gal. 5:19–21), some Christian young people feel that anything short of coitus is acceptable. However, is a young woman who engages in heavy petting with numerous young men any more virtuous than a young woman who once engaged in coitus with her husband-to-be before her marriage?

Addressing the issue of how far a Christian should go in physical intimacy before marriage, H. Norman Wright suggests:

> Given our conviction to refrain from sexual intercourse until marriage, the question remains: How far shall we go, short of sexual intercourse, before marriage?

The answer to this question depends upon how far along you are in your relationship (first date or engaged) and upon your abilities to withstand the very strong temptation to have sexual intercourse.

However, a general principle which we feel applies to everyone is the following: That which has its natural end in sexual intercourse should be held to your wedding night.... This means at the very least, that heavy petting, direct stimulation of each other's sexual organs, and mutual masturbation should be out.... This also means that you should not engage in any physical activity which will build up the other person's sexual drives to the point of no return. (1977a:197)

I personally go along with what Wright advocates. In fact, an even slower approach might be advocated. It is not enough to stop only at the right point but also at the right stage of the relationship. As was pointed out earlier, very early in their relationship many Christian couples go as far as they believe right. It is my contention that couples ought to move slowly in the area of physical intimacy. Rather than engage in every permissible behavior early in their relationship, they ought to save various expressions of physical intimacy to celebrate various stages of their relationship. For example, most Christian couples have no new act of physical intimacy left with which to celebrate their engagement. Using the same format as in figure 4.1, figure 4.2 presents a possible progress of physical intimacy for a Christian couple.

FIGURE 4.2	Friendship	Dating	Going Steady	Engaged	Married
	L T	h H	k K	K fk	B SO SI
Suggested Levels of Intimate Activities	Key is in figure 4.1				

Remember that our sexuality and sex drives are not wrong or sinful. They are not part of our fallen nature but are part of the original creation that God called "good" (Gen. 1:26–28, 31). It is only the misuse and abuse of them that is sinful. When the Christian uses his or her sexuality and sex drive as God intended and directed, it is a beautiful thing, God's gift of life and love.

On a practical level there are several things a couple can do to avoid temptations in the area of sexual behavior. One is to do a lot of "public dating"; that is, a couple should spend time in public places such as restaurants and parks rather than in a parked car or alone in a living room. A couple can have all the privacy they need to talk and get to know each other in a public place without the temptations of a secluded setting. Another suggestion is "double dating" or "group dating"; again, there is security in numbers. A couple should also avoid those places and activities that either stimulate sexual desire or provide opportunity for sexual activity. Perhaps the best safeguard for a Christian couple is to have a close walk with the Lord and maintain both a Spirit-filled life and a Spirit-filled relationship. Prayer and Bible study should be a regular part of a couple's relationship.[1]

Masturbation

Some years ago the dean of students at a Christian college told me that the number one source of spiritual problems on his campus was masturbation. Research indicates that 90 percent of males and 60 percent of females have engaged in masturbation by age 24 (Strong et al. 1998:221). Research I conducted at a Christian college where I taught found that 90 percent of males and 60 percent of females had engaged in masturbation. Thus, there was no difference between students at this Christian college and the findings on secular campuses.

For purposes of our discussion, masturbation will be defined as "deliberate and conscious self-stimulation so as to produce sexual excitement with the goal of orgasm" (Seamands 1977:104). It is not achieving an orgasm that defines masturbation, but rather the attempt, whether or not the goal is reached.

The question facing Christian young people is whether or not masturbation is a sin. While hosts of evangelical writers have condemned it as such, in recent years some evangelicals have taught that a limited practice of masturbation for the purpose of self-control in relating to the opposite sex may be permissible (e.g., Dobson 1978; Miles 1971; Seamands 1977; Shedd 1976; White 1977).

In attempting to answer the question of whether or not masturbation is sinful, we must begin by recognizing that the Scriptures do not address the issue directly. Two passages that some writers have used to condemn masturbation are Genesis 38:8–11 and 1 Corinthians 6:9–10. However, on closer examination it will be seen that they do not address the issue. In Genesis 38:8–11, Onan's sin was not masturbation or even practicing coitus interruptus, but disobeying God's command to raise up seed for his dead brother. In the King James Version the term "abusers of themselves" appears in the Corinthians passage. While some understood this phrase to

---

[1]This does not mean a couple needs to have "devotions" on every date, but they should have some regular pattern of spiritual interaction.

refer to masturbation, it refers to homosexuality and is so translated in later versions (i.e., NIV; NASB; TEV). Because the Bible does not discuss masturbation directly, it is an issue concerning which Christians may come to different conclusions. It is one of those areas in which we must be careful not to judge others and to be faithful to our own conscience and understanding of God's Word.

While recognizing the right and need of every believer to settle this issue for himself or herself, I would like to share three reasons why I believe that masturbation is best avoided by Christian young people. First, there is no biological necessity for masturbation. Females have no need for a biological release. In mature males the testes continually produce sperm, and the prostate gland produces semen. The sperm is deposited in the seminal fluid and stored in the seminal vesicles. When these fill with seminal fluid, there is a need for release. A certain amount of seminal fluid may be drained off during urination. Another mechanism for releasing the seminal fluid is the nocturnal emission. While the male sleeps, the bladder fills and presses against the seminal vesicles. The male has an erection and experiences an ejaculation.[2] God has provided the mechanism for release of seminal fluid.

Second, masturbation is a solo act, and God created us as sexual beings in order to bring men and women together (Gen. 1:26–28; 2:24–25). Our sexuality was meant to be a coupling mechanism rather than to lead to an act conducted in isolation. Masturbation can easily become an emotional substitute for normal interpersonal relationships. It can become a means of avoiding meaningful relationships with members of the opposite sex.

Third, and perhaps the strongest argument against masturbation, is the thought that accompanies the act. Research studies have found that nearly all men and two-thirds of all women fantasize when they masturbate, with the fantasies providing part of the stimulus (Strong et al. 1981:237). While the Scriptures do not directly address the act of masturbation, the Bible does speak to the issue of our thought life (Matt. 5:27–28). Because of this, if the sin does not lie in the act of masturbation, it often lies in the thoughts.

For the person who concludes that masturbation is wrong for himself or herself and is trying to control the practice, I would like to offer a

---

[2]Nocturnal emissions are often accompanied by dreams with sexual content. In some of these dreams the male may be engaging in sexual activity in which he would not engage when conscious. No guilt should be felt over these dreams since one does not have control of unconscious brain activities such as dreams.

few practical suggestions. First, avoid the time and places where masturbation has been practiced. We are all creatures of habit, and a good procedure for breaking a habit is changing your routine. Second, avoid sexual stimuli, whether it be certain types of music, movies, television programs, magazines, or whatever. As the apostle Paul advises, "Whatever is true, whatever is noble, whatever is right, whatever is pure . . . think about such things" (Phil. 4:8). Third, do not fight your thoughts related to masturbation; when you fight them, you are thinking about them. Instead, replace those thoughts with something else. Fourth, take it a day at a time. Just try for victory the next time you are tempted. A habit is defeated one step at a time. Fifth, and most important, commit the matter to God in prayer. Get other believers to pray for you—you do not have to tell them specifics. Also spend time in God's Word. As with all sexual temptations, remember the words of James: "Submit yourselves, then, to God. Resist the devil, and he will flee from you. Come near to God and he will come near to you. Wash your hands . . . and purify your hearts" (James 4:7–8).

D I S C U S S I O N   Q U E S T I O N S

1. What is your reaction to Cox's assertion that "intimate physical contact of any kind between male and female is sexual behavior"? Why?

2. Do you believe that the media more often reflect current sexual attitudes or shape them? Why?

3. Why do you think more unwed mothers are keeping their babies? Do you believe it is best for an unwed teenage mother to keep her baby or put it up for adoption? Why?

4. Why do you think there is such a difference between people's permissive attitudes toward premarital sex in general and their desire to date and marry someone who has been chaste?

5. What is your reaction to the author's suggestion that dating couples practice a "go slow" approach to physical intimacy and save permissible expressions of intimacy to celebrate significant stages of their relationship? Why?

6. In your opinion, why does the Bible take such a strong stand against premarital sexual relations?

S U G G E S T E D   R E A D I N G

Robert Michael et al., *Sex in America: The Definitive Survey* (Boston: Little, Brown, 1994). Based on a random, cross-sectional survey of over three thousand men and women involving personal interviews, this study presents an informative look at sex and sexual activity in America.

Bill Sanders, *Life, Sex and Everything in Between* (Grand Rapids: Revell, 1991). The author writes about the sexuality and sexual activity of teens. He deals with the tough issues from a biblical perspective.

Jim Tally and Bobbi Reed, *Too Close, Too Soon,* 2d ed. (Nashville: Thomas Nelson, 1990). Written by two psychologists, this book deals with premarital intimacy from a Christian perspective. There is a built-in study guide at the end of the book.

Singlehood

I am content to live by myself. I enjoy my freedom and not needing to be accountable to someone else.

A SINGLE CAREER WOMAN

While nearly 90 percent of all American adults will marry, some 55 percent of them will be single at any given time (U.S. Bureau of the Census 1996a). Because the *sex ratio* (the number of men per 100 women in the population) in America is ninety-five (that is 95 males for each 100 females), there are more single women than single men. Singlehood also varies by race and ethnicity. While 37 percent of white adults are single, 42 percent of Hispanic adults are single and 58 percent of black adults are single (U.S. Bureau of the Census 1995).

SINGLE POPULATION

The single population is made up of three groups: the never-married, the divorced, and the widowed. While these three groups share the experience of being single, singleness is different for each of them.

Never-Married

Those who have never been married make up the largest group of singles. The reason this group is so large is delayed marriage. In 1960 the age at first marriage was 20.3 for women and 22.8 for men; by 1994 the age at first marriage had risen to 24.5 for women and 26.7 for men (Strong, DeVault, and Sayad 1998:189).

Delayed marriage has resulted from several factors. One factor is extended education. With well over half of all high school graduates going on to college or other higher education, and with growing graduate school enrollment, marriage is being postponed to complete schooling. Another factor is the growing acceptance of cohabitation that was discussed in

Pairing and Singlehood

	WHITE		HISPANIC		BLACK	
	Men	*Women*	*Men*	*Women*	*Men*	*Women*
Never Married	24.9%	17.1%	35.4%	24.2%	42.4%	36.2%
Divorced	8.0%	10.1%	6.2%	8.7%	8.7%	12.4%
Widowed	2.4%	11.4%	2.0%	6.9%	3.0%	11.0%

Source: U.S. Census Bureau 1995

Chapter 4. Still another factor is economic. Many of those completing college are graduating not only with a degree but with a large student loan debt. Marriage is being postponed to get established in careers and to achieve financial stability. While most of the never-marrieds will eventually marry, about 10 percent of them will never marry.

Divorced

Divorced persons find themselves single again. With 50 percent of all marriages ending in divorce, many married adults will be single adults once more. While over half of all divorced people are remarried within five years, many will remain single. For women who are divorced after age 40, less than one-third will remarry (Yorburg 1993:345). Women with children are also less likely to remarry. Only 25 percent of divorced African Americans and 50 percent of divorced Hispanics will remarry (Yorburg 1993:346). Divorce and remarriage will be discussed further in Chapter 14.

Widowed

The death of a mate also returns a person to singlehood. Because women have longer life expectancy than men, there are four times as many widows as widowers. Three out of four married women will be widowed. While widowed people do remarry, the majority will remain single for the rest of their lives. Widowhood will be discussed in Chapter 13. Table 5.1 shows the percentage of the U.S. population that is single.

TYPES OF SINGLES

Researchers have suggested a variety of ways for typing singles. We will look at two of the more widely used approaches.

Relationships

One approach is to look at the type of relationships in which the person is involved. Using this approach, Robert Staples (1981) has distinguished five types of singles. The first type is the *free floating single.* This person is unattached and dates a number of different people. The second type is the *open-coupled relationship.* This is where the person has a regular partner but the relationship is open and each is free to see others. The third type is the *closed-couple relationship.* This is where the partners have an exclusive relationship and are expected to be faithful to each other. The fourth type is *committed singles.* These individuals are either engaged or are living together in a committed relationship. The fifth type is the *accomodationist.* This is the person who lives alone and either temporarily or permanently is not dating or romantically involved.

Choice and Circumstances

The second approach looks at whether a person is single voluntarily or involuntarily and whether or not singleness is temporary or permanent (Shostak 1987). The result is four types of singles.

The first type is the *voluntary and temporary singles.* These are younger never-marrieds, divorced, or widowed people who are open to the possibility of marriage or remarriage but who are not actively seeking a mate. They are involved in pursuing an education, a career, or some other interest. Shostak calls these singles the *ambivalents.*

The second type is the *voluntary and permanent singles.* These are people who are committed to being single and have no desire or intention to marry. Roman Catholic priests and nuns would be an example of this group. My own mother has remained single since the death of my father. There was a man who was interested in her, but she had no interest in remarriage. She is content to be single. Women who are successful in demanding careers are often found in this type. These singles are called the *resolveds* by Shostak.

The third type is the *involuntary and temporary singles.* These are never-married, divorced, or widowed individuals who would like to be married or remarried and are seeking a mate. They expect to be married. While some of these people may never marry, it is their desire to be married that puts them in this category. These are the *wishfuls* according to Shostak.

The fourth type is the *involuntary and permanent singles.* These are never-married, divorced, or widowed people who would like to be married

Pairing and Singlehood

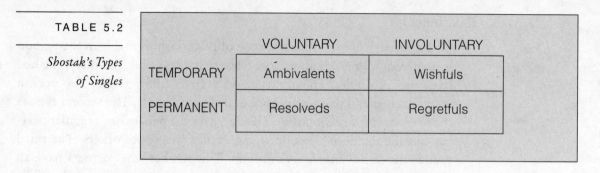

	VOLUNTARY	INVOLUNTARY
TEMPORARY	Ambivalents	Wishfuls
PERMANENT	Resolveds	Regretfuls

but realize they probably never will be married. They are involuntarily single but have accepted the fact that they will probably never marry. This group consists mainly of older divorced or widowed individuals. Shostak calls this group the *regretfuls*.

These four types are really categories, and people can move from one category to another over time. A young woman may be a voluntary and temporary single as she gets her education and launches her career. As the years go by and she moves up the corporate ladder, she may find herself in the involuntary and permanent single category as she realizes the marriage opportunities are dwindling. On the other hand, she may move into the voluntary and permanent single category by consciously deciding to pursue her career rather than marriage.

Regardless of whether people are single voluntarily or involuntarily, being single impacts their lives. After reviewing more than 130 research studies on marital status and personal well-being, Robert H. Coombs (1991) found that singles tend to be in poorer mental and physical heath than married people. Alcoholism and problem drinking is a greater problem for singles. Single people are sick more often and have higher death rates than married people. Singles also have higher incidences of psychiatric problems.

RESIDENCE

While a number of singles live by themselves, most singles are living with other people. Who are singles living with? Basically there are three types of living arrangements.

Parents

More than half of all adults under age 25 are living with their parents, and 12 percent of those between 25 and 34 are still living with their parents

(U.S. Bureau of the Census 1995). Education and the cost of going to school is one reason. More than one-third of all college students and over half of all college freshman are attending community colleges (Farley 1998:349). Many of these students are living at home.

It is interesting that more men than women live at home. In 1993, 59 percent of men age 18–24 lived at home, while only 47 percent of women that age lived at home. Part of the reason for this difference is that parents have often given their daughters less freedom than their sons and required more domestic help from them. Some women have moved out of the home to get out from under their parents' control. Also men tend to be more domestically dependent. Living at home means hot meals and clean laundry.

Roommates

Another living arrangement is a household made up of roommates. The roommates may be of the same sex or mixed sexes. When our daughter was in college, she lived off-campus in an apartment with another female student. When our younger son was in college, he lived off-campus in a house with several other male students. Where we are currently living, a man and woman live next door as roommates. They are not cohabiting or romantically involved, rather they are living together to share the housing costs.

Cohabitation

As we saw in Chapter 4, about four million unmarried couples are living together. Cohabitation is often a short-term living arrangement. One research study found that 39 percent of never-married cohabiting couples lasted less than a year. For cohabiting couples where one or both had been previously married, 30 percent of the relationships lasted less than a year (Bumpass, Sweet, and Cherlin 1991). Another study found that half of cohabiting couples got married (London 1991). So between relationships either breaking up or the couple getting married, cohabitation is generally a temporary living arrangement for singles.

Living Alone

One out of every four households in America consists of a single adult living alone (U.S. Bureau of the Census 1992). About 40 percent of those living alone are males and 60 percent are females. My never-married cousin in his fifties lives by himself. My widowed mother lives by herself as do a couple of my widowed aunts. Senior housing units are over-whelmingly single-adult households.

SINGLE-PARENT FAMILIES

Single-parent families are the fastest growing form of family in the United States. In 1970, 13 percent of children under age 18 lived in a single-par-ent home. By 1995, that number had nearly doubled to 25 percent of chil-dren under age 18 living in single-parent families. Nearly 90 percent of these single-parent families are headed by a female (U.S. Bureau of the Census 1996a).

Creation of Single-Parent Families

Single-parent families are created in three ways: by births to unmarried women, by divorce, and by widowhood. While each of these is a single-parent family, their circumstances differ; therefore we will look at each of them separately.

Unmarried Women

While there are more single-parent families created by divorce, single-parent families created by births to unmarried women are increasing at a higher rate (Burns and Scott 1994). Single women give birth to 30 percent of the babies born in America. Being born to a single mother puts a child at a very high risk for poverty. However, the relationship between being an unwed mother and being in poverty is not as clear as it may seem at first.

The birth rate for single women in poverty is much higher than for single women in general. This is especially true for women between the ages of 14 and 21 (Wu 1996). There are a number of reasons why this is true. One is that poor people are less familiar with, and have less access to, birth control. Another reason is that poor people feel they have less con-trol over their lives, so they tend to take less control. This feeling carries over to pregnancy, so they are less likely to try to prevent a pregnancy. Also poverty affects attitudes toward pregnancy and out-of-wedlock births. To a teenage girl trapped in poverty, having a baby may be a source of self-esteem and respect. It appears that the relationship between poverty and out-of-wedlock births is cyclical.

Singlehood

Divorce

The number one source of single-parent families is divorce. More than 60 percent of all divorces involve couples with children under 18 years of age (Strong, DeVault, and Sayad 1998:529). On the average, white children will spend 30 percent of their childhood in a single-parent family and black children about 60 percent of their childhood.

Divorce generally means a lower income for women with children. Divorced fathers retain almost 90 percent of their predivorce income, whereas household income for divorced women drops about 50 percent (Yorburg 1993:302). The impact of divorce on children will be discussed in Chapter 14.

Widowhood

While widowhood produces the smallest number of single parents, these parents are generally better off than either unwed parents or divorced parents. A divorced mother often receives less help from her own family and little or no help from her former husband's family. Widowed mothers, however, generally receive considerable help from both their own families and their husbands' families. Because our culture still considers unwed mothers as deviant, it is less supportive of never-married mothers. On the other hand, widowed mothers are viewed sympathetically and receive a great deal of support.

Characteristics of Single Parents

Single parents tend to be young: 60 percent are under age 34. They also tend to be less educated: 30 percent have less than four years of high school and another 43 percent have only a high school education. Single parents have lower incomes: 52 percent live below the poverty level, and the unemployment rate for single parents is 42 percent (Yorburg 1993:302–3).

While 25 percent of white children live in single-parent families, 36 percent of Hispanic children and 64 percent of black children live in single-parent families (U.S. Bureau of the Census 1996a). White single mothers are more likely to be divorced, while Hispanic and black single mothers are more likely to never have married. Also Hispanic and black women are more likely than white women to become single mothers by being widowed.

Christians and Single-Parent Families

While Christians believe in premarital chastity and lifelong marriages, the reality is that a number of unmarried Christian women do become pregnant, and the divorce rates for Christians are approaching the national average. The reality is that we are going to see more and more single-parent families in our churches. Gary Collins presents some of the questions single parents face:

1. *How do I parent alone?* This can be stressful and anxiety producing, complicated by concerns about discipline, finding employment, and developing relationships.
2. *Is it okay and normal to feel as lonely as I do? And how long will this last?*
3. *How do I cope with all the demands?*
4. *How will I manage financially?* Single parents who go to many church-based counselors find advice that is long on principles (remember to tithe, don't go into debt) but short on how to manage on a day-to-day basis.
5. *Is there life after divorce?* More than anything else this is an expression of worry about the future.
6. *What will my family become?* Parents worry about the adjustment of their children, how being raised by a single parent will impact their futures, how the family will relate to extended family members, etc.
7. *Am I a strong enough Christian to trust God to meet my needs?* Often single parents feel that their faith is being tested by the pressures, and many wonder if they will fall short.
8. *Will I ever be accepted as a full member of my church? Or will I always carry the label of being different?*
9. *What resources are available to me? Who or what can help me with my finances, finding employment, developing friendships to combat my loneliness, or giving me help with the burdens?* (Collins 1995:195)

What should be our response? Whether the single-parent families are believers or seekers, our response needs to be one of compassion, support, and ministry. Without approving of or condoning out-of-wedlock births or divorce, we can reach out to those who find themselves single parents. The truth is, many of them are already experiencing guilt and remorse.

What they need is acceptance, not of their behavior, but of themselves. They need to hear the good news that God forgives. They need the support and encouragement that a body of believers can uniquely provide.

SINGLES AND THE CHURCH

Single adults need the church, and the church needs single adults. While a church may have a specific singles ministry and special programs and events for singles, it is important not to create a ghetto mentality for singles. They need to be integrated into the life of the church. They need to participate in the church and be involved in its ministry. In every church I have been part of, singles have played an integral role in the church. They have both added to the vitality of the church and personally grown through the experience.

DISCUSSION QUESTIONS

1. If you are single, which of Staple's types of singles are you? Why do you see yourself as that type? If you are not single, think of a single you know. What type is he or she? Why do you see him or her as that type?

2. If you are single, which of Shostak's types of singles are you? Why do you see yourself as that type? If you are not single, think of a single you know. What type is he or she? Why do you see him or her as that type?

3. Why do you think singles tend to be in poorer mental and physical health than married people?

4. When a couple divorce, why do you believe the woman ends up with the children almost 90 percent of the time? Do you believe it should be this way? Why?

5. What do you believe could be done to lower the birth rate for single teenagers?

6. With 44 percent of the adult population single at any given time and single-parent families on the rise, how can the church respond to the needs of singles?

SUGGESTED READING

Greg Cynaumon, *Empowering Single Parents* (Chicago: Moody, 1994). Written by a Christian psychologist, the book deals with handling common problems and issues faced by single parents. The author uses both psychological and biblical insights.

Carolyn N. Koons and Michael J. Anthony, *Single Adult Passages* (Grand Rapids: Baker, 1994). This work is based on a 1,400-person survey that studied single Christians and their adult life stages. The authors bring a biblical and theological perspective to their analysis.

Stacy Rinehart and Paula Rinehart, *Choices,* 2d ed. (Colorado Springs: NavPress, 1996). The authors deal with the issues faced by singles in dating, sex, and courtship. Written from a biblical perspective, the book discusses healthy dating relationships, celibacy, and courtship. The authors recount their own experience as singles who dated, courted, and married.

Harold Sala, *Joyfully Single in a Couples World* (Camp Hill, Pa.: Horizon Books, 1998). The author deals with loneliness, temptation, finances, relationships, and other issues that singles wrestle with. He brings a biblical perspective to these topics.

Marriage

Husband-and-Wife Relationship

The man said, "This is now bone of my bones and flesh of my flesh; she shall be called 'woman,' for she was taken out of man." For this reason a man will leave his father and mother and be united to his wife, and they will become one flesh.

GENESIS 2:23–24

The institution of marriage received a good deal of bad publicity in the 1990s. We have all read the accounts of the rising divorce rate and the stories of wife abuse. We are constantly hearing about the demise of the family. All of this negative press may lead us to question the future of marriage. However, while there are serious problems with many marriages in our society, these problems do not seem to have turned people away from marriage. In fact, today a greater percentage of Americans marry than at any other time in history.

EXTENT OF MARRIAGE

Approximately 90 percent of all Americans will eventually marry, according to the U.S. Census Bureau. This means that most of those reading this book either are married or will be married. While the percentage of Americans who eventually marry has risen steadily since the founding of our nation, the age at which first marriages take place has fluctuated. The median age at first marriage in the United States was 26.1 for men and 22.0 for women in 1890. By 1950, the ages had dropped to 22.8 for men and 20.3 for women. However, since 1960 the age has been climbing steadily, and by 1994 it had reached 26.7 for men and 24.5 for women (see table 6.1).

Marriage

TABLE 6.1	YEAR	MEN	WOMEN
	1890	26.1	22.0
Median Age At	1950	22.8	20.3
First Marriage	1960	22.8	20.3
	1970	23.2	20.8
	1978	24.2	21.8
	1988	25.9	23.6
	1994	26.7	24.5

Season and day also affect the occurrence of marriage. In the United States twice as many marriages occur in June as in February. After June, the next two most popular months for weddings are August and September. January and March have almost as few weddings as February. It is also interesting to note that age at marriage and season interact. It seems that younger couples prefer June, middle-aged couples prefer December, and older couples choose July (Eshleman 1981:406–7). Nevertheless, no matter the age or season, the most popular day, by far, for getting married is Saturday. Over half of all weddings (55 percent) occur on this day.

MARRIAGE AS A CONTRACT

When we think of marriage, we generally think of "being in love" and of romance. We think of commitment and of "becoming one." While marriage may well be all of those things, it is also as much a legal contract as a sales agreement, a promissory note, a deed, or a job contract. In fact, it often has aspects of all of these types of contracts. Marriage is a legal contract between two people and between those two people and the state.

A Contract with the State

We will first consider the contract between the couple and the state. State laws control whom we may marry and under what circumstances. These laws have changed over the years. For example, interracial marriage was prohibited in over half the states until 1966. In that year the Supreme Court struck down such prohibitions. But state laws still control marriage. All states have incest laws that prohibit marriage between close blood relatives—parents and children, brothers and sisters, uncles and nieces, aunts and nephews, and grandparents and grandchildren. Many states do not allow marriage between a half brother and sister or between first cousins. Some states prohibit the marriage of second cousins and in-laws. However, every state prohibits polygamy.

The state also determines the minimum age for marriage, whether there is a waiting period for a marriage license and/or a waiting period after the issuing of the license, and whether or not a blood test is required. State laws are summarized in table 6.2.

State laws also control the financial relationship between a husband and wife. Some states have communal property law where all the assets of the couple, regardless of which person acquired them or whose name they are in, are communal property of the couple. Other states see the assets of each party as separate and belonging to that party. When a couple moves from one state to another, it is the laws of the state in which they reside that apply, not the laws of the state in which they were married.

As a result of the rise of divorce rates, a new type of marriage law called *covenant marriage* has been passed in two states, Louisiana and Arizona, and is being considered by other states. This is an optional form of marriage in those states that have passed the law. A couple may opt for marriage under existing law, or they may opt for a covenant marriage. Covenant marriages require premarital counseling and a two-year separation before divorce or specific grounds for divorce, such as adultery or abuse.

The state also controls the termination of the marriage contract through divorce laws. These laws prescribe the circumstances under which the marriage contract may be terminated. They also direct the distribution of property, the custody of children, and other matters pertaining to the termination of the marriage contract.

A Contract Between Individuals

While marriage is a contract between a couple and the state, it is also a contract between two individuals. In their marriage vows, a couple make certain promises to each other. The nature of these promises varies from ceremony to ceremony. For example, in the traditional wedding vows the woman promises to "love, honor, and obey" her husband. Modern vows used by many couples today usually substitute the phrase "love and cherish." In fact, today many couples write their own vows. Some couples even

TABLE 6.2

State Marriage Laws as of 1997

State or Other Jurisdiction	Age At Which Marriage Can Be Contracted Without Parental Consent		Age At Which Marriage Can Be Contracted With Parental Consent		Maximum Period Between Examination and Issuance of License (Days)	Blood Tests and Other Medical Requirements		
	Male	Female	Male	Female		Scope of Medical Inquiry	Waiting Period Before Issuance of License	Waiting Period After Issuance of License
Alabama	18	18	17(a)	14(a)	30	(b)	…	…
Alaska	18	18	16(c)	16(c)	30	(b)	3 da.	…
Arizona	18	18	16(c)	16(c)	30	(b)	(d)	…
Arkansas	18	18	17(c)	16(c)	30	(b)	3 da.	…
California	18	18	18(a,c)	16(a,c)	30	(b,e,f,g)	…	…
Colorado	18	18	16(c)	16(c)	30	(b,f,h)	…	…
Connecticut	18	18	18(c)	16(c)	35	(b)	4 da.	…
Delaware	18	18	18(c)	16(c)	30	(b)	…	(i)
Florida	18	18	16(a,c)	16(a,c)	30	(b)	3 da.	…
Georgia	18j	18j	16(c,j)	16(c,j)	30	(b,e)	3 da.(k)	…
Hawaii	18	18	16	16(c)	30	(b,f)	(m)	…
Idaho	18	18	16(c)	16(c)	…	(f)	…	…
Illinois	18	18	16(c)	16(c)	15	(b,e)	3 da.	…
Indiana	18	18	17(c)	17(c)	30	(b,e)	3 da.	…
Iowa	18	18	16	16	20	(b)	3 da.	…
Kansas	18	18	18(c)	18(c)	30	(b)	3 da.	…
Kentucky	18	18	(a,o)	(a,o)	15	(b,e)	3 da.	…
Louisiana	18	18	18(c)	16(c)	10	(b)	3 da.	72 hrs.
Maine	18	18	16(c)	16(c)	60	(b)	5 da.	…
Maryland	18	18	18(c)	18(c)	…	…	48 hrs.	…
Massachusetts	18	18	(r)	16	30	(b,f)	3 da.	…
Michigan	18	18	18	16(q)	33	(b)	3 da.	…
Minnesota	18	18	18	16	…	…	5 da.	…
Mississippi	21	21	17(c)	15(c)	30	(b)	3 da.	…
Missouri	18	18	15(c)	15(c)	15	(b)	3 da.	…
Montana	18	18	18(c)	18(c)	20	(b)	5 da.	…
Nebraska	19	19	17	17	30	(b,f)	2 da.	3 da.
Nevada	18	18	16(a,c)	16(a,c)	30(r)	(b)	…	…
New Hampshire	18	18	14(q)	13(q)	30	(b)	3 da.	…
New Jersey	18	18	16(c)	16(c)	30	(b)	72 hrs.	…
New Mexico	18	18	16(c)	16(c)	30	(b,e)	72 hrs.	…
New York	18	18	16	14(s)	30	(b,f,u,v)	…	24 da.(t)
North Carolina	18	18	16	16(c)	30	(b,w)	…	…
North Dakota	18	18	16	16	30	(b)	…	…
Ohio	18	18	18(c)	16(c)	30	(b)	5 da.	…
Oklahoma	18	18	16(c)	16(c)	30	(b)	(m)	…
Oregon	18	18	17	17	30	(b)	…	(a,b)

State								
Pennsylvania	18	18	16(c)	16(c)	30	(b,y)	3 da.	...
Rhode Island	18	18	18(c)	16(c)	40	(b,f,v)	24 hrs.	...
South Carolina	18	18	16(c)	14(c)	...	...	...	...
South Dakota	18	18	16(c)	16(c)	20	(b)	...	...
Tennessee	18	18	16(c)	16(c)	30	(b)	3 da.(ab)	
Texas	18	18	14(c)	14(c)	21	(b)	...	
Utah	18	18	16(a)	14(a)	30	(b)	...	
Vermont	18	18	16(c)	16(c)	30	(b)	...	5 da.
Virginia	18	18	16(a,c)	16(a,c)	30	(b)	...	
Washington	18	18	17(c)	17(c)	...	(b,r,aa)	3 da.	
West Virginia	18	18	(q)	(o)	30	(b)	3 da.	
Wisconsin	18	18	16	16	20	(b)	5 da.	
Wyoming	19	19	17(c)	16(c)	30	(b)	...	
District of Columbia	18	18	16(a)	16(a)	30	(b)	3 da.	
Puerto Rico	21	21	18(c)	16(c)	10(ab)	(b,aa)	...	

(a) Parental consent not required if previously married.
(b) Venereal diseases.
(c) Legal procedure for younger persons to obtain license.
(d) Blood test must be on record at least 48 hours before issuance of license.
(e) Sickle cell anemia.
(f) Rubella immunity.
(g) Tay-Sachs disease.
(h) Rh factor.
(i) Residents, 24 hours; nonresidents, 96 hours.
(j) Parental consent is not needed regardless of age in case of pregnancy or when couple has a living child born out of wedlock.
(k) Unless parties are 18 years of age or over, or woman is pregnant, or applicants are the parents of a living child born out of wedlock.
(l) Generally no, but may be recognized for limited purposes, e.g., legitimacy of children, workers' compensation benefits, etc.
(m) Three days if parties are under 18 years of age.
(n) However, contracting such a marriage is a misdemeanor.
(o) No minimum age.
(p) No provision in the law for parental consent for males.
(q) Permission of judge also required.
(r) Maximum period between blood test and date of intended marriage.
(s) If under 16 years of age, consent of family court judge also required.
(t) However, marriage may not be solemnized within 3 days of date on which specimen for blood test was taken.
(u) Mental competence.
(v) Tuberculosis.
(w) Some marriages prohibited if a party is severely retarded.
(x) License valid 3 days after application signed and valid for 30 days thereafter.
(y) Court order needed if party is weak-minded, insane, or of unsound mind.
(aa) Affidavit of mental competence required. Also, no epilepsy in Puerto Rico.
(ab) Maximum time from blood test to expiration of license.

Source: World Almanac and Book of Facts 1998:735

Marriage

enter marriage with written contracts stating responsibilities, property distribution, and other matters. The legality of these contracts, particularly if they are not consistent with state law, is still very much in question.

The thing that is of interest to me is that most people enter a marriage in total ignorance of their state's laws and the specific things they are contracting to perform. Usually a couple's only concern is with minimum ages (if they are young), blood tests, and waiting periods. Most couples think of their marriage as a romantic and religious occasion and are unaware that they are also entering a legal contract with each other and with the state.

Frequently, Christians also see marriage as a contract between a couple and God. They view their vows not only as promises to each other but also as promises to God. These Christians see God, through his Word, giving responsibilities and principles for the couple to carry out in their life together. I believe that marriage is a commitment made before God and that he has given believers guidelines for living together. Some of these guidelines will be explored in this chapter, and others will be examined in later chapters.

GENDER ROLES

That men and women often think differently, behave differently, and respond differently is beyond debate. Such best-selling books as *Men Are from Mars, Women Are from Venus* (Gray 1992) and *He Says, She Says* (Glass 1992) document these differences. The debate involves how much of this difference is genetic and how much is cultural.

Sociologists distinguish between the terms *gender* and *sex*. *Sex* refers to the biological differences between males and females. *Gender* refers to the socially learned or cultural differences that produce masculinity and femininity. The behaviors that are learned and expected of persons based on their sex are called *gender roles*.

The nature versus nurture debate has raged in the behavioral sciences through the years. How much of our behavior is genetically determined, and how much is socially shaped? This debate carries over into the differences between women and men.

Masculinity and Femininity

While our sex—that is, maleness and femaleness—is innate, our gender—that is, masculinity and femininity—is learned. While there are biologi-

Husband-and-Wife Relationship

cal differences between males and females (see table 6.3), the ongoing debate concerns the effect of these differences on behavior. Sandra Bem, a social psychologist, developed a test for measuring masculine and feminine trait characteristics (1977). The test consists of twenty traditionally masculine characteristics and twenty traditionally feminine characteristics. The test also contains twenty neutral characteristics as filler items (see table 6.4 for all the items). American college students rated the items as masculine, feminine, and neutral. Are these characteristics innate or learned?

Sociologists are generally agreed that the characteristics listed in table 6.4 are primarily learned. One of the strongest evidences supporting this conclusion is that behaviors considered masculine in one culture may be

TABLE 6.3

Normal Biological Sex Differences

MALE	FEMALE	CHARACTERISTIC
XY sex chromosomes	XX chromosomes	Sex is determined by sperm bearing X or Y chromosome uniting with X bearing ovum
Androgens (testosterone)	Estrogens	Male and female sex hormones
Penis	Clitoris	Erectile genitals
Scrotum	Vulva	Sensitive, soft external genitalia
Testes	Ovaries	Paired gonads producing male and female hormones and germ cells
Spermatozoa	Ovum	Germ cells produced by testes and ovaries
Vas deferens	Fallopian tubes	Tubes for carrying germ cells from gonads
Facial, body, and pubic hair	Pubic hair	Adult characteristics
Strong, heavy muscles	Fatty layer beneath skin over smaller muscles	Adult body development
Narrow hips, broad shoulders	Broad hips, sloping shoulders, developed breasts	Adult body shape
Source: Adapted from Duvall 1977:6		

	MASCULINE ITEMS	FEMININE ITEMS	NEUTRAL ITEMS
TABLE 6.4	Acts as a leader	Affectionate	Adaptable
	Aggressive	Cheerful	Conceited
Masculine, Feminine,	Ambitious	Childlike	Conscientious
and Neutral Items	Analytical	Compassionate	Conventional
on the Bem Sex-Role	Assertive	Does not use harsh	Friendly
Inventory		language	
	Athletic	Eager to soothe	Happy
		hurt feelings	
	Competitive	Feminine	Helpful
	Defends own beliefs	Flatterable	Inefficient
	Dominant	Gentle	Jealous
	Forceful		Gullible
	Likable		
	Has leadership abilities	Loves children	Moody
	Independent	Loyal	Reliable
	Individualistic	Sensitive to the needs	Secretive
		of others	
	Makes decisions easily	Shy	Sincere
	Masculine	Soft-spoken	Solemn
	Self-reliant	Sympathetic	Tactful
	Self-sufficient	Tender	Theatrical
	Strong personality	Understanding	Truthful
	Willing to take a stand	Warm	Unpredictable
	Willing to take risks	Yielding	Unsystematic

Note: Items in each column are listed alphabetically.

Source: Adapted from Bem 1977:208

considered feminine in another culture. For example, among the Tchambuli of Indonesia, women are dominant and impersonal, while men are dependent and emotional. In the Marquesas Islands, males are the primary child-care agents because they believe "women are not maternally inclined" (Vander Zanden 1979:330). If sex determined behavior, masculinity and femininity should be the same in every culture. The fact that gender roles vary greatly from culture to culture indicates that most behaviors we consider masculine or feminine are learned.

Gender Role Socialization

We have seen that while sex is determined by birth, masculinity and femininity are learned. We acquire our gender roles by the process of socialization. This process begins at birth. I have two sons and a daughter. When my sons were born, they were wrapped in blue blankets, whereas my daughter was wrapped in a pink blanket. Why was this done? Was it so the hospital personnel would know how to treat them? Researchers have found that caretakers will play rougher with a male infant than with a female infant. On the other hand, they will talk more with a female infant than with a male infant. However, male infants receive more physical contact than female infants (Orthner 1981:170). When my infant sons were brought home from the hospital, friends and relatives gave them trucks and balls. When my daughter arrived home from the hospital, she received dolls and frilly outfits.

Television plays a significant role in the socialization of children. If you observe television programs, and particularly commercials, you will see a great deal of gender-role stereotyping. What different roles do women and men play? As long as children see men fixing cars, driving trucks, and performing surgery and women preparing supper, washing clothes, worrying about "static cling," and working as secretaries and nurses, they will be socialized to accept these traditional gender roles.

Parents, teachers, and peers also play important roles in the socialization process. The roles and attitudes of parents have a profound effect on children. Parents are the earliest role models children are exposed to. Teachers also have a profound influence. Research indicates that many teachers and guidance counselors continue to direct students into courses and programs that will prepare them for traditional gender roles and occupations (Farley 1998:123). While gender roles are changing, socialization is the major determiner of the direction and extent of the change.

Traditional Roles

Traditional husband/wife roles are based on what sociologists call division of labor. In traditional roles, division of labor is highly specialized. That is, certain jobs are considered women's work and certain jobs are considered men's work. Generally, men's work consists of tasks such as maintaining the family car, cutting the grass, shoveling the snow, making major repairs of the house, paying the bills, and being the final decision-maker. Women's tasks consist of primary child care, meal preparation, maintaining the home, and being submissive. The more traditional couples are in their roles, the more specialized the roles become. I know a college professor who will not even load a dishwasher because he believes that it is his wife's responsibility. The next time you are visiting in someone's home, observe who prepares and serves the meal and who cleans up after the meal. Is there any discussion of who should do it, or does one person automatically assume it is his/her responsibility?

Changing Roles

While many people are content with traditional husband-wife roles, others are not. They see traditional gender roles as limiting. They would prefer to see marriage as a partnership in which both the husband and wife provide the support and both keep the home and care for the children.

For several years I have administered to my sociology classes the Attitudes Toward Women Scale, a test that indicates a person's attitudes toward the roles of women. Each year the females have indicated significantly more liberated attitudes toward female gender roles than the males. However, on the whole, the attitudes of both males and females have become more liberated each year. It will be interesting to see the types of husband-wife roles that develop as these students begin to marry.

The most fundamental change in roles in marriage has been the number of married women in the workforce. Nearly 70 percent of married women are employed outside the home. With women in the workforce, their role as mothers is changing. Traditionally, mothers provided primary child care for their children. When mothers enter the workforce, they share this responsibility with baby-sitters, child-care workers, camp counselors, and other service personnel and agencies.

Another change is that husbands have taken on more domestic responsibilities. In most families, wives are seen as primarily responsible for domestic chores. However, husbands are getting more involved and picking up more responsibility. Also power and decision making are becoming more equal. While marriage is moving from a hierarchical relationship to more of a partner relationship, the husband is still often seen as the senior partner.

While some attitudes and areas of the husband-wife relationship have changed in recent years, very few couples have a truly equal marriage. Most marriages still carry over many of the vestiges of traditional marriages. Ellen Goodman catches the subtleties of it for us in an editorial that appeared in the October 30, 1981, issue of the *Minneapolis Tribune:*

> The TV ad is cheerfully maternalistic, a mother and daughter special. In a mere 60 seconds, we see the passing of eternal wisdom from one generation of women to the next.

It begins as we discover that the girl has bought—gasp!—a bargain bleach. This turns out to be more a cause of pity than for censure. Mother, who knows best about washing, explains gently that a bargain is not always a bargain, especially when it is used on a favorite blouse.

By the end of the commercial, the girl has become wise in the ways of brand-name bleaches, and we have become wise in the ways we really live in our changing families.

The commercial is not more inane than any other, but there is a new character in the advertising soap opera: the commercial geared to the teenage girl as family shopper. The advertising people are hip to something. As more and more mothers go to work, we are looking for more and more help at home . . . from our daughters. . . .

In this laundry-room scene, there is neither father nor brother. Mother and daughter share the laundry and the shopping. It is still women's work . . . and girl's work. . . .

And in that scenario, a great deal more is passed down from mother to daughter than the brand name of a bleach.

Looking at the social research and observing marriages around us, we find that marriages are changing. We conclude that husbands are becoming more involved in household tasks, that more wives are entering the labor force, and that child care is being shared or delegated. However with all these changes, the traditional model of marriage still prevails in American culture. When a husband does household chores or child care, he generally sees himself as helping his wife as opposed to meeting his responsibilities. Many women in the labor force are seen as supplementing the family income rather than pursuing a career. In other words, while a great deal of observable behavior has changed in recent years, it appears that changes in attitudes and beliefs and thus significant role changes are following more slowly.

HUSBAND AND WIFE ROLES AND THE BIBLE

As Christians, we turn to God's Word to find principles to guide us in establishing our norms and values. However, there seems to be a great deal of disagreement among Christians on what the Bible teaches about the husband-wife relationship. Some believers understand the Scriptures to teach a traditional model of family life; others find support for a partnership model of marriage. We will examine both perspectives and their implications.

Traditional Marriage

Those who believe that the Scriptures teach that the traditional marriage is the model for Christians hold a position that sees the husband as the head of the home, the final authority, and the leader, while the wife is to be submissive to that authority and leadership. Larry Christenson explains this position:

> God has ordered the family according to the principle of "headship." Each member of the family lives under the authority of the "head" whom God has appointed.
>
> The husband lives under the authority of Christ and is responsible to Christ for the leadership and care of the family. The wife lives under the authority of her husband, and is responsible to him for the way she orders the household and cares for the children.... The authority over the children, however, remains essentially one ... the authority of the mother is a derived authority. She exercises authority over the children on behalf of and in the place of her husband....
>
> Thus God has structured the family along clear-cut lines of authority and responsibility.... God has made the well-being and happiness of the family absolutely dependent upon the observance of His divinely appointed order. (1970:17–17)

There are a number of Scripture passages to which those holding to this position appeal. One of these is Genesis 2:18: "And the LORD God said, It is not good that the man should be alone; I will make him an help meet for him" (AV). It is argued that the husband is in authority both because he was created first and because the woman was created to be his helper (i.e., assistant).

Another verse in Genesis that is appealed to is 3:16: "Your desire will be for your husband, and he will rule over you." This verse is understood as a commandment setting up God's order for family life after the Fall.

The mainstay of the traditionalists' argument from Scripture, however, is Ephesians 5:22–31:

> Wives, submit to your husbands as to the Lord. For the husband is the head of the wife as Christ is the head of the church, his body, of which he is the Savior. Now as the church submits to Christ, so also wives should submit to their husbands in everything.
>
> Husbands, love your wives, just as Christ loved the church and gave himself up for her to make her holy, cleansing her by the washing with water through the word, and to present her to himself as a radiant church, without stain or wrinkle or any other blemish, but holy and blameless.

Husband-and-Wife Relationship

In this same way, husbands ought to love their wives as their own bodies. He who loves his wife loves himself. After all, no one ever hated his own body, but he feeds and cares for it, just as Christ does the church—for we are members of his body. "For this reason a man will leave his father and mother and be united to his wife, and the two will become one flesh." This is a profound mystery—but I am talking about Christ and the church. However, each one of you also must love his wife as he loves himself, and the wife must respect her husband.

Let us see how those that hold to a traditional view of marriage understand these verses. Gene Getz writes:

> Though Eve was created as Adam's counterpart, it was God's plan that man was to be the head administrator in the home. Throughout the Old Testament days, this was the pattern for governing family affairs. During the New Testament times, this principle was reaffirmed and illustrated by Christ's relationship to the church. (1972:25)

Kenneth Gangel believes that a biblical husband is a ruler. He says, "All arguments regarding the equalization of the sexes fade into nonsense when one looks into the Word of God" (1972:39). He adds, "The quality of 'headship' certainly refers to the deciding voice in the family" (1972:40). Henry Brandt and Phil Landrum follow the same line of reasoning. Discussing Ephesians 5:22, they say that in any family decision "the husband has the last word" (1976:98). They go on to say, "It is the husband's duty to see to it that objectives, policies, procedures and rules are set up and carried out" (1976:100).

Those who hold the traditional position argue that while the husband is to be the leader and the final authority in the home, this does not mean that he is to be an autocratic dictator or his wife a servant. They point out that this passage teaches that the husband is to exercise his authority in love. Howard Hendricks summarizes this view for us:

> The husband is to be the head of the home; he is also to be the heart of the home. It is his leadership which provides authority; it is his heart that provides affection. One without the other always leads to distortion. He is to be a leader; he is to be a lover.
>
> If the husband is a leader without being a lover, he is an autocratic individual; if he is a lover without being a leader, he will be a sentimentalist. If he has leadership with love, no woman in her right mind resists placing herself willingly and submissively under a man who loves her as Christ loved the Church. (1973:34)

Marriage

Jack Taylor writes in his book *One Home Under God:*

> No organization can function properly without submission. Submission suggests authority. The whole of nature operates on authority and submission. To take these factors away would be to destroy the whole realm of nature. God has ordered the wife to be submissive to her husband, that is to yield to his authority. That is her God-given role. Wife, don't try to figure out this matter of submission. Lead with your heart and receive the capacity of submission as a perfect gift from God. (1974:24)

Another passage that those with the traditional view hold to is 1 Peter 3:1–7:

> Wives, in the same way be submissive to your husbands so that, if any of them do not believe the word, they may be won over without words by the behavior of their wives, when they see the purity and reverence of your lives. Your beauty should not come from outward adornment, such as braided hair and the wearing of gold jewelry and fine clothes. Instead, it should be that of your inner self, the unfading beauty of a gentle and quiet spirit, which is of great worth in God's sight. For this is the way the holy women of the past who put their hope in God used to make themselves beautiful. They were submissive to their own husbands, like Sarah, who obeyed Abraham and called him her master. You are her daughters if you do what is right and do not give way to fear.
>
> Husbands, in the same way be considerate as you live with your wives, and treat them with respect as the weaker partner and as heirs with you of the gracious gift of life, so that nothing will hinder your prayers.

Commenting on this passage as it relates to marriage in our day, Kenneth Gangel reasons as follows:

> There is no question that the fifty-fifty marriage makes sense in terms of today's social mores and cultural values. It remains to be demonstrated, however, that such an emphasis can fit in harmony with the pattern of the Word of God. This is not to say that Scripture suggests that the husband is a brutal dictator in his home. The husband honors his wife as "the weaker vessel," loves her as part of his own body, and her proper response is a regular submission to his leadership. (1972:44)

Summarizing the position of those that hold a traditional view of marriage, we see that they understand the Scriptures to teach that it is God's plan for the husband to be the final authority in the home and that the wife is to submit to that authority. While the traditionalists believe that his authority is to be exercised in love, they still see it as final and absolute. Some exponents of the traditional view also associate role behavior with their understanding of this position. They will advocate, for example, that the husband should handle the family finances, since he is the "head" of the home.

On the other hand, when we examine the views of those who hold to a partnership model of marriage, we discover that they also appeal to the Bible and often to the same passages as the traditionalists.

Partnership Marriage

Those holding to a partnership marriage begin the defense of their position with the creation accounts as do the traditionalists. However, they generally begin with Genesis 1:26–28:

> Then God said, "Let us make man in our image, in our likeness, and let them rule over the fish of the sea and the birds of the air, over the livestock, over all the earth, and over all the creatures that move along the ground." So God created man in his own image, in the image of God he created him; male and female he created them.
> God blessed them and said to them, "Be fruitful and increase in number; fill the earth and subdue it. Rule over the fish of the sea and the birds of the air and over every living creature that moves on the ground."

Believers holding the partnership position note that both men and women are created in the image of God, both are blessed by God, both are given the commission to procreate, and both are given dominion over nature. Pat Gundry, commenting on these verses, points out that "there is no differentiation of power or position, no order or hierarchy established here" (1980:82).

We have seen that those who hold to a traditional view of marriage appeal to the creation account recorded in Genesis 2:18–24. The exponents of partnership marriage counter that this passage in general and verse 18 in particular have been misinterpreted. Gundry helps us understand verse 18 when she writes:

> The words *help* and *meet* in the King James Version translate two Hebrew words, *ezer* and *neged*. The word *ezer* ("help") is never used in the Bible to refer to a subordinate helper but is used in reference to God as our Helper as in Psalms 121:1, 2. The word *neged* is a preposition in Hebrew, but the most accurate way to translate it into English is by giving it a meaning such as "corresponding to." ... The idea is that Eve was an appropriate, fitting partner for Adam. (1977:20)

It is interesting to note that these two Hebrew words are translated *paraclete* in the Septuagint (a Greek translation of the Old Testament in use at the time of Christ). This word, *paraclete,* is the same word Jesus uses in John 14:16 to speak of the Holy Spirit as a helper.

Looking at the larger context, Scanzoni and Hardesty (1975:26) say that God brought all the animals to Adam, not because he thought the man might find a "helper" among them, but rather to demonstrate to the man that he would never be satisfied with an inferior creature. When the man realized that he would be satisfied only with an equal, God created the woman for him.

Looking at the "one flesh" concept in verse 24, Herbert and Fern Miles write:

> One flesh is a total relationship of the whole person of the husband to the total person of his wife, and the whole person of the wife to the total person of her husband. One flesh affects the whole self of both husband and wife. The two become one, yet they remain two separate individuals. Each and every succeeding act of intercourse continues, maintains, and renews the one-flesh unity. . . .
>
> It is difficult to imagine how the hierarchy doctrine of husband-dominant/wife-submissive relationship could make any contribution to this sacred act. Equality, on the other hand, tends to encourage sharing and giving, and thereby eliminates problems and discord prevalent where one mate is dominant. The one-flesh unity is in direct conflict with the dominant/subordinate concept. (1978:165)

Some traditionalists agree with those holding the partnership view up to this point, but they argue that the Fall brought into being a new order according to Genesis 3:16. Responding to the traditionalists' argument, Prohl explains:

> God is not here issuing a special commandment, "Be thou ruled by him!" or, "Thou shalt not rule!" But here in Genesis 3:16 we have a statement, a prediction, a prophecy, of how man, degenerated by sin, would take advantage of his headship as husband to dominate, lord it over, his wife. Nowhere in the Bible is Genesis 3:16 quoted or referred to as establishing a general subordination of woman to man. (1957:39, in Scanzoni and Hardesty 1975:35)

Those holding the partnership view point out that people who use Genesis 3:16 to teach the subordination of women to their husbands never address Genesis 3:18–19 in relation to the use of herbicides, air conditioning, and other devices for overcoming the consequences of the Fall.

Next we will turn to Ephesians 5. As we have seen, the traditionalists begin their discussion with verse 22. This is not hard to understand since some translations begin a new paragraph with verse 22 (e.g., NASB, NIV) and most translations begin a new sentence at that point. Supporters of the partnership position are quick to point out that this is a bias in the translation. In the Greek text the word *submit* is not found in verse 22, for that verse is a subordinate clause without a verb. The translators have added the verb from verse 21, which reads, "Submit to one another out of reverence for Christ." Grammatically, it is very difficult to separate verse 21 from 22. Gundry explains, "Mutual submission was a principle given to guide relationships between all believers. The verses following verse 21 tell how to work it out" (1980:95).

Those interpreting this passage to support partnership marriage appeal to a basic rule of hermeneutics—a passage must be understood in light of its cultural context. Examining the cultural context, we find that "Ionia was a conquered province, under sway of Rome, and the law of *Patria Potestas* held the husband responsible for the conduct of his wife; he was amenable for her offenses.... Roman law made the husband the sole and absolute head of his wife. His will was her law; from his decision there was no appeal (Starr 1955:246, in Gundry 1977:72). Commenting on this cultural context, Gundry says:

> If a wife was already subject, why say it to her at all? The answer is in "as to the Lord."... The extent of their subjection was already legally established; it was their *manner* Paul was talking about.... If the wife imitated the manner of the church in serving Christ, it would be a loving, respectful service without evil motive or hidden barb.... The husband was to also work out his mutual submission to his wife by using his absolute legal power over her, not to his own advantage, but as Christ exercises His power over the church, as Savior of the body. Again, it was his manner that would turn his advantage into service and loving protection, not dictatorship or authoritarianism. The "headship" concept expressed here is one of loving service and care, not one of domination. (1977:73)

Stewart deals with this passage in the following way:

> Does one interpret this that man is lord of the creation and woman his slave?... It is better, I believe, to see in the analogy of the servanthood of

Christ, the authority which the male has with his wife.... The man does not dominate the woman but ministers to her, as Christ ministers to the church. So the wife may also minister having a stake in leadership.... The motive is not power but love, and finds its source in Christ, whose suffering service blots out our sins, our aggrandizement, and our status-seeking. (1970:207)

Finally, we will look at 1 Peter 3:1–7 and see how those who hold the partnership position understand this passage. Again, the cultural context needs to be examined. According to 1 Peter 1:1 this epistle is written to those who reside as aliens, "scattered throughout Pontus, Galatia, Cappadocia, Asia and Bithynia." These aliens were Jewish Christians living outside of Palestine in a Greek province with Greek customs, but under Roman law and government. The time is, most likely, after the destruction of Jerusalem (A.D. 70), and the believers are suffering much persecution (1 Peter 1:6; 2:12, 20; 3:17; 4:12–16; 5:10). Apparently they were also being falsely accused of many evil practices (1 Peter 2:12, 20; 4:14–15).

Looking at the passage under consideration, Gundry interprets 1 Peter 3:1–2 as follows: "Roman law placed women under the complete control of their husbands. Thus, Christian wives were in a position to be easily persecuted and mistreated by unbelieving husbands. A woman might greatly desire to see her husband converted but have little power to influence him in religious matters. Peter says, in effect, 'Actions speak louder than words'" (1977:82).

In verses 3 to 5, Peter seems to be saying, "Be as concerned with your personhood as with your appearance." He was telling the women that they should attempt to impress their husbands not so much with their physical appearance as with their personhood. It has been suggested that this is the opposite of what is advocated in some works such as *The Total Woman* (Morgan 1973).

Commenting on verse 6, Gundry states: "The reference to Sarah is unfortunately not translated accurately in most versions, so the import is lost. The word usually rendered 'lord' or 'master' is better translated 'sir,' for it was a term of respect, not servitude. Sarah treated her husband with respect and addressed him with respect" (1977:82–83).

In verse 7, Peter is saying to husbands that in spite of their physical and legal (in that culture) advantage over their wives, they were to treat them as "fellow-heirs." Again, what from a twentieth-century American perspective looks like a teaching of hierarchy, when studied in its cultural context becomes a teaching of husband-wife equality, according to the partnership perspective.

Summarizing the partnership position, we see that those holding this view believe that the Scriptures teach husband-wife equality. They understand the Bible to teach mutual submission as opposed to dominance-submission. They believe that it is God's intention for married couples to live together as partners.

It is important for us to realize that the debate is not between those who accept God's Word as authoritative and those who reject it. Those in both camps believe in the inspiration of Scripture and its authority. The debate does not involve the *authority* of the Bible; it involves the *interpretation* of the Bible. It is my conviction that many in both camps are sincere Christians seeking to follow God's Word.

Equality and Submission

John C. Howell, in a book entitled *Equality and Submission in Marriage* (1979), sees the traditional marriage and the partnership marriage as two ends of a continuum rather than as a dichotomy. He says that a couple may be anywhere along that continuum in their relationship (see figure 6.1). He then makes what I consider to be a significant point. He says:

> Generally couples establish their pattern of relating during the first eighteen months of marriage. Many couples will continue to live out the style of relationship they found satisfactory in those early months. . . . If the relationship has been formed on the independent-dependent style but has retained the essential characteristics of love and respect, the couple can be very happy in the marriage. . . . This marriage is toward the right end of the marital spectrum. If the relationship has been formed on a mutually interdependent style with full affirmation of the equality of the mates in status and role definition, it will be at the left of the spectrum. But many marriages will result in a blending of these styles in such a way that they will not be fully traditional or fully companionship. . . . Its actual position will be subject to some fluctuation based on differing role expectations. The important consideration is that [each of these marriages is] Christian. Under the guidance of the Holy Spirit and in their commitment to building a Christian marriage, couples are free to work out role relationships which meet their own personality needs. (1979:129–30)

I appreciate the point that Howell makes. I believe that as Christians we should not attempt to force our own personal model of marriage on

Marriage

FIGURE 6.1

Marital Spectrum

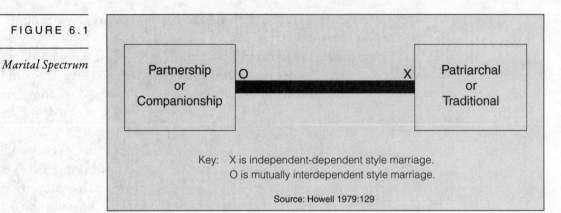

Key: X is independent-dependent style marriage.
O is mutually interdependent style marriage.

Source: Howell 1979:129

others. Nor should we question a couple's motives or spirituality based on the position on the spectrum where their marriage is located. My wife and I are a little more to the partnership end of the spectrum. That is the model of marriage that works best for us and that we are most comfortable with. However, I have friends who have a more traditional marriage. They appear to be as happy and satisfied as we are, and they also seem to be fine Christians. The point is that before God we need to develop a model of marriage with our spouse that we believe honors God and meets our needs. True liberation does not consist of moving people from one set of role expectations to another set. That is only exchanging one prison cell for another. True liberation allows people to pick the place on the spectrum where they are most comfortable. In this whole area, Paul's advice in Romans 14:4 is quite appropriate: "Who are you to judge someone else's servant? To his own master he stands or falls. And he will stand, for the Lord is able to make him stand."

At this point I can imagine the frustration that some readers may be experiencing. They may be saying, "Partnership marriage and traditional marriage cannot both be taught in Scripture. If one is right, then the other is wrong." Which one is right? It is my conviction that God gives us more latitude in conducting our lives than we allow ourselves and each other in many cases. I really appreciate Paul's discussion in Romans 14. One person abstains from eating meat, whereas another eats meat; one person observes certain days, and another does not. Paul's concern is not with who is right and who is wrong. His concern is with their motivation. If they are doing it to honor the Lord, God will accept it (Rom. 14:3–6). I am not arguing that the ends justify the means. There are things in the

Bible that are clearly wrong, and if they are done God will never honor them. However, in areas where there are sincere differences of interpretation between believers who are faithfully attempting to follow God's Word as they understand it, I believe that even in cases where one view may be in some absolute sense "more correct" than another, God will accept both parties. Rather than being divided on which model of marriage is most accurate, we should be united in the effort of developing and strengthening Christian homes.

DISCUSSION QUESTIONS

1. Why do you think the age of first marriage has been rising since 1960?

2. Do you believe a husband should be the primary wage earner in the family and that the wife should be primarily responsible for the home and child care? Why?

3. To what extent do you believe television in general and commercials in particular influence gender roles? To what degree do you believe they reflect current values? Why?

4. In your opinion, why do college females have more liberated attitudes toward gender roles than college males?

5. How do you account for the fact that today more couples are moving away from the traditional model of marriage toward a partnership model? Is this trend good or bad? Why?

6. What is your understanding of the Bible's teaching on the husband-wife relationship?

SUGGESTED READING

Kaye Cook and Lee Lance, *Man and Woman* (Grand Rapids: Baker, 1996). The authors look at modern gender roles in the home and the workplace. They discuss gender roles in the dating relationship and the marriage relationship.

Marriage

Peter DeJong and Donald R. Wilson, *Husband and Wife: The Sexes in Scripture and Society* (Grand Rapids: Zondervan, 1979). Written by evangelical sociologists, the book deals with the biological and social antecedents of gender roles from a Christian perspective. The authors support a partnership model of marriage.

Patricia Gundry, *Heirs Together* (Grand Rapids: Zondervan, 1980). This book represents the partnership model of marriage. The author explores what she sees as the inadequacies of the traditional position and lays out her arguments for husband-wife equality from a biblical perspective.

John C. Howell, *Equality and Submission in Marriage* (Nashville: Broadman, 1979). The author examines the concepts of equality and submission from a biblical perspective. While he favors the partnership model, he argues for understanding and acceptance among believers over this issue.

Human Sexuality

How delightful is your love, my sister, my bride!
*   How much more pleasing is your love than wine,*
and the fragrance of your perfume than any spice!
You are a garden locked up, my sister, my bride.
Let my lover come into his garden
*   and taste its choice fruits.*

SONG OF SONGS 4:10, 12, 16

Marriage is both a legal and a social relationship, as we saw in the preceding chapter. However, it is more than that; it is also a physical relationship. The Bible says that a husband and wife "become one flesh" (Gen. 2:24). Sex is an important aspect of our humanity and a foundational aspect of marriage. The Bible has a great deal to say about human sexuality in general and sex in marriage in particular. In dealing with a topic such as human sexuality, we need to begin with a biblical perspective.

THE BIBLE AND HUMAN SEXUALITY

We have already seen that God has created us as sexual beings: "Male and female he created them" (Gen. 1:27), and that he ordained sex: "Be fruitful and increase" (Gen. 1:28) and "A man will . . . be united to his wife, and they will become one flesh" (Gen. 2:24). All of these pronouncements were made *before* the Fall. Sex is not a consequence of sin or an accommodation to our sinful nature. Sex is part of the original design; it is part of what God declared "very good" (Gen. 1:31). It is true that the Fall and human sinfulness have resulted in the perversion, misuse, and abuse of sex; however, that does not diminish its original purpose.

Sex is a physical bonding between a husband and wife; it is a physical act that expresses their spiritual and social unity. Sex is a means for them to give and receive pleasure; it is the most intimate and personal sharing of one another. Speaking of the one-flesh experience, the Penners explain, "The scripture is talking about that mystical union between husband and wife that includes the emotional, physical, and spiritual—*the total person*" (1981:41).

God created us as sexual beings to enjoy and find pleasure in each other as husband and wife. The LaHayes write, "The idea that God designed our sex organs for our enjoyment comes almost as a surprise to some people" (1976:11). The Wheats expand on this point:

> God's plan for our pleasure has never changed, and we realize this even more as we consider how we are "fearfully and wonderfully made" (Psalms 139:14). When we discover the many intricate details of our bodies which provide so many intense, wonderful physical sensations for husbands and wives to enjoy together, we can be sure that He intended for us to experience full satisfaction in the marriage relationship. (1977:17)

The Old Testament speaks of the pleasurable nature of sex in Proverbs 5:18–19: "May your fountain be blessed, and may you rejoice in the wife of your youth. A loving doe, a graceful deer—may her breasts satisfy you always, may you ever be captivated by her love." The New Testament has the same emphasis. In 1 Corinthians 7:3–4 Paul writes, "The husband should fulfill his marital duty to his wife, and likewise the wife to her husband. The wife's body does not belong to her alone but also to her husband. In the same way, the husband's body does not belong to him alone but also to his wife." It is interesting to note that both husband and wife have a marital duty to each other, and both are to enjoy each other.

The sanctity of sex in marriage is emphasized in Hebrews 13:4: "Marriage should be honored by all, and the marriage bed kept pure." Commenting on this verse, the LaHayes (1976:13) point out that the Greek word for "bed" is *koite* and means "cohabitation by implanting the male sperm." Sex in marriage is God-sanctioned and God-ordained. Our sexuality and our sexual organs were created by God to unite a man and woman in marriage.

HUMAN REPRODUCTIVE ANATOMY

As we have seen, God created us as sexual creatures. Foundational to understanding our sexuality and the role of sex in marriage is a basic understanding of our reproductive systems. Also, a grasp of proper terminology will facilitate later discussions.

The Male Reproductive System

The male reproductive system consists of the male genitals, the penis and the scrotum; and internal glands, the testicles and the prostate gland. Each of these organs will be briefly described and their functions explained. See figure 7.1 for a cross-sectional view of the male reproductive system.

Penis

The *penis* contains three columns or tubes of spongy erectile tissue. Two larger tubes, the *corpora cavernosa,* sit astride the third, the *corpus spongiosum.* The *urethra* runs through the corpus spongiosum. When a male becomes sexually aroused, these three columns fill with blood from the many arteries that permeate the penis. At the same time, the veins in the penis constrict, trapping the blood in the columns and causing the penis to become erect. While the size of flaccid or unstimulated penises varies significantly, erect penises are usually about the same size, approximately six inches in length (Strong et al. 1981:42). God created males with the

FIGURE 7.1

Cross Section of the Male Reproductive System

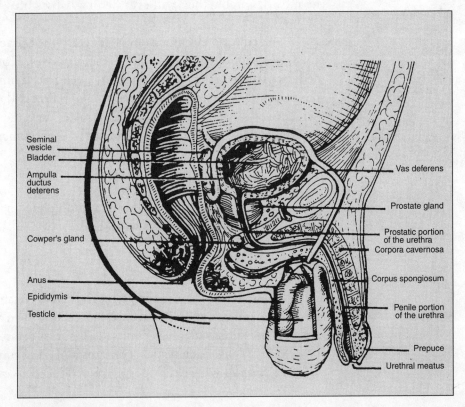

capacity for erection of the penis to permit penetration of the vagina during sexual relations.

Externally the penis consists of two distinct parts. The first is the *shaft* that is covered by loose skin that permits expansion during an erection. The second is the *glans* or the head of the penis. The glans contains many nerve endings and is very sensitive to tactile stimuli. It is the focal point of sexual stimulation. At birth, all males have a fold of skin that extends from the shaft over the glans. This fold of skin is called the *prepuce* or foreskin. A surgical procedure, known as circumcision, is used to remove the prepuce. Over 90 percent of male infants born in American hospitals were circumcised in 1975. By 1990 the number had dropped to 59 percent according to the National Center for Health Statistics.

The Old Testament Hebrews practiced circumcision as a sign of their covenant relationship with God (Gen. 17:9–14). God commanded that the circumcision be performed on the eighth day after birth. Ed Wheat, a medical doctor, has made the interesting observation that the eighth day is "the very day when blood-clotting and infection-prevention factors are the most favorable they will ever be in a baby's life" (Wheat and Wheat 1977:66).

In our culture, circumcision is generally not practiced as a religious ritual, except by Jews, but for hygienic purposes. However, recently the medical profession has questioned the need for circumcision of males. It is argued that with normal hygiene an uncircumcised male has no greater incidence of disease than a circumcised male. With the exception of Israel, the United States has the highest rate of male circumcision among developed countries.

Scrotum

The *scrotum* is a pouch, divided into a double sac, that hangs behind the penis. The scrotum consists of wrinkled, elastic skin. The function of the scrotum is to carry the testicles.

Testicles

The *testicles* are the primary male reproductive organs. The testicles are egg-shaped and one and a half to two inches long in an adult male. In firmness they are similar to a flexed muscle. Testicles produce sperm, the male reproductive cells. Each testicle contains a mass of tiny tubes called *seminiferous tubules* where the sperm are produced. A pair of testicles can produce over one hundred million sperm cells each day. The testicles continuously produce sperm cells, not just when a male is sexually stimulated. The seminiferous tubules of each testicle deposit their sperm into a duct called the *epididymis*. The epididymis, which is folded back and forth against itself, straightens into a tube called the *vas deferens*. With one from each testicle, the vas deferens ascend into the abdomen and loop over the bladder and form the *ampullae*, a series of ducts. These lead to the *seminal vesicles* where the sperm are combined with a lubricating secretion. From the seminal vesicles, the ampulae then enter the prostate gland.

Prostate Gland

The *prostate gland* is located between the bladder and the base of the penis and surrounds the urinary passage from the bladder to the penis. The prostate gland is about the size and shape of a large walnut.

One function of the prostate gland is to produce *semen*, a milky and slightly gelatinous fluid that is primarily protein. A typical *ejaculation*, the forceful discharge of about a teaspoon of semen from the penis, contains 250 to 500 million sperm cells. Another function of the prostate gland is to close off the urinary duct from the bladder during sexual intercourse. The urinary duct from the bladder joins the ducts from the seminal vesicles to form the *urethra*, a single tube running from the prostate gland through the penis. The urethra is used for both the elimination of urine and the discharge of semen. When a male becomes sexually aroused and has an erection, the prostate gland closes off the duct from the bladder.

Just below the prostate gland are located a pair of glands called *Cowper's glands*. About the size of a pea, these glands produce a clear, sticky fluid. This fluid is secreted prior to ejaculation and oozes from the erect penis. This fluid neutralizes acids in the penis and vagina that might affect the sperm. The fluid also functions as a lubricant for intercourse. The fluid from the Cowper's glands contains thousands of sperm cells—one of the reasons that the withdrawal method of birth control is less effective. Fertilization may result even if the penis is withdrawn before ejaculation.

The Female Reproductive System

Like the male reproductive system, the female reproductive system consists of both external genitals and internal organs. We will begin our discussion with the external female genitals, collectively called the *vulva* (see figure 7.2), and then deal with the internal female organs (see figure 7.3).

Marriage

FIGURE 7.2

*External Female
Genitalia*

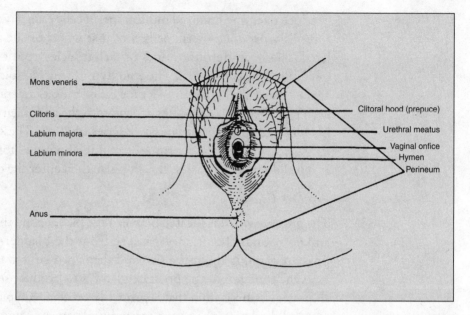

Mons veneris

Clitoris

Labium majora

Labium minora

Anus

Clitoral hood (prepuce)

Urethral meatus

Vaginal onfice

Hymen

Perineum

FIGURE 7.3

*Cross Section of the
Female Reproductive
System*

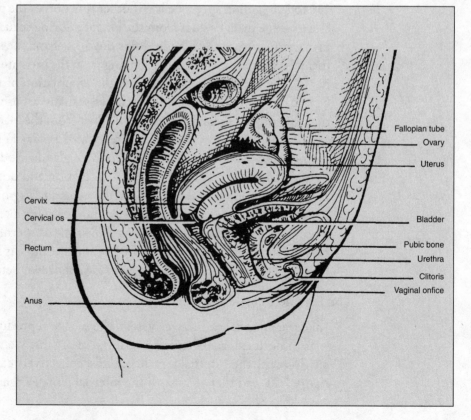

Cervix

Cervical os

Rectum

Anus

Fallopian tube

Ovary

Uterus

Bladder

Pubic bone

Urethra

Clitoris

Vaginal onfice

Mons Veneris

Located about six inches below the navel is a fatty mound known as the *mons veneris,* Latin for "Mount of Venus." In postpubic females the mons veneris is covered y a triangular growth of pubic hair. This fatty mound functions as a shock absorber to protect the genital area.

Labia Majora

The *labia majora,* Latin for "major lips," are two mounds of flesh, running parallel with each other from the mons veneris, along the midline between the legs, to the anus. They normally join over the vaginal opening to provide protection for the other organs. When a woman is sexually aroused, the lips pull back from the vaginal opening and flatten.

Labia Minora

Latin for "minor lips," the *labia minora* are two folds of hairless, smooth, soft tissue within the fold of the labia majora. They connect to the hood over the clitoris and run parallel on either side of the vaginal opening. When a woman becomes sexually aroused, the labia minora become engorged with blood, swell to two or three times their normal size, and protrude from the labia majora. Nerve endings in the labia minora are connected to pleasure centers in the brain and stimulation produces sexual enjoyment in most women.

Clitoris

The *clitoris* has been called the trigger for female sexual arousal. The unaroused clitoris is partially hidden by a hood of flesh, called the *prepuce,* which is located at the peak of the labia minora. The clitoris consists of two *corpora cavernosa* that fill with blood when sexually aroused. In some women the clitoris will become noticeably enlarged, in others it will not. The clitoris is generally between a quarter of an inch and an inch in length. The tip of the clitoris, called the *glans clitoris* contains a high concentration of touch-sensitive nerves. As far as current medical and biological researchers have ascertained, the only function of the clitoris is sexual stimulation and the triggering of the orgasm. Based on this finding, some Christian scholars have suggested that this is evidence that God intended sex not only for reproduction, but also for pleasure (Penner and Penner 1981:59–60).

Urethral Meatus

While not part of the reproductive system, the *urethral meatus* is part of the vulva. Located between the clitoris and the vaginal orifice, the sole function of the urethral meatus is the elimination of urine.

Vaginal Orifice

Located at the rear juncture of the labia minora, the *vaginal orifice* is the opening of the vagina. The vaginal orifice may be partially closed by a membrane named the *hymen* after the mythical god of marriage. The lack of an intact hymen is not necessarily a sign of loss of virginity. It may be stretched or torn under a variety of circumstances, including strenuous physical activities and accidents. Two small glands, called *Bartholin's glands,* are located on either side of the vaginal opening. These glands produce a secretion during sexual arousal.

Inner Vagina

The first of the internal female reproductive organs to be discussed is the *vagina,* Latin for "sheath." An elastic, tubular canal, the vagina extends up and back in the abdomen. The inner walls of the vagina consist of folds of elastic mucous tissue. Normally three to five inches long, the vagina can expand both to receive the penis and to allow the passage of a baby during childbirth. Glands in the folds of this tissue produce secretions during sexual arousal to lubricate the vagina for sexual intercourse.

Uterus

Firm, muscular, and about the size and shape of a pear, the *uterus* is located behind the bladder at the upper end of the vagina. The small end of the uterus, called the *cervix,* extends into the upper end of the vagina. The *os,* a narrow opening in the cervix, joins the uterus and the vagina. The uterus is elastic as well as muscular and can expand to accommodate up to seven babies (septuplets).

The inner lining of the uterus, called the *endometrium,* consists of red, velvety tissue permeated by tiny blood vessels. When fertilization occurs, the zygote is implanted in the endometrium, which provides nourishment for it. When a woman does not become pregnant, the endometrium, which has been thickening in readiness for the possible arrival of an embryo, degenerates, resulting in monthly periods of menstrual flow consisting of endometrial blood and tissue. We will discuss the menstrual cycle in more detail later in this chapter.

Ovaries

The *ovaries* are the primary female reproductive organs. They produce *ova* (eggs) as well as the female hormones *estrogen* and *progesterone.* Each ovary is about the size and shape of a robin's egg. The two ovaries are located on either side of the uterus, one on the left and the other on the right. Females are born with about two hundred thousand follicles in each ovary. Each follicle contains an immature egg, or ovum, which is the female reproductive cell. Every month after a female reaches puberty, one ovary or the other releases a mature ovum. Occasionally more than one ovum may be released. If all the ova are fertilized, multiple births (twins, triplets, etc.) will result. The ovum is released from the ovary about midway through the monthly menstrual cycle. The releasing of the mature ovum is called *ovulation.* A woman will ovulate about four hundred ova during her fertile years.

Fallopian Tubes

The *Fallopian tubes,* or *oviducts,* provide the passage for the ova from the ovaries to the uterus. Made primarily of muscle, each tube is approximately four inches long and resembles a miniature saxophone. Contractions of the muscles in the Fallopian tubes move the ova down to the uterus. Fertilization takes place in the Fallopian tubes, and the fertilized ova is deposited in the uterus.

Menstrual Cycle

As we have seen, each month the endometrium of the uterus thickens in preparation to receive a fertilized ovum. If fertilization does not occur, this lining is shed and the cycle begins again. The menstrual cycle is calculated from the first day of menstrual flow, which is considered day one.[1] On the first day of menstrual flow the endometrium is twice as thick as it is at the end of the flow. Menstrual flow generally lasts for four or five days. During this time the typical flow amounts to two or three liquid ounces. Ovulation occurs approximately ten days after the cessation of menstrual flow. About fourteen days later the next menstrual cycle begins (see figure 7.4).

If an ovum is not fertilized by the time it reaches the uterus, the secretion of two hormones, estrogen and progesterone, is discontinued. Within

---

[1]The days of the menstrual cycle given here are for an average cycle. A normal female may have a cycle that varies from this. An average consists of shorter and longer cycles.

Marriage

FIGURE 7.4

Female Menstrual Cycle

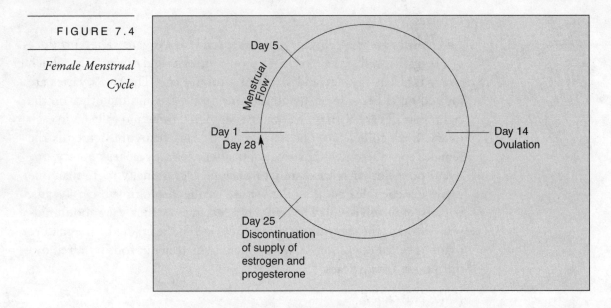

two or three days the network of blood vessels in the endometrium begin to contract. With the loss of nourishment, the surrounding tissue begins to shed and the weakened blood vessels open. When the tissue has been shed, the blood vessels return to normal size and are sealed.

SEXUAL RESPONSE

A widely accepted scheme for understanding human sexual response has been developed by Masters and Johnson (1966). They have divided the sexual response pattern into four segments or phases. We need to understand that this division is somewhat arbitrary and the phases flow into each other. However, this division is a useful model for studying human sexual response patterns. We should also recognize that the phases are generalizations from which individual deviations are normal and expected. The four phases are the excitement phase, the plateau phase, the orgasmic phase, and the resolution phase (see figure 7.5). We will look at each of these phases individually.

Masters and Johnson's Phases of Sexual Response

Excitement Phase

A person may become sexually stimulated by various sensory inputs, such as the sight of one's sex partner, a touch, a kiss, the words of another,

Human Sexuality

music, even certain odors, such as a particular perfume. While one may be sexually stimulated through any of the senses, the most basic and direct means of sexual stimulation is touch (Strong et al. 1981:55). Areas of the body that produce a sexual response when touched are called *erogenous zones*. Some of these responses are *subcortical*—that is, the stimulus does not pass through the brain, but responses are produced in both primary and secondary sex organs without the individual being conscious of being sexually stimulated. However, most sexual responses involve awareness.

With the onset of sexual arousal, the changes that occur in the primary sex organs result from the process of *vasocongestion,* the engorgement of sex organ tissues with an increased supply of blood. The physiological changes that take place in the primary sex organs of males and females when they are sexually aroused have been discussed above. During the excitement phase, a woman's breasts may enlarge and the nipples may become erect and increase slightly in diameter.

FIGURE 7.5

Phases of Sexual Response

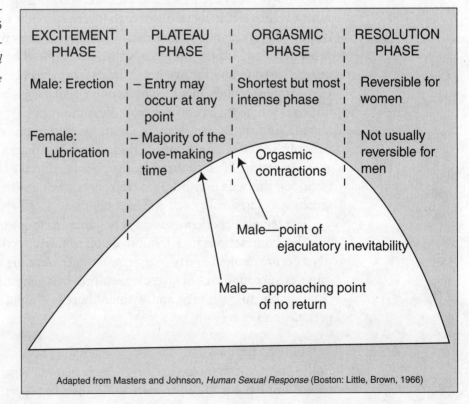

EXCITEMENT PHASE	PLATEAU PHASE	ORGASMIC PHASE	RESOLUTION PHASE
Male: Erection	– Entry may occur at any point	Shortest but most intense phase	Reversible for women
Female: Lubrication	– Majority of the love-making time	Orgasmic contractions	Not usually reversible for men

Male—point of ejaculatory inevitability

Male—approaching point of no return

Adapted from Masters and Johnson, *Human Sexual Response* (Boston: Little, Brown, 1966)

Plateau Phase

The excitement phase merges into the plateau phase, which is a more highly aroused state of sexual stimulation. In this phase penile erection reaches its maximum. The glans swells and darkens. The Cowper's glands begin their secretion, and a few drops may flow from the urethra. The vagina continues to lengthen and balloons into a saclike receptacle for the seminal fluid at the base of the cervix.

During this phase increased *foreplay,* stimulation of the erogenous zones, takes place. This is a period of heightened excitement and enjoyment. It is also during this phase that penile penetration of the vagina takes place, and genital stimulation continues as the couple move rhythmically. As the level of excitement increases, both heart rate and breathing become more rapid, vasocongestion increases, and sexual sensitivity becomes more intense.

Orgasm Phase

In many ways the orgasmic response is similar for both men and women (Green 1978:86; Strong et al. 1981:57). Orgasm is characterized by a series of contractions of the pelvic muscles accompanied by pleasurable sensations of release, usually lasting five to fifteen seconds. In the male, orgasm begins with contractions of the seminal vesicles, the vas deferens, and the prostate gland, which compresses the seminal fluid behind the sphincter muscle surrounding the urethra. The male experiences a sensation, lasting two or three seconds, in which he knows ejaculation is about to take place, but over which he has no control. Next the sphincter muscle opens the urethra, and the semen is pumped out by contractions of muscles at the base of the penis. These contractions occur less than a second apart and are pleasurable. Most of the semen is ejaculated in the first three contractions, but the male may have a dozen contractions with lesser amounts of semen ejaculated with each contraction.

The female experiences reactions similar to those of the male. However, her contractions may last longer, up to thirty seconds. Her contractions occur simultaneously in the muscles surrounding the vagina and the muscles surrounding the uterus, resulting in a sensation of total pelvic contraction. In both men and women there is a rapid increase in blood pressure and heart rate.

Resolution Phase

Following orgasm, men enter a *refractory period,* which lasts at least five to ten minutes for younger men and longer for older men. During the refractory stage, men are incapable of restimulation and an erection. On the other hand, females do not have a refractory lapse and are capable of immediate rearousal to orgasm. With continued stimulation, most women are capable of multiple orgasms, in rapid succession.

In the resolution phase, following orgasm, the physiological characteristics of sexual arousal generally recede more quickly in males than females. If the female has not achieved orgasm, the resolution phase can last as long as two hours before the genitals return fully to a prearoused state. The resolution phase has been called the *afterglow.* It should be a time of intimacy for a married couple.

Kaplan's Sexual Response Cycle

A decade after the work of Masters and Johnson, Helen Singer Kaplan (1974) carried out research on human sexual response. She describes the sexual response cycle in three phases: the desire phase, the excitement phase, and the orgasm phase.

Desire Phase

The desire phase is psychological and can occur apart from a physical sexual response. This phase involves erotic sensations or feelings that lead a person to seek a sexual encounter. A romantic candlelight dinner, a moonlight ride on the bay, watching a romantic movie, and any number of other experiences can cause a person to desire sex. The desire usually abates after orgasm.

Excitement Phase

This is the physical phase of sexual arousal. When a person is sexually aroused, a number of physiological changes take place. In the male this involves an erection. The testes may also enlarge. In the female the vagina becomes lubricated and the clitoris enlarges. The breasts may also enlarge and the nipples may become erect.

Orgasmic Phase

The release of physical tension after the buildup of sexual excitement is called orgasm. In the male it involves muscle contractions in the vas deferens, the seminal vesicles, and the urethral bulb resulting in ejaculation. There are also contractions of the sphincter muscle. In the female, orgasm involves rhythmic contractions of the uterus, orgasmic platform, and rectal sphincter muscles. Following orgasm males experience a refractory period during which further orgasms are not possible. Females do not have a refractory period and are capable of multiple orgasms.

SEXUAL DYSFUNCTIONS

The term *sexual dysfunction* refers to problems in giving or receiving sexual satisfaction. Sexual dysfunctions can have psychological and physical causes. Diseases such as prostatitis, hepatitis, diabetes, and epilepsy may interfere with sexual functioning. Sexual dysfunction may also result from hormonal deficiencies. We will look at some of the more common male and female sexual dysfunctions and then examine some of the common psychological causes of these dysfunctions.

Male Sexual Dysfunctions

Male sexual dysfunctions are generally found in two forms: impotence and ejaculatory dysfunctions.

Impotence

The inability of a male to achieve and maintain an erection during sexual intercourse is referred to as *impotence.* This is a common problem experienced by most married men at one time or another. As an isolated occurrence, it is not serious. However, when a man has experienced impotence several times in succession, it can become more serious. Frequently a cyclical effect develops. The male becomes anxious about not achieving an erection, and the anxiety blocks the sexual response needed for an erection, resulting in further anxiety and further blocking.

Impotence is usually classified into two types. The first type, *primary impotence,* refers to a man's never having experienced an erection. The second type, *secondary impotence,* refers to a man's temporary inability to have an erection though he has experienced erections in the past.

Until recently it was thought that the cause of most secondary impotence was psychological. Most men experience erection at night while sleeping and often awaken with an erection. If a man were capable of a nocturnal erection, it was thought that the inability to have or retain an erection during sexual activity was due to psychological causes. However, medical research has found that the cause is often physiological. The most common cause is hardening of the arteries in the penis. This is quite common in men over 50 years of age. The popularity and success of the impotence drug Viagra™ confirms the extent of this physiological cause.

Ejaculatory Dysfunctions

There are two ejaculatory dysfunctions: *premature ejaculation* and *retarded ejaculation*. The most common complaint of men receiving sexual therapy is premature ejaculation (Strong 1981:268). Premature ejaculation refers to a male's inability to delay orgasm until his partner has achieved orgasm. That is, the male ejaculates and the penis becomes flaccid before his partner has been sufficiently aroused to experience orgasm. Therapeutic techniques have been developed to help a man learn to control his ejaculatory response until his partner has been aroused.

Less common than premature ejaculation but still occurring with some frequency is retarded ejaculation. In this condition a male achieves and maintains an erection, but is unable to ejaculate. This problem tends to be transitory.

Female Sexual Dysfunctions

Female sexual dysfunctions are generally found in three forms: general sexual dysfunction, female orgasmic dysfunction, and vaginismus.

General Sexual Dysfunction

The term *frigid* has widely been used to label sexually unresponsive women. Because of its negative connotations and accusatory nature, this term is not clinically accepted. Kaplan (1974) has introduced the term *general sexual dysfunction* to replace it. This term has been generally accepted in the social sciences. General sexual dysfunction refers to both a lack of sexual feelings and stimulation and the lack of physical response such as vasocongestion and lubrication. The cause of general sexual dysfunction is usually psychological, often resulting from learning a negative view of sex.

Female Orgasmic Dysfunction

Some women who are able to become sexually aroused and experience vasocongestion and lubrication never achieve orgasm. Wheat and Wheat (1977:103) refer to such women as preorgasmic. They feel this is a healthier term because it implies the potential for orgasm. As with the male problem of premature ejaculation, therapeutic techniques have been developed to assist a woman in achieving orgasm.

Vaginismus

The involuntary spasmodic contraction of the muscles around the vaginal opening when the penis attempts to penetrate the vagina is called *vaginismus.* The reaction precludes the possibility of intercourse. A female may experience vaginismus as the result of a traumatic experience such as rape. It may also develop from strong inhibitions toward sexual intercourse formed from a repressive upbringing marked by excessive prohibitions. Vaginismus may also result from a woman's strong feelings of anger or resentment toward her partner. Again we see that many of the causes of sexual dysfunctions are psychological.

Psychological Causes

There are many psychological causes of sexual dysfunctions. We will examine a few of the more common causes in this section.

Stress

"Long-term stress can contribute to lowered sexual drive and responsiveness" (Strong et al. 1981:259). Stress related to family matters, health, one's job, or other areas of life may adversely affect one's sexual functioning. The problem often compounds itself because when persons are under stress, they need closeness and intimacy. However, if a person is not able to function sexually, he or she may become upset and experience additional stress. When one partner is under stress, the other partner may need to provide a kind of closeness and intimacy that does not demand sexual functioning.

Faulty Learning

Many people have been taught false or misleading ideas about sex. A number of women have been taught when they were young that sex is basically evil, or that it is a man's "pleasure" and a woman's "duty." Some women have been taught that only "bad girls" enjoy sex, while "good girls" endure it. Some men have been taught that sex is something you do *to* a woman instead of *with* a woman. They have learned only to satisfy themselves. Many men have been led to believe that a "real" man should always be ready to perform, and should be able to please a woman every time.

People bring many false and misleading ideas into marriage. Some of these ideas can be quite destructive and rob a couple of the sexual pleasure and oneness God intended for them to experience. This is why it is so important for parents to provide a healthy, proper, accurate, and biblical view of sex for their children.

Human Sexuality

Sexual Anxiety

A common male myth is that a man should be able to function sexually anytime and anywhere. When a man—because of stress, physical exhaustion, or other causes—experiences impotence, he may become anxious about it, and that anxiety may inhibit future functioning. Until recently, women were not under as much pressure to perform, since their function is more passive. However, with the current proliferation of sex manuals and sex research, women are experiencing pressure to be "complete women" by experiencing orgasm each time they engage in intercourse. This pressure is described by a wife interviewed in the Hite study:

> I resent the pressure placed on me and other women to have orgasms. Every time I read a survey that says Masters and Johnson or other researchers have found that X percent of women almost always have orgasms, I feel psychologically inadequate. (1976:117)

Anxiety about the inability to function sexually in one instance may inhibit functioning in another instance, generating further anxiety and further inhibition. The physiological effect of anxiety on sexual performance is explained by Strong et al.:

> The autonomic nervous system is composed of sympathetic and parasympathetic subsystems. The sympathetic subsystem controls the release of adrenaline which stimulates our "fight or flee" behavior, preparing us for danger or adversity. Among men, it controls the physiological responses involved in ejaculation; with women, the sympathetic nervous system governs the motor aspects of orgasm. The parasympathetic subsystem governs not only sleep, digestion, and relaxation, but erection, vaginal lubrication, and vasocongestion, as well as erotic sensations accompanying orgasm. (Strong et al. 1981:260)

Marital Problems

Various problems in marriage may result in sexual dysfunction. Kaplan (1974) has suggested that there are six areas of marital problems that are common causes of sexual dysfunctions. The first of these problems is *transferences.* It is common for us to transfer feelings about one person to another person, particularly if these persons are significant in our lives. Generally, a man transfers some of the feelings he had for his mother to his wife, and a woman transfers some feelings she had for her father to her husband. To some extent this is normal and healthy. However, when the feelings that are transferred are negative or when the transference is so extensive that one's partner is confused with one's parent, sexual dysfunctions may result.

A second problem is *lack of trust.* Marriage is based on trust. When a man and woman trust each other, they can expose themselves to each other emotionally, psychologically, and physically. Emotional intimacy is intricately related to physical intimacy. When trust is broken, emotional intimacy is destroyed, and physical intimacy is affected.

Kaplan's third problem area is *power struggles.* When a man and woman are struggling for dominance in a relationship, they usually resort to whatever weapons are needed to win. The power struggle itself may thwart one or the other partner's sexual drive, and performance or sex itself may become a weapon in the power struggle. This may happen unconsciously. One partner may not respond sexually to the other, unconsciously seeking revenge or concessions.

The fourth problem area is called *contractual disappointments.* Everyone enters marriage with assumptions and expectations; these are often unspoken and sometimes unconscious. Each partner believes the other partner has agreed to these unstated expectations by entering the marriage. For example, he expects her to come to bed at night all made up in a flimsy negligee, and she comes to bed in flannel pajamas with curlers in her hair. On the other hand, she expects romantic evenings together, and he hides behind the newspaper. Then each wonders why the other partner is not sexually responsive.

Another problem is *sexual sabotage.* This occurs when one partner demands sex in a manner, at a time, or in a situation that the other partner is not responsive to. This behavior may be due to insensitivity or it may be unconscious. In either case, it has an adverse effect on the person's sexual functioning.

The final problem area, and the most important area, is *communication failure.* Marriage partners are not mind readers. One's partner cannot know what is arousing and what is annoying without being told. Even in our enlightened age, many people are inhibited about discussing sexual matters. However, if a husband and wife want to have a fulfilling and satisfying sex life, they need to discuss it. In therapeutic settings, many sexual dysfunctions are cleared up through communication between the partners. We will examine the area of sexual communication to see how it can enrich a couple's relationship.

Human Sexuality

SEXUAL COMMUNICATION

"Communication is the means by which relating takes place.... Good communication is the ability to transmit and receive meanings; it is the instrument for achieving that mutual understanding which is at the heart of marital intimacy" (Clinebell and Clinebell 1970:87). However good their communication may be in other areas, many couples have a difficult time communicating about sex—particularly their needs and desires. Someone has said, "While a couple may have good sex without having a good marriage, they cannot have a good marriage without good sex." Whether that is entirely true or not, we recognize that sex is an important aspect of marriage; therefore, good communication in this area is essential for marriage to be all it can be.

Communication takes place on two levels, verbal and nonverbal. Nonverbal communication includes touch, facial expressions, tone of voice, posture—any means of communicating beyond words. Verbal communication, of course, is communication by means of words. There is potential for miscommunication at both levels.

Communication in marriage will be discussed in Chapter 9, and many of the principles discussed there also apply to sexual communication. In addition, there are some practical things a couple can do to increase their ability to communicate in this area. First, they need to understand human reproductive physiology and the correct terminology for the various organs. One reason couples are afraid to discuss sexual matters is ignorance and the lack of adequate vocabulary. Second, they need to talk in terms of their needs and desires and not in terms of accusations. For example, a wife should not say to her husband, "You don't satisfy me," but rather, "I need more satisfaction from our relationship." The one response creates defensiveness, the other openness. Third, a couple should read together some good books on the sexual side of marriage (see Suggested Reading). One partner may want to try a variation but be afraid to mention it, thinking the other will consider it "weird." But when they discover a new technique in a book, they can discuss it, since the book raised the topic. There are many other ways a book on sex can help a couple communicate about sex.

Sex in marriage can be all God intended it to be, or it can be a source of frustration, embarrassment, and contention. If couples want their sex life to be all it can be, they need to live in accordance with God's principles for marriage and sex, maintain open and honest communication, and be willing to seek competent help when needed. Sexual dysfunctions should be discussed, and medical and/or psychological assistance sought. We need to remember that one of God's purposes for sex is to draw a couple together into an intimacy that can only be expressed as "one flesh."

DISCUSSION QUESTIONS

1. What do you believe the biblical phrase "one flesh" means? Why?

2. In your opinion, why are so many people embarrassed and afraid to discuss sexual matters?

3. Why do we need to understand sex as more than just a biological function?

4. What similarities do you see between the male and female reproductive systems?

5. Why do you believe it is important for parents to teach their children a healthy and biblical view of sex? Did your parents do this for you?

6. What do you see as the main truths being taught in Proverbs 5:15–19?

SUGGESTED READING

Tim and Beverly LaHaye, *The Act of Marriage*, 2d ed. (Grand Rapids: Zondervan, 1998) and Clifford and Joyce Penner, *The Gift of Sex* (Waco, Tex.: Word, 1981). Two Christian sex manuals. Both deal with the basics of human sexuality, sexual response, sexual dysfunction, and sexual techniques. They have contributed to a new and healthy openness about sex in marriage among Christians.

Kevin Leman, *Sex Begins in the Kitchen* (Ventura, Calif.: Regal, 1981) and Rusty and Linda Wright, *Dynamic Sex* (San Bernardino, Calif.: Here's Life, 1979). These two books deal with the emotional and psychological aspects of sex in marriage. They point out that sex is a twenty-four-hour activity, not just a thirty-minute exercise in bed at night.

Human Sexuality

William H. Masters, Virginia E. Johnson, and Robert C. Kolodny, *Human Sexuality*, 5th ed. (New York: HarperCollins, 1995). This is considered by many to be the definitive work on the subject of human sexuality. The book covers male and female anatomy, sexual behavior, sexual dysfunctions, sexually transmitted diseases, and cultural perspectives.

Bryan Strong and Christine DeVault, *Human Sexuality: Diversity in Contemporary America*, 2d ed. (Mountain View, Calif.: Mayfield, 1997). A secular text on human sexuality, well written and tastefully handled. In addition to covering the topics in this chapter, it deals with sexually transmitted diseases, sexual development, sexual identity, and social issues.

Economics

I have learned to be content whatever the circumstances. I know what it is to be in need, and I know what it is to have plenty. I have learned the secret of being content in any and every situation, whether well fed or hungry, whether living in plenty or in want. I can do everything through him who gives me strength.

PAUL IN HIS LETTER TO THE CHURCH AT PHILIPPI (4:11– 13)

Both Dave and Gwen have full-time jobs and earn approximately the same amount of money. They have just bought a new house and are in the process of furnishing it. Dave feels they can get by with the hand-me-down furniture they had in their previous apartment and that shades are all they need for the windows at this time. He wants to wait and save for new furnishings. On the other hand, Gwen wants to charge new furniture and drapes. She argues that they should enjoy their new home completely. She points out that they are both working, that the payments will fit their budget, and that inflation will raise the cost of the furnishings faster than their money will earn interest.

Dave says he can enjoy the new house without new furnishings, and anyway, his parents always saved for major purchases. The only thing they ever borrowed for was a mortgage. Gwen argues that she is working and contributing equally to the budget and that she should be able to enjoy "the fruits of her labor."

Both Dave and Gwen had been willing to work hard and save for the down payment on the new house, but now they disagree on how to handle their finances. They find themselves constantly arguing with each other. Their disagreement over spending seems to be spreading to other areas of their marriage.

One of the major sources of conflict in marriage is money. Research indicates that married couples disagree more over financial issues than any other single issue (Lasswell and Lasswell 1982:403; Strong, DeVault, and Sayad 1998:162). Summarizing the research, one sociologist said, "Studies indicate that couples quarrel over money more than anything else, that economic factors are closely related to marital stability and critical to marital adjustment, and that economic stress is a major cause of marital failure" (Saxton 1980:547). This conclusion is confirmed by Gary Collins (1995:65–66). In Chapter 3 we saw the relationship between income and divorce. As income increases, divorce decreases. However, conflicts about money often cannot be reduced to dollars and cents. Money has many meanings in our society.

THE MEANING OF MONEY

Money is defined as "something accepted as a medium of exchange"; however, we are all aware that it is more than that. On a monetary level a twenty-dollar bill is just twenty dollars; its exchange value is the same for everyone in our society. To an upper-class business executive it may be only pocket change; however, to a five-year-old boy from a lower-class family it may be a small fortune. Let us look at some of the common meanings money has in our society. Belkin and Goodman (1980) suggest that, beyond its exchange value, money represents at least three things: power, love, and status. To this list we can add a fourth, security.

Money as Power

We are all familiar with expressions such as "Money talks" or "Everyone has a price." While we are all aware of the power of money in society in general, we may not be as aware of its power in marriage. Based on research studies, sociologists have come to a number of conclusions about the power of money in marriage. One conclusion is that a husband's power over his wife increases with his income. In effect, he buys the right to make decisions. On the other hand, a wife's power increases as the share she contributes to the budget increases. Another finding was that employed women are more likely to influence family financial matters and to share in all major decisions in the family (Orthner 1981; Lamanna and Riedmann 1997). Parents also use money as a means of control over their children.

Because money is power, marital disputes over money may in fact not be over dollars and cents—but over power. Many times a couple will fight over how money should be spent, not so much because either one really cares that much for the thing they are arguing for, but to see who will control the spending. When a family's financial situation changes because a wife enters or leaves the workforce, or when either husband or wife receives a major raise, the balance of power frequently is tipped and a period of tension follows. This tension will continue until the power relationship is back in balance.

Ideally, in a Christian family money should not be a source of power but rather a shared resource. In reality, however, money becomes a source of power and therefore of problems even in Christian families. As a couple becomes aware that money is often seen as power and used to control others, they can begin to deal with the problem in their marriage.

Money as Love

One of the ways we show we love a person is by giving presents. Parents give their children presents as tokens of their love. When I am out of town on business, I always buy little presents to bring home to my children because I love them. In dating and courtship, a man and woman frequently give presents to each other. In marriage, husbands and wives give presents to each other. These presents, which cost money or even consist of money, become associated with love. Therefore, the withholding of something may be seen as a withholding of love.

In our opening anecdote, Gwen may accuse Dave of not loving her anymore, since he does not want to get the new furnishings at this time. Gwen may interpret Dave's position not as a monetary policy but as a lack of concern and love for her. She may feel that if he really loved her, he would want her to be happy. Even the Bible recognizes the relationship between love and money. Jesus told a parable about a moneylender who had two debtors. One owed the equivalent of two years' wages, and the other the equivalent of two months' wages. The moneylender forgave them both, in essence giving them the money. Jesus said the one who was given the most would love the most (Luke 7:41–43). What we do with our money reveals what we love. Jesus said, "For where your treasure is, there your heart will be also" (Matt. 6:21).

Money as Status

In the first chapter *status* was defined as a place or position in a social system with its rights and duties. The statuses in a social system are generally ranked; that is, some are seen as higher, and others as lower. For example, we see the president of a bank as having a higher status than a teller in the bank. The ranking of statuses is known as *stratification*. In studying stratification, sociologists use a concept called *socioeconomic status* (SES). A person's SES is determined by an index that includes education, occupation, and income. Of these three indicators, income is regarded as the most important. In fact, a person's SES is often calculated solely on the basis of income.

One marriage counselor writes that money "is an instrument used in our society to calibrate the individual's character and functioning while at the same time shaping the person's self-perception of adequacy and worthwhileness" (Feldman 1976:3). A sociologist writes, "In our society people are often judged by how much money they have. Thus, one's self-esteem can be tied in with one's finances" (Belkin and Goodman 1980:382).

Since we do not wear our financial statements or bank accounts on our sleeves, we generally communicate our financial status by things we purchase. These things are called *status symbols.* Common status symbols are cars, homes, and clothes. Status symbols also include membership in a country club or even the "right" church. Because how a couple spends their income communicates their status, many disagreements over money are really disagreements over status. The husband wants to spend extra money on an expensive car to increase his status, whereas the wife wants to spend the extra money on more expensive furniture to increase her status.

Money as Security

Even the Bible recognizes that people look to money for security. The longest section of Jesus' Sermon on the Mount deals with money and security (Matt. 6:19–34). In Luke 12:16–21, Jesus told a parable about a rich farmer who was placing his security in his wealth. The truth is that most of us find security in having some savings, in having financial reserves. Most advertisements for mutual funds and retirement accounts stress financial security. Because money represents security, when couples are discussing finances, they may really be discussing security.

As we have seen, money is more than a medium of exchange. It represents power, love, status, and many other things such as security, confirmation of one's worth, and opportunities for oneself and one's family. It is no wonder that finances are such a source of problems in marriage.

Economics

That is why two people, somewhere in the process of becoming a couple, need to explore the topic of money in depth. It also helps us understand why, all other things being equal, the closer in SES partners are, the greater the potential for a successful marriage.

BIBLICAL VIEW OF MONEY

It is interesting to notice that half of the parables of Jesus recorded in the Gospels deal with money and possessions. In fact, Jesus said more about money than about heaven and hell combined. There are about five hundred verses in the Bible dealing with prayer and about five hundred verses on faith, whereas there are over two thousand verses in the Bible concerning money and possessions (Dayton 1979:10). Consider the following topics:

- God the provider for our needs: Deut. 8:18; Matt. 6:31–33; Luke 12:30–31; 1 Cor. 4:7
- Being good stewards of what God provides: Gen. 1:28; Ps. 8:6; 1 Cor. 4:2
- Debt and how to handle it: Ps. 37:21; Prov. 3:27–28; 22:7; Matt. 5:25–26; Rom. 13:8
- Cosigning loans: Prov. 6:1–5; 17:18; 22:26–27
- The acquisition of money by work: Prov. 6:6–9; 13:4; 1 Thess. 2:9; 1 Tim. 4:14; 2 Peter 1:10
- Being ethical in our financial dealings: Deut. 5:19–21; Prov. 10:2; 11:18; 20:10, 23; 28:12; 29:14; Isa. 33:15; Zech. 8:16–17; Matt. 7:12; Luke 12:15; Rom. 13:9–10
- Saving: Prov. 21:20; 30:24–25
- Investing: Prov. 21:5; Matt. 25:14–29; Luke 19:12–24
- Inheritances: Num. 27:8–11; Prov. 13:22
- Giving to God: Gen. 28:22; Mal. 3:8–10; Matt. 23:23–25; 1 Cor. 16:2; 2 Cor. 8:3
- Giving to others: Deut. 18:1–5; Prov. 28:27; Rom. 12:13; 1 Tim. 5:17–18

However, the basic concern of the Bible seems to be with our *attitude* toward money. Greed and the love of money are particularly addressed. Paul warns Timothy that "the love of money is a root of all kinds of evil" (1 Tim. 6:10). In his letters to the Ephesians and the Colossians, Paul equates greed with idolatry (Eph. 5:5; Col. 3:5). In the story of the rich young ruler, we see that the ruler's love of money stood in the way of his following Christ (Matt. 19:16–22). And Jesus taught, "Be on your guard against all kinds of greed; a man's life does not consist in the abundance of his possessions" (Luke 12:14). Jesus went on to teach:

> Do not worry about your life, what you will eat; or about your body, what you will wear. Life is more than food, and the body more than clothes.... And do not set your heart on what you will eat or drink; do not worry about it.... your Father knows that you need them. But seek his kingdom, and these things will be given to you as well.... For where your treasure is, there your heart will be also. (Luke 12:22–23, 29–31, 34)

The society we live in has a much more complicated economic system than societies had in Bible times. However, the principles of Scripture are just as applicable today. As we go on to discuss budgeting, credit, insurance, savings, and wills, we need to keep these principles in mind.

BUDGETING

There is something about the very mention of the word *budget* that sounds restrictive and limiting. A budget is something that everyone says a couple should have—but no one wants to have. Why does the thought of a plan for using money bring up negative reactions in most people? I believe it is because most of us do not want to be restricted and limited in the use of our money. However, that is exactly what a budget should *not* do. Instead, it should free us to get the most for our money. A budget is a master that no couple can faithfully serve, but a servant that every couple should have.

If a couple allows their budget to control them, it will never work. But, if it allows them to control their money, it will work. Let me illustrate. Suppose my wife and I have eighty dollars a week budgeted for groceries and sixteen dollars a week for entertainment. Let us further suppose that we learn of a concert we both want to attend this week, and two tickets cost thirty-two dollars. Now if our budget is our master, it will only allow us sixteen dollars for entertainment, so we cannot go to the concert. However, if it is our servant, we can take sixteen dollars from the grocery money, go to the concert, and have soup and crackers for supper a couple of evenings. When the budget is our servant, it allows us to make trade-offs. But we know what we are trading off. Without a budget, couples also make trade-offs. But they may end up with the least desirable option.

What exactly is a budget? Basically, it is a flexible, workable plan for spending money that channels a couple's cash flow into areas that provide the greatest benefit to them. Notice that the two key aspects of the plan are *flexible* and *workable*. It must be flexible. If not, it quickly becomes a master rather than a servant. The plan must also be workable. The best budget in the world is no good if it does not meet a couple's needs. The basic test of a budget is how it performs, and the basic function is to help people get the most for their money.

Purpose of a Budget

Green (1978) suggests at least four purposes or values of budgeting for couples. He points out that a budget (1) maximizes income, (2) provides a realistic view of financial status, (3) opens communication, and (4) reduces tensions. Let us examine each of these purposes.

Maximizes Income

A well-planned budget helps a couple get the most for their income. A couple has a given income. Without a budget, they find their money is leaking away, and they have no idea where it has gone. Most of us are familiar with families that have about the same income, and yet one family has a significantly higher standard of living than the other. A budget allows a couple to invest in those things that they value most.

Provides a Realistic View of Financial Status

A budget supplies a couple with a realistic view of their income and expenditures and lets them know where they are and where they are going. In addition, it can help keep a couple out of debt and aid them in developing a program of saving and investment. Frequently couples wake up one day to discover that their bills have become larger than their income. A budget allows them always to be aware of their financial status.

Opens Communication

Developing a budget encourages a couple to discuss their financial plans. It allows them to discuss their goals, desires, and needs. Together they can decide on a lifestyle and their financial future. A budget provides the basis for communicating about their values, for it is basically a statement of values. Figure 8.1 presents a questionnaire that is useful in uncovering one's financial values.

Reduces Tensions

We have already seen that finances are the number-one cause of tension in marriage. Couples fight about money more than any other topic. As we saw above, a budget allows a couple to discuss how they want to spend their money. It aids them in developing a financial plan together. Then once a financial plan acceptable to both of them has been developed, they can work together toward that common goal. A marriage should be a partnership, not an adversarial relationship. A budget helps a couple function as partners.

FIGURE 8.1					
Financial Values Questionnaire	Circle the letter that describes how you feel about the following: (L = Luxury, D = Desirable, U = Useful, N = Necessity)				
	Cellular Phone	L	D	U	N
	Large Screen TV	L	D	U	N
	New furniture	L	D	U	N
	A will	L	D	U	N
	A CD player	L	D	U	N
	A second car	L	D	U	N
	Owning a home	L	D	U	N
	Tithing	L	D	U	N
	Owning stock	L	D	U	N
	Pets	L	D	U	N
	Vacation once a year	L	D	U	N
	Retirement plan	L	D	U	N
	Credit cards	L	D	U	N
	Eating out	L	D	U	N
	Life insurance	L	D	U	N
	Hobbies/sports	L	D	U	N
	Medical insurance	L	D	U	N
	Latest fashions	L	D	U	N
	Snack food	L	D	U	N
	Home computer	L	D	U	N
	Internet access	L	D	U	N

Adapted from Wright 1977a:201

Economics

Developing a Budget

Developing a budget is relatively simple. There are three basic steps. The first is to determine your monthly income. This includes wages (minus regular deductions such as taxes and social security), royalties, dividends, interest, and any other sources. The second step is to determine your fixed or nondiscretionary expenses. These include items such as rent or mortgage payments, car payments, installment loan payments, utilities, insurance, stewardship, and other fixed items. The third step is to list variable or discretionary expenses. These include items such as food, clothing, furnishings, entertainment, savings, and personal allowances. The difference between your income and your fixed expenses is the money you can allot to discretionary spending. A sample budget form for following these steps is presented in figure 8.2.

It should be noted that the term *fixed expenses* is only relative. If a couple wants more money for discretionary expenses and cannot increase their income, they can lower their fixed expenses. They could find less expensive housing, drive a less expensive car, or do without some item on their fixed-expenses list. That is the value of a budget; it allows a couple to make rational decisions about how they want to spend their money.

A question I am frequently asked when discussing budgeting is what percentage of a person's income should be spent on housing or food or other categories. While this has to be an individual decision and will vary from person to person and situation to situation, there are some guidelines we can follow. Howard Dayton (1979:88–89) offers a suggested breakdown for a budget as shown in table 8.1.

TABLE 8.1	CATEGORY	PERCENT OF INCOME (after taxes and stewardship)
Recommended Budget Allotments	Shelter	20–35
	Food	15–25
	Transportation	10–15
	Clothing	4–8
	Insurance	3–5
	Medical	3–5
	Entertainment and recreation	3–5
	Debts (credit purchases)	0–10
	Savings	5–10
	Miscellaneous	3–5

Marriage

FIGURE 8.2

Sample Budget Form

SOURCES OF MONTHLY INCOME   AMOUNT

Wages $_____

Interest   _____

Dividends   _____

Other:_____

_____

_____

Total monthly income: $_____

FIXED EXPENSES   AMOUNT

Housing (rent or mortgage) $_____

Utilities (monthly average)   _____

Insurance   _____

Automobile payments   _____

Automobile operating expenses   _____

Installment payments   _____

Stewardship   _____

Medical and dental (average)   _____

Other:_____   _____

_____   _____

_____   _____

Total monthly fixed expenses: $_____

DISCRETIONARY EXPENSES   AMOUNT

Groceries $_____

Household items   _____

Furnishings   _____

Clothing   _____

Entertainment   _____

Savings   _____

Personal allowances   _____

Other:_____   _____

_____   _____

_____   _____

Total discretionary expenses: $_____

CREDIT

What is credit? We may define *credit* as goods or services received with payment deferred. Or simply put, it is possess now and pay later. Credit is widely used and is an integral part of the American economy. Americans have over one billion credit cards, including cards for stores such as Sears, Ward's, Macy's, and Penney's; gasoline companies; and bank cards such as Visa and MasterCard, as well as cards such as American Express and Diners Club. In 1996 consumer debt was 1.2 trillion dollars. In 1985 there were 297,885 personal bankruptcies. By 1996 the number of personal bankruptcies had more than tripled to 989,172, the majority as a result of consumer debt (U.S. Bureau of the Census 1997).

Types of Credits

Saxton (1980) classifies credit into three categories: open credit, profit-making credit, and non-profit-making credit. We will examine each of these types of credit.

Open Credit

By *open credit* Saxton is referring to credit advanced with no finance charge. Common examples of open credit include medical and dental treatment for which we are billed at the end of the month; newspaper delivery for which we pay at the end of the week; and utilities, which bill us monthly for the amount of service used. In these cases we use the service or product and then pay for it later.

Most department store, gasoline, and bank credit cards also extend open credit. That is, we may make a purchase today, and if we pay the balance in full within thirty days of being billed, we will not be charged interest. In other words, the store, oil company, or bank is lending us the amount of the purchase without interest if we pay in full when billed.

There are several advantages to using open credit. One of these is the elimination of the necessity of carrying around large amounts of cash. Another is that the charge slip or bill provides a convenient receipt, especially when dealing with tax-deductible items. A third advantage of open credit is that it gives us leverage with the seller if the product is faulty. When we pay in cash, the seller may not be anxious to make the purchase right. But if we have not yet paid, the seller may be more willing to correct the situation. Under recent federal legislation, this is even true for bank credit cards. Still another advantage of open credit is that it allows us to take advantage of sales. If I need something that I already had budgeted to take out of next week's paycheck and it goes on sale for this week only at half price, I can take advantage of that savings.

A final advantage of open credit is that our money can be drawing interest in savings or other short-term investments while we use the retailer's or bank's money interest-free to make our purchase. For example, if I want to buy a washer and dryer from a major department store chain for $700, it would be best to use my credit card for the purchase even though I have the cash. The bill would come approximately fifteen days later[1] and would need to be paid within thirty days of the billing. That means I can use the store's money for about forty-five days interest-free. If I put $700 in a money-market fund paying 12 percent annual interest, I could make $10.50 in interest for those forty-five days.

While there are obvious advantages to open credit, there are also pitfalls. The major pitfall is spending money we do not have. If I operate on a cash basis, then when I see something I want, I can get it only if I have the money in hand. But if I have a credit card, I can purchase something without the means to pay it off in full. Open credit should be used only for planned and budgeted purchases. If a bill cannot be paid in full, we cease to have open credit because we will be paying a finance charge that generally ranges from 16 to 24 percent annually.

Profit-making Credit

Saxton considers a loan or an extension of credit to be *profit-making credit* if the return on the use of the credit will equal or exceed the interest paid. For example, I buy a lawn mower on credit and use the mower to start a lawn-cutting business. If the profit from my lawn cutting exceeds the interest paid on the loan, it would be profit-making credit. Saxton considers educational loans as profit-making credit because education increases one's earning power. Also, loans to start a business, purchase tools for a trade, or other income-producing causes would fall into this category. A home mortgage might also fall into this classification if the tax advantages and increasing value of the home offset the interest payments.

---

[1] A usual billing cycle is thirty days. Purchases made early in the cycle give you more time; purchases made later in the cycle provide less time.

Non-profit-making Credit

The interest paid exceeds the monetary value of the purchase in *non-profit-making credit*. An example of this type of credit is taking out a two-year loan to finance a vacation to Europe. Saxton does not argue that one should not use credit in this way, but only that there is no monetary profit to this type of purchase. This type of credit allows people to enjoy something now rather than waiting to save.

Non-profit-making credit may even save a couple money in some instances. For example, a couple decides they would like a new refrigerator that will cost $500. They decide to save $50 a month for ten months in order to purchase it. The next week the refrigerator goes on sale for $400. If they buy the refrigerator for $400 and finance it at 18 percent interest for ten months, the interest would be $22 if they paid $40 on the principle each month. Therefore, their total cost would be $422 as opposed to $500.

Some basic rules a couple or individual should keep in mind if they want to use credit wisely and stay out of financial trouble include:

1. Do not make impulse purchases on credit. If you see something you really would like to have, wait thirty days and see if you still feel the same way.
2. Use credit cards only for planned or budgeted purchases. Leave credit cards at home except when making a planned purchase.
3. Make sure the monthly payment on a credit purchase will fit the family budget.
4. When possible, save for an item rather than purchasing on credit.
5. Make sure the value of an item is always greater than the amount owed on the item.

INSURANCE

Insurance is a program for pooled risk. In the case of automobile insurance, a group of car owners contribute to a pool of funds generally handled by an insurance company, and if any of them is involved in an accident, that one is reimbursed from the pool. Insurance is basically a means of sharing risks. There are many types of insurance. Anything from automobiles to lives to business ventures can be insured. We will look at three areas of insurance that are important for all families: life, health, and property insurance.

Life Insurance

Life insurance provides funds in the event that a member of the family dies. Generally these funds are used to replace the income or services that had been provided by that family member. It is usual for the breadwinner in a family to have enough life insurance so that, in the case of death, the income can be replaced for a given period of time. There are many factors that go into determining the amount of coverage a breadwinner should have. These include number and ages of children, Social Security, other sources of income, and financial goals. There are four basic types of life insurance: term, whole life, hybrid, and universal life.

Term Life Insurance

Term life insurance covers a person for only a specific period of time. Term insurance generally is issued for terms of five, ten, or twenty years, although some policies can be written for any term desired. Since only a period of a person's life is insured, there is a probability that the person will not die during the term, and the insurance company will not have to pay. On the other hand, the insurance company knows it will have to pay sooner or later on a whole life policy. Since the insurance company will not have to pay on all term policies, term insurance is significantly less expensive. The value of term insurance, besides cost, is that insurance needs vary throughout the life cycle. When children are young, more protection is needed; when they are grown and just the couple are home, less protection is needed. During the young years when the most coverage is needed, the probability of death is lower, so greater coverage at lower cost is available through term insurance. The major drawback to term insurance is that premiums go up for the same level of coverage as a person gets older. A person can maintain a level premium by lowering coverage.

Whole Life Insurance

Whole life insurance, which is also referred to as ordinary life or straight life, is a lifetime policy with a fixed premium. That is, a person pays the same premium until death or on some policies until age 65 or other agreed-upon age when the policy is paid up. Most whole life policies have a cash value based on interest paid on premiums. This interest is only paid on part of the premium, and the interest rate is generally quite low. When the policyholder dies, the cash value is added to the face value of the policy. If the policy is canceled by the policyholder, the accumulated cash value is refunded. Often the policyholder may also borrow money from the policy up to the accumulated cash value at reasonable interest rates. For some people this type of policy functions as a forced savings plan.

Hybrid (Whole Life/Term Combination) Life Insurance

Hybrid life insurance is a combination of whole life and term insurance. Part of the policy is term insurance, and part is whole life, with the percentage of each determined when the policy is written. The cash value on the whole life part of the policy is used to buy paid-up life insurance, which replaces the term part of the policy. The premiums are higher than a term policy but lower than a whole life policy. The disadvantage is that the cash value does not build up. It is used to buy paid-up insurance.

Universal Life

Universal life insurance is a flexible form of life insurance with both the premiums and death benefits being flexible. This is actually an investment vehicle and term policy. The policy builds up cash value as interest is paid on the premiums minus the cost of the term insurance. The larger the premiums the larger the cash value and the greater the death benefit. The danger with this type of policy is that if the premiums paid are too low, all the cash value could be used up paying for the term insurance and the policy could expire.

Which type of insurance is the best buy? That really depends on a person's age and life circumstances. For most people one- or five-year renewable term insurance is the best buy. Such a policy insures your life for one or five years at a time with renewal guaranteed. That allows you to pay the lowest rate at any given period. It also pays to shop around for insurance; the rates vary widely. Saxton (1980:585) found that for a 30-year-old white male, the premiums varied from $3.85 to over $8.00 for each $1,000 of coverage. Many times lower rates can be obtained through professional associations or other groups. Also, some companies offer lower rates to nondrinkers and/or nonsmokers.

While most people think of life insurance for the primary breadwinner (traditionally the husband), life insurance for the rest of the family is often considered a luxury. However, life insurance for every family member is a practical idea. When a wife is employed outside the home, what would happen to the family's lifestyle if her income was lost? Whether or not the wife is employed outside the home, how will the services she provides in child care, housecleaning, laundry, and other domestic services be replaced? Domestic help costs between six and ten dollars an hour. If a wife dies from a lingering illness, what about medical bills not covered by health insurance? What about burial expenses? It becomes readily apparent that life insurance for a wife and mother is a necessity.

Life insurance for children is also a good idea. Again, if a child suffers a lingering illness, there will be medical expenses. When a child dies, burial expenses are the same as for an adult. The death of a child involves enough grief and emotional distress without adding indebtedness. Another advantage of insuring children is that you can also insure their insurability. Most children's policies have a conversion feature whereby when the child reaches a certain age, usually 19 or 21, he or she can purchase up to a specified amount of life insurance regardless of his or her insurability. That is, even if they have cancer, heart problems, or any other medical difficulty that would normally prevent them from being issued a policy, they can convert their policy at the current rates for their age group. A policy with a face value of 10,000 dollars and convertibility up to 50,000 dollars has annual premiums of only about 36 dollars for a one-year-old child.

Health Insurance

Hospital and medical expenses have been rising much faster than the general rate of inflation. Medical expenses are such that a serious illness would bankrupt all but the wealthiest families. Many people receive medical insurance as part of a benefit package where they are employed. It is important to ascertain if the plan covers one's family as well. For individuals who do not have medical coverage through their employer, it is important to purchase a private plan.

Major Medical

A popular form of personal insurance is *major medical*. It is often referred to as "tragedy" insurance. Major medical is coverage that takes over where regular health coverages end. It is designed to cover serious accidents and prolonged illnesses. Frequently there is a deductible, ranging from 100 to 1,000 dollars. After the deductible is satisfied, major medical will provide benefits to as much as 100,000 dollars depending on the policy.

Property Insurance

Property insurance is insurance that covers one's property against damage or theft. The two most common types are collision and comprehensive insurance on automobiles and home-owners insurance on houses. *Collision insurance* on a car provides for repair or replacement of the car in case of accident, regardless of who is at fault. *Comprehensive insurance* covers theft, storm damage, vandalism, and other hazards. *Home-owners insurance* covers a house from loss due to fire, storm, vandalism, or other sources of damage. It also covers the contents of the home from theft and damage. Home-owners insurance usually provides liability coverage also. That is, if a person is injured on one's property or in one's home, the insurance will cover the costs.

Many renters do not have property insurance. They believe that the building owner has insurance. While that is usually true, the insurance covers only the building. The personal property of the renter is not covered. The cost of replacing the wardrobes and furnishings of a typical couple can easily run over 10,000 dollars. Also, if someone is injured in an apartment, the renter—not the owner—is liable. *Renter insurance* is available at very reasonable rates and will cover these risks. It is important for families to have their property insured, since most are not in a position to replace items stolen or damaged.

WILLS

Half the people who die in the United States each year do not have a will. Many people put off making a will, thinking they will do it when they get closer to death. However, over one-third of all Americans die before age 65. Others argue that they have little or nothing, so a will is not important. However, there are several important reasons for couples to have a will.

Perhaps the most important reason, if a couple has children, is to designate who will raise the children in the event that both mother and father should die. If a couple does not have a will, the courts will decide who receives custody of their children. A couple may think that everyone in the family is agreed on what will happen if they die, but as many lawyers can tell us, strange things happen in families after a death. A will insures that one's children will be cared for as one desires in the event of death.

Even if a couple does not have children, a will insures that the surviving spouse has access to communal property in the event that the other dies. In many states when a person dies, checking and savings accounts are impounded and personal property is placed under court control. If there is a will, it can usually be speedily probated and funds and property released.

Marriage

Death is enough of a trauma without leaving the survivor with legal problems as well. That is why every couple should have a will. In the case of simple estates, a will is relatively inexpensive. As with any other product, shop around for lawyers' services. Some lawyers' fees are much more reasonable than others.

STEWARDSHIP

The Bible clearly teaches that the material blessings God gives us are not merely for our personal benefit. They are a stewardship to be used for furthering his kingdom and benefiting his children. The Bible teaches that we should have a regular pattern of stewardship: "On the first day of every week, each one of you should set aside a sum of money in keeping with his income" (1 Cor. 16:2). The Bible also addresses the attitude with which we should give: "Each man should give what he has decided in his heart to give, not reluctantly or under compulsion, for God loves a cheerful giver" (2 Cor. 9:7).

How much should one give? This is a matter of some controversy. I personally believe the tithe, which is 10 percent, should be the starting point. The tithe is mentioned in Scripture before the Law of Moses was given (Gen. 14:20; 28:22). The tithe is, of course, an integral part of the Mosaic Law (Lev. 27:30; Deut. 14:22; 26:12). Tithing is also mentioned in the New Testament (Matt. 23:23; Luke 11:42; 18:12; Heb. 7:8–9) and was commended by Jesus (Matt. 23:23). Nowhere in the New Testament is the tithe done away with, but proportional giving is encouraged (1 Cor. 16:2). The main problem I have with tithing is not the basic concept, but that many people who tithe feel they have done their part. They believe 10 percent is God's and 90 percent is theirs. Actually, it is all God's. The tithe should be the beginning point of stewardship—not the end.

Regardless of whether one agrees with my views on tithing or not, I think we can all agree that stewardship should be a prominent part of family financial planning. As God blesses us, we should be sharing with others. The Bible teaches that the use of our money is a good indicator of our spiritual condition. Our material resources are given to us in trust. We are stewards of what we possess.

Economics

DISCUSSION QUESTIONS

1. What else do you think money might represent in addition to love, power, status, and security?

2. In your opinion, why are there so many biblical references to money?

3. Do you see life insurance for a newly married couple as a necessity or a luxury? Why?

4. Why do you believe so many people have trouble making and keeping a budget?

5. In the opening anecdote, who do you side with—Dave or Gwen? Why?

6. What do you see as the major biblical principles for guiding a couple in financial decisions?

SUGGESTED READING

Thom Black and Paul Lewis, *Money Sense: Gaining Control of Your Family's Finances* (Grand Rapids: Zondervan, 1997). Written to help families deal with financial issues and get their finances under control.

Ron Blue, *Master Your Money*, 2d ed. (Nashville: Thomas Nelson, 1991). This book covers biblical principles of money management, budgeting, debt, financial planning, stewardship, and setting financial goals. There are charts for the reader to use and many examples.

Larry Burkett, *Debt-free Living* (Chicago: Moody, 1989). The author deals with the problems of indebtedness and how to get out of debt and stay out of debt. He uses numerous examples and presents several practical strategies for family finances.

Gail Liberman and Alan Lavine, *Love, Marriage, and Money* (Chicago: Dearborn, 1998). This practical book covers budgeting, investing, saving, insurance, estate planning, and the other basic issues in family financial planning.

Living and Growing Together

It is not love that sustains the marriage, but from now on, the marriage that sustains your love.

DIETRICH BONHOEFFER

Almost 90 percent of all Americans will marry, and nearly half of those marriages will end in divorce. What is the difference between those marriages that survive and those that do not? In Chapter 3 we looked at courtship and saw that a number of demographic factors, such as age and social status, are good predictors of marital success. Yet we all know of couples whose marriages defy all the predictors. The predictors indicate only the situations under which divorce is more likely to result. They do not tell us why some marriages are successful while others fail under similar conditions.

Lasswell and Lasswell report on a study they did with 130 strong, cohesive, and functional families (1982:18–19). While there were many differences among these families, six qualities clearly stood out in all of them. The first quality was that *the family members appreciated each other.* They supported each other and made each other feel good about themselves. Criticism was generally absent in these homes. Rather, the members showed appreciation for each other and enjoyed being together.

The second quality that characterized these successful families was that *the members arranged their personal schedules so they had time to be together as a family.* While these families had spontaneous times together, they made a strong effort to have planned times together. They were willing to make an effort to be together.

A third quality of these 130 families was *positive communication patterns.* This involved openness, honesty, patience, respect, concern, and a willingness to discuss differences. The objective is not necessarily the quantity of communication, although it must be adequate, but the *quality* of communication. The family members in the study talked *to* each other, not *at* each other. They listened to hear what the other person was saying and feeling. The family members worked on the quality of their communication.

A high level of commitment to their family was a fourth quality that characterized these family members. The family is a small group, and in the study families, group dynamics were positive. There was a cohesiveness, a sense of belonging, a feeling of being part of a team. The members were willing to invest time and energy in the family.

Another quality of the families was a *spiritual orientation*. This does not mean they were religious and regular church attenders, although many were. Rather, this refers to values or morals associated with religion or spiritual experiences. Strong families have a value system or a moral base to which they can turn and on which they build their lives.

The final quality that characterized these strong families was their *ability to deal positively with crises.* First of all, they were able to face their problems realistically. They did not engage in denial or repression. Second, they were adaptable and able to nurture and care for each other during crises. Crises pulled them together, rather than apart.

It is obvious that these six qualities are not isolated characteristics, but are interrelated. They fit together like a mosaic, supporting and complementing each other. In this chapter we will look more closely at some of these qualities and how they can be developed and maintained.

COMMUNICATION: KEY TO A GROWING RELATIONSHIP

Marriage counselors are generally agreed that communication is the key to a successful marriage and that lack of communication is one of the major problems in marriages that are failing (Black 1982; Clinebell and Clinebell 1970; Collins 1995; Lee 1976; Sanford 1982; Sperry 1978; Wright 1974). Communication involves both the sending and receiving of messages. Of these two, receiving may be the more important. James advises us, "Everyone should be quick to listen, slow to speak" (1:19). The book of Proverbs also speaks of the importance of listening (12:15; 21:28). Listening is a particularly important skill for marriage partners.

Keys to Effective Listening

There are a number of skills that we can develop to become better listeners. While these suggestions may be applicable to many different types of communication settings, we will apply them to communication in marriage. The first suggestion for effective listening is to *establish eye contact and assume a posture that clearly indicates the other person has your complete attention.*

I do a lot of reading, and every spare minute I have my nose in a book or magazine. When my wife and I were first married, she would speak to me while I was reading, and I would stop reading to listen. However, I kept the book or magazine in front of me with my eyes on the page. My wife interpreted that as lack of attention and concern for her. I had to learn to put down my reading material, turn, and look at her. That little action has done a great deal to improve our communication. The cartoon showing the husband at the breakfast table with his face in the newspaper is not a joke. Nonverbal communication is at least as important as the words spoken. By establishing eye contact and good posture, we are communicating that we are listening, are interested, and care.

A second suggestion is to *pay attention to nonverbal cues,* as well as to verbal communication. Imagine a husband coming home from work late and his wife greeting him with the words "I've been waiting for you." How do we interpret her words? We have to look at the nonverbal cues. Is she crying? If so, she may be indicating worry and concern, possibly fear he had been in an accident. Is she scowling? In that case she may be indicating anger and displeasure, possibly upset he did not call saying he would be late. Is she smiling and warm? Then she may be indicating affection. Possibly she has missed him and is glad he is home. Attention to nonverbal cues is critical to effective communication.

Reflective listening is another skill that enhances effective listening. Reflective listening involves hearing the other person's meanings and feelings and reflecting them back. There are two values to reflective listening. One is that it lets the other person know we have heard and understood what he or she is feeling. The other value is that the other person can correct our understanding if it is inaccurate. For example, I arrive home from work one evening and my wife says, "My mother is just impossible." A reflective response might be, "It sounds like your mother has been giving you a hard time about something." If that is the case, it lets my wife know I understand. If it is not the case, she can correct my incorrect impression.

Another skill, which is related to reflective listening, is learning to give *open responses.* Open responses reflect the other person's feelings and allow him or her to continue to discuss the issue. Unfortunately, many of us frequently use closed responses that are judgmental or instructive and lead to conflict. When my wife tells me, "My mother is just impossible," I can give an open or a closed response. An example of a closed response would be, "How many times have I told you to put your foot down with your mother and not let her interfere in our home!" That response is judgmental and will bring a defensive response from my wife, and soon we will be involved in a heated disagreement. On the other hand, an open response such as, "Your mother must have done something to really upset you," allows my wife to discuss the matter. She can tell me what her mother did and what happened. As long as I continue to practice reflective listening and give open responses, she can discuss the situation with me as an ally rather than an adversary.

An additional characteristic of effective listening is to *allow the other person to resolve the problem.* Probably the greatest temptation we face is to immediately offer a solution, especially if a solution appears obvious to us. We need to avoid that temptation and help the other person think through the alternatives. If the other person comes up with the solution, he or she will be more likely to follow through on it. Again, returning to the example of my wife and her mother, the fact may be that she needs to stand up to her mother. But if I impose that solution, she is not likely to follow through. However, if I can help her come to that conclusion, she most likely will follow through. After using reflective listening and open responses to help her talk out the situation, I should not offer a solution, but rather say something like, "What do you think we can do about this problem?" Now it is the two of us against the problem rather than the two of us against each other. As we practice these listening skills, we will find that our communication improves.

Keys to Effective Sharing

As we have seen, there are two aspects to the communication process—sending the message and receiving the message. We have already examined the listening process, but what about the sending process? Norm Wright has presented a number of biblical principles of communication:

1. Be a ready listener and do not answer until the other person has finished talking (Prov. 18:13; James 1:19).
2. Be slow to speak. Think first. Don't be hasty in your words. Speak in such a way that the other person can understand and accept what you say (Prov. 15:23, 28; 21:23; 29:20; James 1:19).

3. Speak the truth always, but do it in love. Do not exaggerate (Eph. 4:15, 25; Col. 3:9).

4. Do not use silence to frustrate the other person. Explain why you are hesitant to talk at this time.

5. Do not become involved in quarrels. It is possible to disagree without quarreling (Prov. 17:14; 20:3; Rom. 13:13; Eph. 4:31).

6. Do not respond in anger. Use a soft and kind response (Prov. 14:29; 15:1; 24:14; 29:11; Eph. 4:26, 31).

7. When you are in the wrong, admit it and ask for forgiveness (James 5:16). When someone confesses to you, tell him you forgive him. Be sure it is forgotten and not brought up to the person (Prov. 17:9; Eph. 4:32; Col. 3:13; 1 Peter 4:8).

8. Avoid nagging (Prov. 10:19; 17:9).

9. Do not blame or criticize the other, but restore, encourage, and edify him (Rom. 14:13; Gal. 6:1; 1 Thess. 5:11). If someone verbally attacks, criticizes, or blames you, do not respond in the same manner (Rom. 12:17, 21; 1 Peter 2:23; 3:9).

10. Try to understand the other person's opinion. Make allowances for differences. Be concerned about his or her interests (Phil. 2:1–4; Eph. 4:2). (Wright 1974:188–89)

In addition to these practical suggestions, there are a few other points on sharing that are worth considering. One of these is the finding that American women use more nonverbal communication than American men do. That is, women load more of the message into the tone of voice, facial expression, gestures, and body movement, whereas men put more of the message into the words. The result is that a woman may believe that she has clearly communicated something to her husband, and he has missed the point.

When we were first married, my wife and I had some disagreements because she had sent me a message primarily with nonverbal communication. I missed the message and did not respond as she desired. She thought I did not respond because I did not care, and she became upset. We have both worked on this. She has made an effort to put more of the message into words, and I have made an effort to pay better attention to her nonverbal cues.

Problems can arise also when one message is given verbally and another is given nonverbally. We used to have a dog that would both wag its tail and growl at the same time when strangers came to the house.

People did not know which end of the dog to believe (actually he was honest; he loved to bite people). We need to be certain that we send the same message verbally and nonverbally.

Good communication also involves knowing when to be quiet and when to bring things up. It is generally unwise to raise important topics just before going to bed or just before leaving the house. If there is an important matter to be discussed, a couple should set aside time to deal with it. *When* something is said may be as critical as *what* is said. If a couple can develop patterns of open and honest communication, practice effective listening, and be sensitive in their sharing, they have the basis for dealing with any problem.

KEYS TO CONSTRUCTIVE COMMUNICATION

John Gottman has published the results of fifteen years of research on married couples in his book *Why Marriages Succeed or Fail* (1994). He found that by analyzing the way couples argue, he could predict with a high degree of accuracy which marriages would succeed and which would fail.

Gottman categorized couples in conflict into three styles: validators, volatiles, and avoidants. *Validators* calmly work out their differences, frequently using compromise. *Volatiles* yell and shout, fighting on a grand scale, then making up on an even grander scale. *Avoidants* usually agree to disagree and rarely confront issues head-on. The interesting thing about Gottman's findings is that all three styles of conflict can be found in both successful and failing marriages. The issue is not the style of conflict, but the ratio of positive to negative comments. He found that in successful marriages, there was a five-to-one ratio of positive to negative comments. Those couples who divorced during his study had more negative than positive comments.

Gottman found nine types of positive communication: compliments, affection, caring, appreciation, concern, empathy, acceptance, good-natured teasing, and sharing joys. He also found four types of negative communication that were particularly destructive. One is *condemnation*, which involves blaming and attacking another's personhood. Gottman says that in healthy marriages, couples focus on the behavior that is causing the problem, whereas in unhealthy marriages they focus on personalities. A second type of negative communication is *contempt*. This involves insulting the other person by name-calling, mocking, belittling, and other tactics. A third type is *defensiveness*. This involves denying, excusing,

Living and Growing Together

cross-blaming, and other strategies. The fourth type is *stonewalling*. This is withdrawal, whether physical or psychological.

HANDLING CONFLICT IN MARRIAGE

In a relationship as intimate as marriage, conflict is bound to arise. Two normal, healthy persons cannot live together without having some areas of disagreement. This is true for Christian couples as well as non-Christian couples. When Christian couples claim to have conflict-free marriages, I like the response of a friend who said, "When a married couple tells me they have a conflict-free relationship, I can tell you one of three things is true of them: either they are liars, one's an idiot, or the other is dead." The fact is each of us is a unique person, and that very uniqueness will lead to conflicts in a relationship.

Conflict in marriage is not wrong, necessarily bad, or a sin. The critical issue is how the conflict is handled. Conflict may destroy a marriage or it may strengthen a marriage. A number of writers have presented useful suggestions for handling conflict in marriage (Bach and Wyden 1968; Dale and Dale 1978: Scanzoni 1979; Shedd 1968; Wright 1977b). Many of the suggestions of these writers overlap each other. Therefore, these ideas will be combined and summarized so we can discuss them.

Timing

One suggestion made by all the writers is that *timing* is critical to constructive resolution of conflicts. As Bach and Wyden write: "Far too many fights become needlessly aggravated because the complainant opens fire when his partner really is in an inappropriate frame of mind or is trying to dash off to work or trying to concentrate on some long-delayed chore that he has finally buckled down to. Indeed there are times when failure to delay—or to advance—the timing of a fight can have cataclysmic consequences" (1968:70).

While emergencies may arise that need to be dealt with at the moment, most conflicts have developed over time. These conflicts usually do not require an immediate resolution but can be temporarily put off until there is adequate time to deal with them. This is regularly done in business, at church, on committees, and in most other settings. It can also be done in a marriage.

A basic rule related to timing in handling conflict is not to raise controversial issues "just before." Conflicts should not be raised just before going to bed, just before sex, just before leaving the house, or just before anything that will not allow adequate time to deal with the issue.

Communication

One of the basic purposes of conflict is to improve communication. It is for partners to let each other know how they feel and think about an issue. Part of communication is listening. The principles of effective listening discussed earlier are especially critical in handling conflict. Yet when dealing with conflict, it is often most difficult to apply the principles of effective listening. In most cases, while one party is talking, the other is not listening carefully but is thinking about how to respond. An exercise that sounds tedious, but in practice is quite effective, is to have one party have his or her say. Then the other party has to repeat back to the first party what was said. The first party then either acknowledges that the second party has it correct or corrects any misunderstandings. Only when both parties agree that the second party fully understands what the first party said, does the second party get his or her say, and the process is repeated.

Stick to the Issue

A woman complained that her husband became historical every time they had an argument. Her friend corrected her by saying, "You mean he becomes hysterical." "No," replied the woman, "I mean *historical*. Whenever we have an argument, he brings up every related problem we have had since we have been married."

All the writers agree that it is important to stick to the issue at hand. When other issues are brought into the discussion, it hampers resolution of the current conflict. It also opens old wounds and confuses the issue. Bach and Wyden recommend that couples "keep all arguments not only fair but up-to-date so that the books on a marriage can be balanced daily, much as banks keep their debits and credits current by clearing all checks with other banks before closing down for business every evening. Couples who fight regularly and constructively need not carry gunny sacks full of grievances, or [drag] the totally irrelevant past into the argument" (1968:19).

Fight Fair

The object of conflict is not to win but to resolve the problem. Marriage is meant to be a cooperative effort, not a competitive sport. When there is a problem, the goal is not to find fault or assess blame but to find a solution. The attitude of partners should not be a win/lose approach—that is, every solution involving a winner and a loser. Rather, the attitude of partners should be a win/win approach. The couple faces the problem together and when a solution is found, they both win.

When a couple has a win/lose approach to conflict resolution, they will often resort to unfair tactics in order to win. Unfair tactics may involve anything from emotional outbursts to withholding sexual intimacy. Unfair tactics may also involve setting power traps. It is important to remember that the one who "wins" the argument may be advocating the least advantageous solution to a problem. The ability to "win" an argument does not necessarily make one right. When winning and losing become more important than finding the best solution to a problem, regardless of whose idea it is, both partners become losers in the long run.

Compromise Is Not a Dirty Word

In a given situation it is rare that one party is entirely wrong and the other party entirely right. Usually the truth lies somewhere in between. Even if a compromise is not the "best" solution, if it works and both parties can live with the compromise, it is a successful solution. The willingness to give in, modify, and negotiate is the secret to successful solutions.

Scanzoni sees negotiation as the key to compromise. He defines *compromise* as "a process of give and take between two parties, aimed at arriving at a solution . . . in which each gets something, but not all, that each originally wanted" (1979:28–29). Negotiation involves both partners placing their desires on the table and attempting to harmonize them in a way that both receive as much as possible. For example, a wife may want to go out for an evening to a concert that is rather expensive. Her husband may feel they cannot afford to attend the concert. The wife may offer to give up something else to save money to pay for the concert, or the husband may offer to take her out to a less expensive activity. In either case, both are seeking a compromise.

One word of caution needs to be made about compromises. Individuals sometimes use compromise in place of admitting they are wrong. For example, if my wife and I are in disagreement over a discipline matter with one of our children, I may begin to realize that she is right and I am wrong. Rather than admitting I am wrong, I may exploit the use of compromise. That is, I could say, "Okay, I am willing to give in this time, but remember, you owe me one." What I should do is admit she is correct. I should say, "As we have been discussing this, I have realized my approach is not too wise. I think we should try what you have been suggesting." It is important that compromise be used honestly.

DIFFERENCES

When a couple marries, it is like the meeting of two cultures. Each brings values, norms, traditions, and expectations to the marriage. The partners have been raised in different homes with different ways of family living. They bring different personalities to the marriage. In fact, they bring many differences to the relationship, and how these differences are handled will have an important bearing on the success of the marriage.

Types of Differences

While the areas of difference between a couple are limitless, they can be categorized into five types—those related to taste, habits, values, thinking, and temperament.

Taste

We all have our likes and dislikes, our preferences—what we call our tastes. We have tastes in food, music, dress, and many other areas. Frequently in dating and courtship, a man and a woman are either not aware of each other's tastes or do not recognize the implications of those differences for marriage. Even in areas such as food, differences may not be recognized. When they went out to eat while dating and courting, he ordered steak and potatoes every time, whereas she ordered quiche one time and crepes another, enjoying a variety of dishes. As long as each ordered his or her own meal, their differences of taste in food did not matter. But after marriage, when they both have to eat the same dinner, it can be critical. He came from a home where dinner meant meat and potatoes. She came from a home where her mother was always experimenting with new recipes.

Frequently in the flush of the romance of dating and courtship, people are willing to "put up" with differences in taste. They may even find the differences interesting when they are encountered occasionally. However, in the day-to-day living of marriage, their differences in taste can become annoying sources of irritation.

Habits

Do you squeeze the toothpaste tube in the middle or roll it from the end? Do you unroll the toilet paper from the top or bottom? Do you sleep with the bedroom window open or shut? Do you shower at night or in the morning? Do you drink from the bottle or can instead of using a glass? Habits, many developed over a dozen or more years, are such an integral part of us that we are not even aware of them most of the time. Yet habits control most of our routine behaviors. Because they do, we notice when something interferes with our habits.

While many habits are readily apparent, there are three areas of habits that a courting couple may not be exposed to that can have a significant impact on married life. One area is habits related to *hygiene.* Does the woman shower at night and the man in the morning? She may think he goes to bed dirty, while he thinks she goes to work dirty. Does he gargle and spit into the sink? She may find that disgusting. Another area of habits where differences may create problems is *diet*—not only what is eaten, but when it is eaten and how. The third area is *sleep habits.* Most people sleep by themselves before they get married. Unless a couple has cohabited before marriage, they are unlikely to be aware of each other's sleep habits. Should the bedroom door be open or shut? Should the room be perfectly dark or should there be some light? Who sleeps nearest the door or window? Do you go to sleep with music or with quiet? These and many more sleep habits may be deeply ingrained in a person.

Values

One writer defines values as ideas, persons, objects, principles, or behaviors we prize or desire (Elder 1976:36). Another writer says, "Values are whatever an individual within a group considers of importance. In each automatic or consciously made decision some value underlies the choice of one thing over against another" (Mayers 1976:148). In essence, our values determine our priorities. Our values are revealed by our behavior. A person may claim to put God first in his or her life. However, if he or she rarely reads God's Word, frequently engages in recreation rather than attending church, and participates in questionable activities, one would have to conclude that person did not highly value God. Perhaps the two best measures of people's values are what they spend their money on and how they spend their time. As someone said, "Show me a man's checkbook and his datebook and I will tell you what kind of man he is."

While differences in values in some areas may be easily overcome, differences in values in other areas are more difficult to resolve. That is why couples with similar religious and social backgrounds have more successful marriages. Values in the area of religion and finances are concerned with central areas of life.

Thinking

Not everyone thinks in the same way. Different people use different cognitive processes. For instance, some people think dichotomously, dividing problems up into parts and solving the problem by dealing with the parts. Other people think holistically, treating a problem as a unit. Some people use logical reasoning, while others use intuitive reasoning.

Our culture appears to encourage males and females to think differently. Boys are taught to think analytically, whereas girls are pushed to think conceptually. While there are no differences between the *total* scores of males and females on IQ tests, college entrance exams, and Graduate Record Exams, males score higher than females on the arithmetic component of these tests, and females score higher than males on the verbal component (Hedges and Nowell 1995). Since marriage involves a male and a female, two people who have been encouraged to think in different ways have to deal with each other.

In thinking about cognitive activity, we need to distinguish between *process* and *outcome*. For example, if I ask you how many apples would be in a basket if five boys each placed five apples in the basket, you could add five plus five plus five plus five plus five or you could multiply five times five. Both processes would produce the same answer—twenty-five. One process treats the problem by parts, the other treats it as a whole, but both produce the same outcome. It is not uncommon to see couples have conflicts over thinking processes when their concern should be over outcomes. One may arrive at a solution one way, the other a different way, but if both processes produce similar outcomes, then there really is no difficulty.

Temperament

Ron says the glass is half full; Joan says it is half empty. They are looking at the same glass. Both acknowledge the content level is 50 percent. However, Ron focuses on the occupied part of the glass, Joan on the empty part. This may result from differences in temperament. Temperament is basically a predisposition to behave in a particular way.

While early temperament theories saw temperament as inherited and totally biologically based, current theory understands temperament as a product of heredity and the environment (Schultz 1981:358–59). Heredity provides the potential, and environment determines the extent of development. One recent theory postulates four temperaments: emotionality, sociability, activity, and impulsivity. These are seen as the building blocks of personality. People's personalities are composed of differing amounts of each of these temperaments (Schultz 1981:358).

Each person has a unique personality. Some are more optimistic, some more pessimistic; some are more outgoing, some more introspective; some are more cheerful, some more easily despondent. When two people come together in a marriage, each brings to the marriage his or her own unique personality. There are bound to be differences. Some of these differences may not come to light until the couple has been married for several years. Also, people's personalities change, so new areas of difference may crop up in a marriage.

Handling Differences

Differences generally do not destroy a marriage. It is *how these differences are handled* that determines the outcome of the marriage. Dan Lambrides, a marriage and family therapist, suggests five steps for dealing with differences (1982).

Awareness

The first step is to be aware of differences. The more aware a couple are of their differences before they marry, the better their chances are for developing strategies for dealing with those differences. Most marriage counselors use a battery of tests in premarital counseling to uncover and highlight many of these differences. This allows couples to deal with these differences before they cause problems.

It is common for couples not to be aware of differences. They recognize that there is tension and conflict in their relationship but seem unable to put their fingers on the source. Couples need to be aware of their differences before they can deal with them.

Acknowledgment

Not only must a couple be aware of their differences, but they must also acknowledge them. There are couples who are aware of their differences but will not acknowledge them. The husband and wife have conspired to ignore and suppress the differences. They see the differences as the problem, when it is how they handle the differences that is the problem. The couple thinks that if they ignore their differences, maybe the problem will go away. Of course it will not; the problem will only get worse. A couple need to acknowledge their differences to deal with them.

Acceptance

Awareness and acknowledgment are important first steps, but they are not enough. There must also be acceptance. However, acceptance does not necessarily mean approval. It does mean accepting reality as it is. Acceptance recognizes what cannot be changed as well as what can be changed and is willing to live with differences. It is saying differences can be okay. We do not need to be mirror images of each other. We can each be ourselves.

Adaptation

Acceptance is the beginning of change. When we are willing to accept things, we can begin adapting. When I can say it is okay for me to be more concerned with time and my wife to be more concerned with people, then we can begin to adapt to each other.

Appreciation

The step of appreciation may be the key to dealing with differences. Rather than seeing my wife's differences as a source of irritation and problems, I need to see them as opportunities for my enrichment. Before I married her, I saw the world through only one set of eyes, thought about things with one cognitive process. In other words, I had a limited perspective. She provides me with a second set of eyes, with another way of thinking through issues, with a broader perspective. Differences can divide or they can unite. A couple's differences can be assets and enrich their relationship. It is how differences are dealt with that is important, not the differences themselves.

SPIRITUAL DIMENSION

Howard and Charlotte Clinebell write, "Intimacy on the horizontal, person-to-person plane and intimacy on the vertical or spiritual plane complement and reinforce each other" (1970:180). They add, "Growth-producing intimacy is difficult if not impossible without a spiritual center and source" (181). It is obvious that non-Christians can have good marriages. We are all familiar with non-Christian couples that have what certainly appear to be good, happy, and successful marriages. Nevertheless, it is my conviction that those marriages would be better with a spiritual dimension.

A marriage is a relationship between two people; the spiritual dimension of that relationship can be no stronger than the spiritual lives of the individuals. It is obvious that as a couple draws nearer to God, they will draw nearer to each other (see figure 9.1). As we have already seen, research demonstrates that the more "religious" a couple are, the more successful their marriage will be.

Scripture

A husband and wife need to look to the Word of God for guidance in their marriage. They need to study the Bible together to discover God's principles for living together, raising children, and other areas of family life; and the children need to be included in their times of Bible study. They must use the Word of God as a marriage manual as well as a guide to general living.

Prayer

A couple should pray together—and for each other. Prayer should be a regular part of their relationship, not an exercise to be engaged in when crises strike. A couple should pray about their relationship as a whole and each aspect of it specifically. They need to pray about decisions, about

FIGURE 9.1

A Couple's Relationship with God Affects Their Relationship with Each Other.

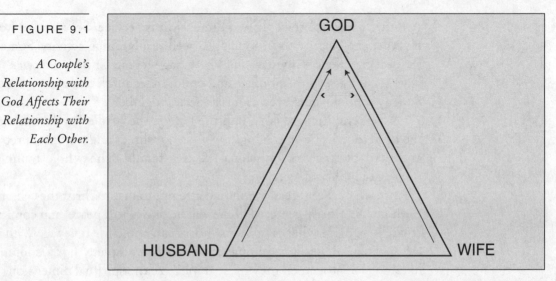

spending—about every area of life. The saying "The family that prays together, stays together" is true.

Values and Ethics

A couple and a family must have a value system to live by. They must have a set of ethics to apply to the various situations that arise in family living. The values and the ethics of a family result from the spiritual lives of the members of that family, individually and collectively. Their values and ethics are forged out of their individual time with the Lord. A family needs to take time to read the Bible and pray together and to discuss the implications of the Scripture they have shared together. How does it apply in their lives individually and as a family?

A family needs to develop a biblical value system and a biblical set of ethics. Values and ethics are best transmitted in the home. Parents have a responsibility to help each other and their children to develop a Christian philosophy of life.

Worship

A couple should also worship together. While it is good and proper for them to structure private worship experiences for themselves as a couple, it is also important for them to participate in corporate worship. They need to find a church in the area where they are living in which they can become involved and have fellowship with other believers.

Service

Another aspect of the spiritual dimension is service. Serving the Lord together can be growth-producing as well as a bonding activity. Some of the best experiences my wife and I have had were in Christian service. We have served as youth sponsors and children's church leaders, co-taught Sunday school, and served as missionaries together.

When children are born into the family, the whole family can serve the Lord together. For example, my wife, our three children, and I prepare and send packages to missionaries as a family. The whole family is involved in Christian service.

In each of these areas, we should attempt to make Christ the center of the home. A Christ-centered home will be one of joy, peace, and comfort. It will be a place where family members can come for renewal. Without the spiritual dimension, a home can never be complete. For a couple to live and grow together, they must emphasize the spiritual dimension.

DISCUSSION QUESTIONS

1. Which of the six qualities of strong marriages, presented by Lasswell and Lasswell, do you believe is the most vital? Why?

2. Which of the keys to effective listening do you see as most essential? Why?

3. Why do you believe men and women differ in their use of nonverbal communication?

4. Suggest some unfair tactics people use in disagreements. Why are they unfair?

5. In your opinion, what is the explanation for the differences in arithmetic and verbal test scores between males and females? Why?

6. Why is the spiritual dimension important to marriage? Can you think of any additional aspects to the spiritual dimension of marriage other than those mentioned? How would they apply?

SUGGESTED READING

Gary Chapman, *Loving Solutions* (Chicago: Moody Press, 1998). The author deals with common problems in marriage such as a workaholic partner, an alcoholic or drug-addicted partner, or an irresponsible partner. He offers practical counsel for dealing with these problems.

John Gottman, *Why Marriages Succeed or Fail* (New York: Simon & Schuster, 1994). A secular book with solid social research and practical insight into marriage. The book deals with styles of conflict and the content of communication.

Willard F. Harley Jr., *Give and Take* (Grand Rapids: Revell, 1996). The author deals with conflict resolution in marriage. A clinical psychologist and marriage counselor, he brings his clinical experience to his writing, offering practical insights and presenting effective strategies for improving communication.

Stanley Scott, *The Heart of Commitment* (Nashville: Thomas Nelson, 1998). Written by a clinical psychologist who specializes in research on marital failure and success, the book discusses seven keys to making a marriage better. Each concept is illustrated with real-life accounts.

PART FOUR

Life Cycle of the Family

Childbearing

Behold, children are a gift of the Lord;
The fruit of the womb is a reward.
Like arrows in the hand of a warrior,
So are the children of one's youth.
How blessed is the man whose quiver is full of them;
They shall not be ashamed,
When they speak with their enemies in the gate.

PSALM 127:3–5 (NASB)

The psalmist writes that children are a gift from God, but they are a gift placed within the mother and father. A couple has the potential to produce dozens of children. How are children conceived? How does a couple decide how many children they want? Should they decide? How can conception be controlled? What about couples who want to have children and are unable to conceive? These are some of the questions that will be dealt with in this chapter.

CONCEPTION

Fertilization or conception takes place in the woman's Fallopian tube or oviduct. Each month, when a woman ovulates, one or more eggs are released. The egg then travels down the Fallopian tube. If the woman engages in sexual intercourse within seventy-two hours before or after ovulation, it is likely that sperm will be present in the Fallopian tube when the egg is there. During ejaculation the seminal fluid, containing millions of sperm, is deposited at the base of the vagina near the cervix. These sperm swim up the cervix, through the uterus, and into the Fallopian tubes. The sperm can survive in the Fallopian tubes for up to seventy-two hours. Of the millions of sperm ejaculated, generally only several dozen make it all the way to the Fallopian tubes.

Life Cycle of the Family

Of the dozens of sperm present in the Fallopian tubes, only one will impregnate the egg. That sperm will penetrate the egg, and as it does so, it loses its tail. Then the head proceeds through the food-rich substance to the nucleus of the egg. When one sperm has penetrated the egg, the egg then rejects all other sperm.

All human cells contain twenty-three *pairs* of chromosomes except germ cells—the sperm and the egg. Germ cells contain twenty-three chromosomes. When fertilization takes place, the twenty-three chromosomes in the sperm pair up to form the genetic heredity of the new child. The twenty-third pair of chromosomes determines the sex of the child. While eggs always have an X chromosome, sperm may have either an X or Y chromosome. If the sperm containing an X chromosome fertilizes the egg, the child will be a female. If the sperm has a Y chromosome, the child will be a male.

PRENATAL DEVELOPMENT

If newborns could remember and speak, they would emerge from the womb carrying tales as wondrous as Homer's. They would describe the fury of conception and the sinuous choreography of nerve cells, billions of them dancing pas de deux to make connections that infuse mere matter with consciousness. They would recount how the amorphous glob of an arm bud grows into the fine structure of fingers agile enough to play a polonaise. They would tell of cells swarming out of the nascent spinal cord to colonize far reaches of the embryo, helping to form face, head and glands. The explosion of such complexity and order—a heart that beats, legs that run and a brain powerful enough to contemplate its own origins—seem like a miracle. It is as if a single dab of white paint turned into the multicolored splendor of the Sistine ceiling. (Begley and Carey 1982:38)

The Bible describes the process this way: "For you created my inmost being; you knit me together in my mother's womb. I praise you because I am fearfully and wonderfully made" (Ps. 139:13–14). Both the authors quoted above and the psalmist describe prenatal development in a literary fashion. The creation of a person is a miracle—fearful and wonderful. Because we can describe it biologically does not mean we can explain it. However, we can study the process. Prenatal development is generally divided into three stages: *germinal, embryonic,* and *fetal* (see table 10.1).

Childbearing

TABLE 10.1

*Prenatal
Development*

STAGE	TIME	CHARACTERISTICS
Germinal		Sperm penetrates egg.
	12 hours	The division of the fertilized egg begins.
	72 hours	The zygote reaches the uterus.
Embryonic	2 weeks	The zygote/embryo is implanted in the uterine wall and is drawing nourishment.
	4 weeks	The embryo is approximately one-fifth of an inch in length. A primitive heart is beating. The head and the tail are established. The mouth, liver, and intestines begin to take shape.
Fetal	8 weeks	The embryo/fetus is now about one inch in length. For the first time it begins to resemble a human being. Facial features, limbs, hands, feet, fingers, and toes become apparent. The nervous system is responsive, and many of the internal organs begin to function.
	12 weeks	The fetus is now three inches long and weighs almost one ounce. The muscles begin to develop and sex organs are formed. Eyelids, fingernails, and toenails are being formed. Spontaneous movements of the trunk can occasionally be seen.
	16 weeks	The fetus is now approximately five inches long. Blinking, grasping, and mouth motions can be observed. Hair appears on the head and body.
	20 weeks	The fetus now weighs about one half pound and is approximately ten inches long. Sweat glands develop and the external skin is no longer transparent.
	24 weeks	The fetus is able to inhale or exhale and could make a crying sound. The eyes are completed and taste buds have developed on the tongue.
	28 weeks	The fetus is usually capable by this time of living outside the womb but would be considered immature at birth.
	38 weeks	The end of the normal gestation period. The fetus is now prepared to live in the outside world.

Adapted from Dworetzky 1981:126

Germinal Stage

Cell division begins about twelve hours after fertilization. The fertilized egg, called a *zygote* at this stage, continues dividing as it travels toward the uterus. By the time the zygote reaches the uterus (about seventy-two hours following fertilization), it consists of about thirty-six cells. The cells form into two layers. The outer layer called the *trophoblast* attaches the zygote to the uterine wall and eventually develops into the placenta, umbilical cord, and amniotic sac. The inner cells, called the *blastocyst,* divide into three layers. The outer layer, the *ectoderm,* will develop into skin, hair, and nerve endings. The middle layer, the *mesoderm,* will become sex glands, kidneys, blood, bone, and muscle. The inner layer, the *endoderm,* will develop into the inner body organs. The *germinal* stage lasts approximately two weeks, ending when the zygote is attached to the uterine wall and is drawing nourishment from the mother.

Embryonic Stage

During the *embryonic stage* the developing child is called an *embryo.* This stage lasts about six weeks. During this time rapid cell division continues and cell specialization appears. After two weeks a tiny vessel, which will eventually become the heart, begins to pump. At this time the embryo is no bigger than an adult's thumbnail.

By the end of the embryonic stage (eight weeks) the embryo is approximately an inch long and resembles a human being. The nervous system as well as many of the internal organs have begun to function.

During the embryonic stage there is a high rate of spontaneous abortions or miscarriages. It is estimated that one-fourth to one-third of all pregnancies are terminated by spontaneous abortions (Dworetzky 1981:127). Many women, not even aware they are pregnant, may believe they are only having an unusually heavy menstrual flow when in fact they are experiencing a spontaneous abortion.

Fetal Stage

The *fetal stage* is the third and longest stage, lasting thirty weeks in the case of a full-term pregnancy. During this period the developing child is called a *fetus.* Cell specialization continues, with the muscular and nervous systems forming rapidly. By the twentieth week of pregnancy the mother is able to feel fetal movement. At about twenty-eight weeks after fertilization, prenatal development has reached a point where survival, in

Childbearing

case of premature birth, is possible. The final weeks of this stage involve weight gain. A full-term pregnancy ends with childbirth at thirty-eight weeks.

TO HAVE OR NOT TO HAVE

Biologically healthy couples are capable of producing one child after another. Throughout most of human history this, in fact, has been the case. Married women have gone from one pregnancy to the next until they died or reached menopause. While at least in theory a woman could bear a child each year, there is a biological mechanism that tends to space children. In societies where women subsist on low fat diets (which includes most primitive societies), a woman will not usually ovulate while she is lactating. This mechanism functions as natural birth control, preventing pregnancy and the birth of another child until the previous one is weaned. However, in societies with higher fat diets, such as North America, this biological mechanism is overridden.

While a healthy woman is capable of bearing many children, throughout history couples have attempted to control the number and timing of their children. Modern birth-control methods have given couples significant control over their fertility. We will examine the issue of controlling the timing and number of children next; in this section we want to deal with the issue of whether or not to have children at all.

Until recently, it was expected that a married couple would have children, and it was considered a tragedy for a couple to be childless. However, in the past twenty-five years that attitude has changed. Today, many couples are deciding not to have children. Among women 18 to 34 who do not have children, 22 percent plan to remain child-free, according to a 1990 U.S. Census Bureau survey. It is generally women with more education and stronger career orientation that choose to remain child-free (Ambry 1992).

Research on the reasons couples choose to remain child-free show they fall into nine categories (Houseknecht 1987). The categories, in the order most often mentioned are:

1. Freedom from child-care responsibility and greater opportunity for self-fulfillment
2. More satisfactory marital relationship
3. Wife's career opportunities

4. Financial advantages
5. Concern over population
6. General dislike for children
7. Negative childhood experiences
8. Concerns about parenting ability
9. Concerns about physical aspect of childbirth

Obviously, the decision to remain child-free has many ramifications. We live in a society that is still family oriented, with children considered an integral part of the family. Parents of child-free couples may apply pressure in a desire for grandchildren. A child-free couple may find they have less in common with their peers as other couples begin to have children and center their lives around the home. One study has found that child-free couples feel negatively stereotyped by society (Somers 1993). The issue of whether or not to have children is a major decision for couples. Table 10.2 suggests some questions a couple might discuss in contemplating this issue.

TABLE 10.2	1. Do you like children—not just cuddly infants but also cranky two-year-olds, curious eight-year-olds, and anxious teenagers?
Parenthood Contemplation Questions	2. Do you view parenthood as a burden or as an enriching experience?
	3. Do you feel your marriage is strong enough for you to take on the responsibility of nurturing another person?
	4. Are you willing to let go of your childhood and really become an adult?
	5. Can you give love without needing an equal amount in return?
	6. Do you respond well to helplessness in others?
	7. Do you have unrealistic expectations about parenthood? Do you believe, for example, that having a child will automatically ensure solace in your old age?
	8. Are you prepared for the profound changes parenthood will bring to your lifestyle—in terms of money, time, and professional goals?
	9. Are you prepared to work out the necessary compromises regarding child care (particularly in a dual-career situation)?
	10. Are you prepared to let a child develop according to his or her bent, rather than according to your predetermined plan?
	11. Are you prepared to depend more heavily on family and friends, as is usually necessary when a couple has a child?
	12. Do you believe that it is consistent with God's leading in your life to have children?

Childbearing

HOW MANY AND WHEN?

Even when a couple decide that they do want to have children, there are still decisions to be made. How many children would they like to have? When do they want to have them? What about spacing? Do they want two in diapers at the same time?

Social research has produced some useful findings that should be considered by a couple making a decision concerning parenthood.

We have already seen the results of research that indicates that the earlier in a marriage a child is born, the greater the probability of divorce (Belkin and Goodman 1980:436). How long should a couple be married before having their first child? While many factors will influence the decision, one authority suggests waiting at least "three years after marriage to get the marriage on solid ground emotionally and financially" (Belkin and Goodman 1980:436).

A significant amount of research has been done on birth order, spacing, and number of children. This research indicates that family size and spacing affect the intellectual development of children (Zajonc 1975:37–43; Steelman and Mercy 1980:571–82; Powell and Steelman 1993; Henry 1995). What this research found was that children who are closely spaced score lower on IQ tests than children with greater spacing between siblings. The research also found that as the number of siblings in a family increases, the average IQ score decreases. One study (see figure 10.1) found a difference of ten IQ points between the scores of children with one sibling and children with eight siblings (Zajonc 1975:43). A leading researcher in this area suggests that if the intellectual development of their children is important to a couple, they should limit their family to two children with at least two years between them (Zajonc 1975:39–43).

Social research shows us the relationship between various factors such as the timing of the first child and divorce rate or number of children and intellectual development. However, we must keep in mind that these are correlational studies and statistical averages. There are always exceptions to these generalizations. A couple should not make family planning decisions based solely on the results of social research. There are many factors that a couple should consider in family planning. Nevertheless, the results of this research should aid a couple in the decision process. The more information they have, the better the possibilities for making wise decisions.

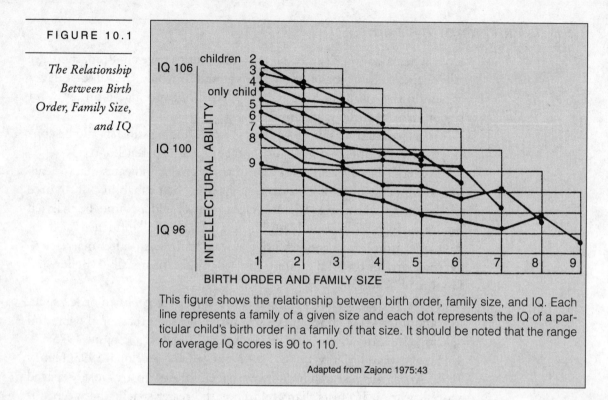

FIGURE 10.1

*The Relationship
Between Birth
Order, Family Size,
and IQ*

This figure shows the relationship between birth order, family size, and IQ. Each line represents a family of a given size and each dot represents the IQ of a particular child's birth order in a family of that size. It should be noted that the range for average IQ scores is 90 to 110.

Adapted from Zajonc 1975:43

BIRTH CONTROL AND THE CHRISTIAN

A number of Protestant scholars (e.g., Grunlan and Mayers 1988:144; Hulme 1962:34–35; Hughes 1969:100–101; Waltke 1969:20) agree that human sexuality has two functions from a biblical perspective. One of the functions of sex is to propagate the race (Gen. 1:27–28). The other function, as Grunlan and Mayers explain, is that it "reinforces the relationship between a man and a woman (Gen. 2:24; Prov. 5:18–19; Eph. 5:22–31). Sex is a sharing of each other, a physical intimacy that expresses the spiritual intimacy between two people. Sex is God-ordained. It is not just for reproduction but also for the expression of love between a husband and wife" (1988:144). Sex is God's gift of life and love to humans.

The task facing a Christian couple is that of harmonizing these two functions of sex. Pregnancy is the natural result of regular sexual activity. The issue is, should a couple continuously produce children as a result of maintaining a one-flesh relationship? William Hulme says:

Childbearing

> "Be fruitful and multiply" still means that the Creator expects children to come out of marriage, and "subdue the earth" still means that man is to exercise dominion over the forces of nature.... In birth control, the theological issue is not whether things work out any better because of conception limitation, but whether conception control is not man's responsibility under God as a part of his elevated status above all other creatures. (Hulme 1962:37–38)

Some argue that birth control is interfering with God. They argue that a couple should engage in sexual intercourse and leave the results to God. They say that we are putting ourselves in the place of God when we use birth control, and they claim a couple should trust God since he knows what is good for them and will bring about what is best for them. As humans we should submit to God. Responding to this type of reasoning, Donald MacKay writes:

> The general attitude they express is, I fear, a false humility. It is more akin to the pagan fear of nature ... than to fear of God in the positive sense that the Bible gives to that phrase.... It is simply bad theology to conclude from this that God places an embargo on taking our share of responsibility for the way things turn out next.
>
> The distinction we need here is between creation (which is God's prerogative) and procreation (which is man's responsibility), ... the process within our created space-time by which human beings bring other human beings into the world.... The sovereignty of God does not at all imply that every aspect of the future is inevitable-for-us. On the contrary, the biblical doctrine is that we are accountable for those decisions and actions that are up to us, precisely because He has made us the determinants of them. (1979:57–59)

Basically, the issue is not whether or not we are going to "interfere" with nature, but to what extent. Every time we visit a physician or dentist, every time we take a drug, every time we build a dam, every time we water a lawn—we are tampering with nature. Most of us do not say when we get a headache, "This must be God's will. When he is ready, he will take it away." Rather, we take an aspirin. The fact is that all of us subdue nature in some way or other every day. The real question is, has God given us the means and responsibility to subdue nature? If he has, we are responsible to do so. As Hulme argues:

> Christianity is no nature cult. We are to subdue nature, not worship it. Instead of submitting helplessly to the processes of nature, the Christian

as a worker together with the Creator channels and subdues these processes to serve the purposes for which God has created and redeemed us. The birth control controversy ... is a theological conflict over whether there is not a higher source for the revelation of God's will than the processes of nature. (1962:39–40)

METHODS OF BIRTH CONTROL

Methods of birth control may be divided into four major categories: (1) natural methods, (2) mechanical methods, (3) chemical methods, and (4) surgical methods. We will examine the basic methods in each category. The advantages and disadvantages of each method will also be discussed. I will not recommend any method. Each couple must weigh the advantages and disadvantages of each method for themselves.

Natural Methods

The methods in this category are called *natural* because they center around natural processes rather than using some form of interference as do the methods in the other categories. The three natural methods we will discuss are the rhythm method, coitus interruptus, and abstinence.

Rhythm Method

The rhythm method is based on the fact that a woman ovulates only once a month. The egg lives in the Fallopian tube for only forty-eight to seventy-two hours, and sperm are not capable of living more than forty-eight to seventy-two hours in the Fallopian tube. Theoretically, therefore, conception can occur only during four to six days of any menstrual cycle. The secret to the successful use of this method is determining when a woman ovulates and then avoiding intercourse for seventy-two hours before and after that time.

There are three common techniques for determining when a woman ovulates. One is the calendar technique. This technique is based on the fact that women with regular cycles ovulate fourteen days, plus or minus two days, before the onset of menses, regardless of the length of the cycle. To use this technique, a woman charts the length of her cycles for at least six months. She can then calculate her fertile days by subtracting eighteen days from her shortest cycle to determine the first unsafe day and subtracting eleven from the number of days in her longest cycle to determine her last unsafe day. For example, if a woman's shortest cycle is twenty-five days and her longest cycle is thirty-two days, her unsafe period extends from the seventh day (25–18 = 7) following the onset of menses to the twenty-first day (32–11 = 21). She needs to avoid sexual intercourse during those two weeks (21–7 = 14 days) to be safe. Obviously, the more regular a woman's cycles, the shorter the unsafe period will be, while the more irregular the longer the unsafe period will be.

The second technique for determining the time of ovulation is the basal temperature technique. Following ovulation, progesterone is produced that results in an elevation of a woman's temperature .4 to .8 degrees. Using this method, a woman takes her temperature each morning immediately upon waking and before getting out of bed. A special thermometer, called a basal thermometer, which records small changes in temperature, is used. If a woman has regular cycles, a pattern may develop that allows her to calculate when she will ovulate.

The third means of determining ovulation is the vaginal mucus technique. Just before ovulation, glands in the cervix secrete mucus. The mucus has the appearance and consistency of the white of a raw egg. The woman performs daily self-examinations, feeling the cervix for the onset of mucus secretion. Frequently, two or more of these techniques are used in combination in determining the time of ovulation.

The advantages of the rhythm method are that little or no cost is involved, neither a physician's services nor prescriptions are required, and there are no medical side effects. There are also several disadvantages to this method. A major disadvantage is that only about 60 percent of women have menstrual cycles that are regular enough for this method to work successfully. Another disadvantage is that it requires discipline in application, involving keeping track of dates, regularly taking one's temperature, and/or engaging in daily self-examinations. A significant disadvantage is that it restricts sex to certain periods of time and forbids sex during a time when many women experience heightened sexual desire (ovulation).

Coitus Interruptus

The method called coitus interruptus, which is also referred to as the *withdrawal method,* requires the male partner to withdraw his penis from the vagina just before ejaculation. Emission of the sperm should take place away from the vagina and external genitalia of the woman. This is an ancient technique and is probably referred to in Genesis 38:9, where it is said of Onan that "he spilled his seed on the ground." Onan was punished by God, not for practicing coitus interruptus, but for failing to obey God's command to raise up children for his brother as the Old Testament levirate law required (Deut. 25:5).

The advantages of coitus interruptus include the following: there is no cost involved, no physician's service or prescriptions are needed, and there are no medical side effects. There are also disadvantages to this method. One disadvantage is that it requires significant discipline on the part of the male partner. Another disadvantage is that it takes away from sexual enjoyment. The natural tendency for a male is to thrust at the time of ejaculation. Also simultaneous orgasms are not possible, and the couple is not able to abandon themselves to the act, but must be monitoring their reactions. The greatest disadvantage to coitus interruptus is that it is not foolproof. A few drops of semen are secreted from the penis before ejaculation. While that semen generally does not contain enough sperm to impregnate a woman, there are always exceptions. Also, if withdrawal is not timed right, the ejaculation may begin before withdrawal is completed, and the first few drops of semen ejaculated at orgasm have the highest concentration of sperm.

Abstinence

Abstaining from sexual intercourse, of course, prevents pregnancy. One form of abstinence, the postpartum sex taboo, is widely practiced in primitive societies. The postpartum sex taboo is a rule prohibiting a woman from having sexual relations with her husband, or any man, for a specified period of time following childbirth. In a study of fifty-six cultures, researchers found that half of them had a postpartum sex taboo that lasted for at least a year (Otterbein 1977:176). The long postpartum sex taboo, according to Otterbein (1977:176–77) is associated with three factors. The first is polygyny. Since the husband has other wives, a long postpartum sex taboo does not deny his sexual gratification. The second factor is clan organization. The spacing of children is important where women must contribute to a group larger than a nuclear family, such as an extended-family household. The third factor is a protein deficiency in the diet, which frequently occurs in tropical areas. Women living in these climates need to space their children in order for their milk to remain rich in protein.

In technological Western societies where monogamy is practiced, abstinence is not an attractive birth control method. With a variety of

Childbearing

birth control methods readily available, most couples are not willing to forego sexual intimacy. In my opinion there is only one group of people for whom abstinence should be the birth control method of first choice—that is single persons.

Mechanical Methods

The methods in this category are called *mechanical* because they either place a mechanical barrier between the sperm and the egg or they mechanically prevent the fertilized egg from implanting in the uterine wall. The methods to be discussed under this category are the condom, the diaphragm, and the intrauterine device.

Condom

The condom is a thin sheath made of latex rubber, polyurethane, or similar material. It is fitted over the erect penis and collects the ejaculated semen so that it is not deposited in the vagina. Other common names for condoms are *prophylactics, safes, rubbers, skins,* and *Trojans* (the name of a popular brand). The condom is applied just before the penile penetration of the vagina. It is unrolled over the erect penis. Many condoms have a receptacle at the end to catch the sperm. When using a condom without

FIGURE 10.2

Condoms

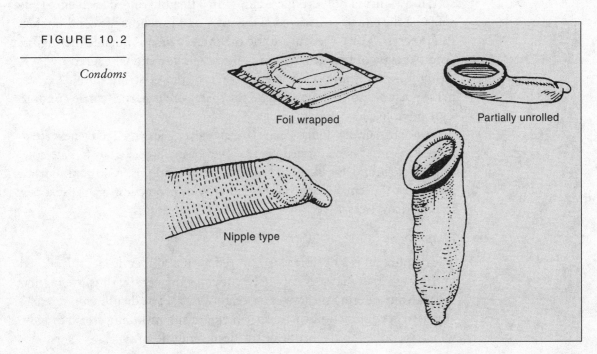

Foil wrapped

Partially unrolled

Nipple type

a receptacle, a little space should be left between the end of the condom and the penis for catching the semen (see figure 10.2). The penis should be withdrawn from the vagina soon after the ejaculation and before the penis becomes flaccid. Care needs to be taken during withdrawal that the condom does not come off and that semen does not spill out in the vagina.

Some of the advantages of the condom are that it is 95 percent effective, the cost is relatively low, no physician's service or prescriptions are necessary, and there are no medical side effects. Another advantage of condoms is that they help prevent the spread of sexually transmitted diseases.

The condom also has a few disadvantages. One of these is that the male often experiences less sensation. This disadvantage may work as an advantage for some males experiencing premature ejaculation. Another disadvantage is that it requires discipline and "breaks the mood." That is, just when foreplay is producing arousal, the couple must stop for the man to apply the condom. Some couples have the wife apply the condom to her husband's penis as part of foreplay. The fact that the penis must be removed so soon after ejaculation is also seen as a disadvantage by some couples. Partners often enjoy lying together coupled following intercourse.

Another form of condom is called the *female condom*. One type is a soft, loose-fitting polyurethane cup with a flexible ring at each end. One ring is at the end to be inserted in the vagina and anchors the condom next to the cervix. The larger ring at the other end remains outside the vagina. Another type of female condom is made of latex and is secured by a G-string. The condom pouch in the crotch of the G-string unfolds as the penis pushes into the vagina. Like the male condom, the female condom is disposable.

Since female condoms are a relatively new product, effectiveness studies have not yet been carried out. However, in clinical trials female condoms were found less likely to leak than male condoms. Also clinical trials found that the female condoms helped provide protection against sexually transmitted diseases.

Diaphragm

The diaphragm is a flexible ring covered with a rubber dome. It is placed in the vagina so that it completely encircles the cervix, thus preventing sperm from entering the uterus (see figure 10.3). The diaphragm is generally used in conjunction with a spermicide, a sperm-killing cream or jelly, which is applied to the inside of the dome and the ring.

FIGURE 10.3

*The Diaphragm and
Its Application*

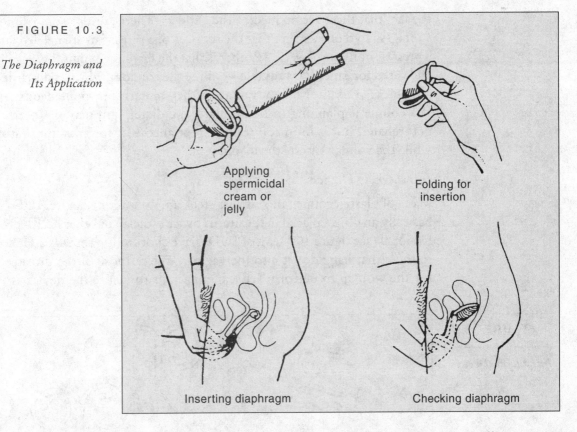

Applying spermicidal cream or jelly

Folding for insertion

Inserting diaphragm

Checking diaphragm

Diaphragms come in different sizes, from 50 to 105 millimeters. A woman must see a physician who will examine and fit her with the proper size. The physician may supply the diaphragm or give her a prescription to purchase one at a pharmacy. A woman should be refitted every couple of years, following the birth of a child, or after significant weight loss or gain. The physician will usually instruct the woman in how to insert and remove the diaphragm and how to care for it.

The diaphragm may be inserted up to four hours before intercourse and must be left in at least six hours following intercourse. Insertion of the diaphragm is not painful, and once in place, it is usually not felt. It does not interfere with either the male's or the female's enjoyment of sex. The diaphragm is the most widely used contraceptive among college-educated women.

The advantages of the diaphragm include its high level of effectiveness (over 98 percent), the fact that it can be inserted well before intercourse and need not interfere with foreplay, its relatively low cost, and the fact that there are no medical side effects. There are also some disadvantages. Two of them are that the services of a physician are needed and a prescription is necessary. Another is that the diaphragm must be cleaned and cared for, since it is reusable—unlike the condom, which is discarded after use. An additional disadvantage is that it interrupts spontaneous sex. If a couple is planning to be intimate, the diaphragm may be inserted beforehand, but if intimacy results spontaneously, foreplay must stop while the woman inserts the diaphragm.

Intrauterine Device

Made of plastic, copper, or stainless steel, an intrauterine device (IUD) is basically an object placed in the uterus by a physician or other health professional (see figure 10.4). Most IUDs have short nylon threads attached to them that hang down into the vagina,. The purpose of the threads is for the woman to perform self-examinations to insure the device is in

FIGURE 10.4

Intrauterine Devices (IUDs)

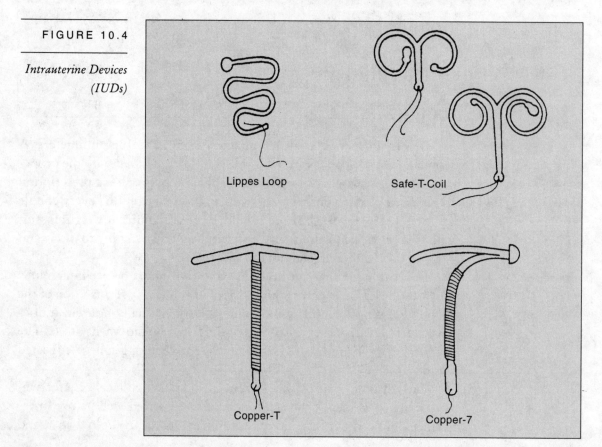

Lippes Loop

Safe-T-Coil

Copper-T

Copper-7

place. The threads do not interfere with intercourse and are not felt by the penis. If the woman desires to have children, a physician can easily remove the IUD.

The IUD is not a *contraceptive* since it does not prevent conception. It is a *contraimplantation* device because it prevents the implantation of the fertilized ovum (zygote) in the uterine wall. It is not known, for sure, how the IUD works, but a widely accepted theory is that it irritates the uterine wall so that the fertilized ovum is rejected. The IUD causes fertilized eggs to be discharged, in fact causing abortions. For this reason many Christians are opposed to the use of IUDs. We will discuss the issue of abortion later in this chapter.

The advantages of the IUD include its high level of effectiveness (about 95 percent); the fact that there is nothing to put on, insert, or care for; and its relatively low cost. There are several disadvantages to the use of IUDs. One is the need to see a physician. Another, more serious disadvantage is the medical side effects, which can include cramping, involuntary expulsion, perforation of the uterus, and pelvic inflammatory disease. Because of these medical side effects and the number of lawsuits which have followed, most IUDs have been withdrawn from the U.S. market. However, the IUD is still widely used around the world, especially in Third World and emerging countries.

Chemical Methods

These methods involve the use of chemical reactions to prevent conception. We will consider two basic methods under this category, the birth-control pills and the spermicides.

Birth Control Pills

The most common form of contraception in the United States is the birth control pill. Approximately ten million women use birth control pills, accounting for nearly one out of four users of contraceptives (Golanty and Harris 1982:313). The most commonly used birth control pills are known as combination pills because they contain estrogen and progesterone. These synthesized hormones inhibit ovulation and thus prevent pregnancy.

In 1973 a second type of birth control pill was introduced, called the "minipill." This pill contains only progesterone. Because it does not contain estrogen, many of the side effects of the combination pill are eliminated or reduced (see table 10.3 for side effects of estrogen). The minipill, unlike the combination pill, does not suppress ovulation, but affects the lining of the uterus so that a fertilized egg will not be implanted. Because the minipill results in fertilized eggs being aborted, its usage is problematic for many Christians.

A third type of birth control pill, the postcoital or "morning-after" pill, contains a large dosage of estrogen. This pill also results in the aborting of the fertilized egg. Because of the side effects of this pill, it is not routinely given. The U.S. Food and Drug Administration has approved it only for "emergency" situations.

TABLE 10.3 *Possible Estrogen* *Side Effects from* *Birth Control Pills*	1. Nausea, bloating, vomiting 2. Fluid retention 3. Breast tenderness 4. Increased skin pigmentation (cloasma), or "mask of pregnancy," on face 5. Increased mucous discharge from glands of cervix, cervical eversion 6. Headaches during days both on and off the pill 7. Worsening of migraine headaches 8. Increase in blood pressure 9. Change in sugar tolerance and insulin requirements in both diabetics and nondiabetics 10. Abnormalities in blood clotting tests 11. Thrombophlebitis (presence of inflamed blood clot in a vein) 12. Pulmonary embolism (passage of blood clot to lung) 13. Cerebral thrombosis (presence of clot in blood vessel in the brain) 14. Myocardial infarction (heart attack due to blood clot in artery of heart) 15. Visual changes, altered contour of the eye and cornea, with contact lenses, discomfort 16. Changes in certain metabolism tests: thyroid, liver, and fat metabolism 17. Increased growth of benign (noncancerous) fibroid tumors of the uterus 18. Increased growth rate of estrogen-dependent cancers of the breast and uterus (however, estrogen does not create new ones) 19. Vitamin deficiencies 20. Possible lowering of the convulsive threshold in sensitive epileptics 21. Urinary tract changes and infection 22. Increased incidence of benign liver tumors and gallbladder disease Adapted from Shapiro 1977:24

Childbearing

Mifepristone, known as *RU-486,* is just being introduced in the United States. This is a post-intercourse pill that "tricks" the body into responding as it would at the end of a menstrual cycle. The uterine lining is shed in what appears to be a heavy menstrual period. This causes the abortion of an fertilized ovum. *RU-486* can be taken up to five to six weeks after intercourse under medical supervision.

The advantages of the combination pill include its effectiveness (over 95 percent), its low cost, and the fact that it does not interfere with sexual activity. Again, there are also disadvantages. Two disadvantages are that the services of a physician are required and a prescription is needed. Another is the discipline required in remembering to take the pill daily. Perhaps the major disadvantage is the frequency of medical side effects (see table 10.3).

Another means of delivering hormones to prevent conception is implants. These are thin capsules about the size of a matchstick that are implanted under the skin of a woman's upper arm. Then progestin is slowly released over a period of up to five years. When the implants are removed, the woman can conceive. Early studies indicate that implants are more effective than pills.

Spermicides

Vaginal spermicides are sperm-killing preparations. They are available in the form of jellies, creams, aerosol foams, and suppositories (see figure 10.5). All of these preparations include two compounds: an inert base that keeps the spermicidal agent in the vagina by the cervix, and a spermicidal agent. The spermicides come with an applicator (see figure 10.5) and must be deposited at the base of the vagina by the cervix in order to be effective. The spermicide should be inserted just before intercourse for maximum effectiveness.

The advantages of the spermicides include an effective rate of 97 percent (99 percent if used in conjunction with the condom), the fact that neither the services of a physician nor a prescription is needed, the cost is low, there are no medical side effects, and the spermicide also functions as a lubricant. There are also disadvantages with this method. One is that the spermicide must be inserted just before intercourse. Another is that this method is messier than other methods. Also, some women have an aversion to placing foreign matter into their vaginas.

Life Cycle of the Family

FIGURE 10.5

*Vaginal Spermicides
and Their
Application*

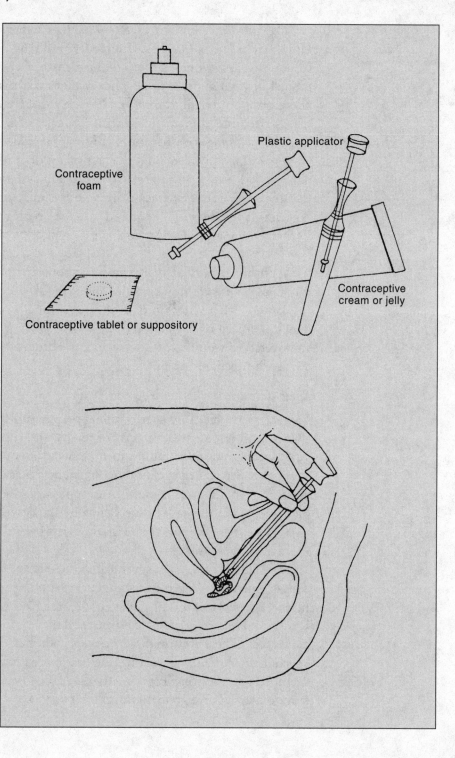

Contraceptive
foam

Plastic applicator

Contraceptive
cream or jelly

Contraceptive tablet or suppository

Childbearing

Surgical Methods

Surgical methods of birth control are those that involve surgical procedures by a physician. We will look at two methods under this category, sterilization and abortion.

Sterilization

The most common form of birth control for couples over thirty is sterilization. Almost 40 percent of all couples choose this method within five years after the birth of their last wanted child (Golanty and Harris 1982:319). While sterilization of females is similar to the sterilization of males in many ways, there are also differences, so we will consider them separately.

The most widely used procedure for the sterilization of women is *tubal ligation,* which involves the cutting and tying of the Fallopian tubes (see figure 10.6). This, of course, prevents the egg and the sperm from meeting. A *tubal ligation* does not affect a woman's hormone production, menstrual cycle, or sexual desire. A tubal ligation should be considered permanent. Although it is possible to surgically reconnect the Fallopian

FIGURE 10.6

Tubal Ligation

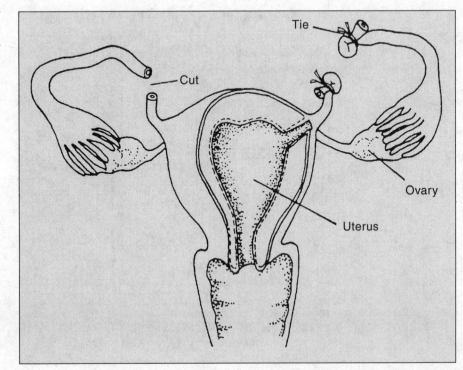

tubes, this does not insure fertility, since scar tissue in the tubes may prevent conception.

The sterilization procedure for a man is called a *vasectomy.* It involves the cutting and tying of the two vas deferens (see figure 10.7). A vasectomy does not affect a man's hormone production, ability to have an erection, or ability to have intercourse. It has no effect on the production of seminal fluid, ejaculation, or orgasm. As with the tubal ligation, a vasectomy is surgically reversible. However, a vasectomy should be considered permanent, since reconnection of the vas deferens does not guarantee the ability to produce children.

FIGURE 10.7

Vasectomy

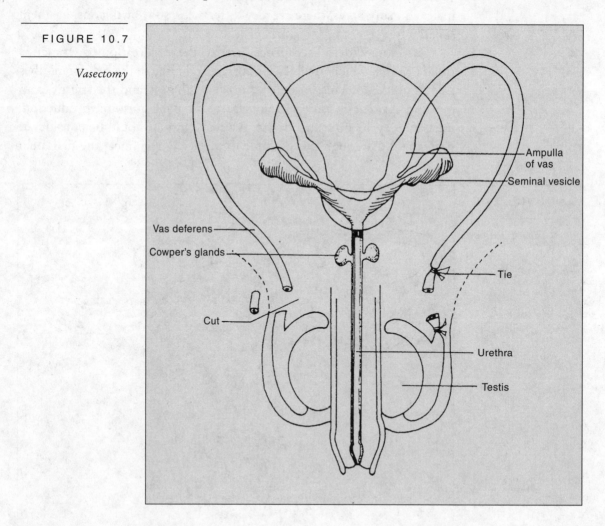

Childbearing

The advantages of sterilization are that it is almost 100 percent effective, it allows sexual freedom, and it has no medical side effects. There are two major disadvantages. One is that the surgical procedures, though relatively simple, are still costly. Fortunately, many medical insurance carriers will cover the cost because it is much lower than the cost of a pregnancy. The other major disadvantage is that it must be considered irreversible.

Abortion

Technically, the term *abortion* refers to the discharge of a zygote, embryo, or fetus. If this occurs naturally, it is referred to as a *spontaneous abortion* or *miscarriage.* If the discharge is produced by artificial means, it is called an *induced abortion.* In our discussion, references to abortion will be to induced abortions.

The three most common methods of induced abortion are the vacuum aspiration, dilation and evacuation, and injection of a saline solution or prostaglandin into the amniotic sac. *Vacuum aspiration* is generally used only during the first trimester of pregnancy. It involves inserting a plastic tube six millimeters in diameter or a twelve-millimeter vacurette through the cervix into the uterus. A suction machine is attached to the tube or vacurette and the embryo or fetus is suctioned out. After the twelfth week of pregnancy *dilation and evacuation* may be used. This is a surgical procedure that involves dilating the cervix and mechanically removing the fetus. After the sixteenth week, the most common practice is to remove the amniotic fluid from around the fetus with a syringe and replace it with a *saline solution.* The uterus reacts to the saline solution by contracting and expels the fetus and placenta within a day. An alternative is to inject a hormonal substance called *prostaglandin* into the amniotic sac. This also causes contractions and expulsion.

The medical side effects to abortion involve the possibility of infection and a slightly higher miscarriage rate after two or more abortions. The psychological side effects vary from individual to individual. One study showed that about 21 percent of the women who had an abortion experienced some guilt or other psychological side effects (Shapiro 1977:175).

ABORTION AND THE CHRISTIAN

Abortion presents a theological problem for Christians. As Montgomery (1981:86) indicates, the basic issue centers around the question of when the developing child receives its soul. The two major positions on this question are called *creationism* and *traducianism.* The creationist position

> regards the soul of each human being as immediately created by God and joined to the body either at conception, at birth, or at some time between these two. The advocates of the theory urge in its favor certain texts of Scripture that refer to God as the Creator of the human soul or spirit as well as the fact that there is a marked individuality in the child, which cannot be explained as a mere reproduction of the qualities existing in the parents. (Bancroft 1976:189)

The traducianist position

> holds that the human race was immediately created in Adam and, as respects both body and soul, was propagated from him by natural generation. All souls since Adam are only mediately created by God, as the upholder of the laws of propagation which were originally established by Him. (Bancroft 1976:190)

We will have to leave the arguments for and against these two positions to the theologians (see, for example, Bancroft 1976:186–91; Berkhof 1949:196–201; Strong 1907:488–97; Thiessen 1951:232–37). However, the implications of these two positions are important for a Christian perspective on abortion. Since those persons holding to traducianism believe the soul is passed on at conception, they generally oppose abortion and see it as the killing of a human soul. On the other hand, those holding to creationism believe God implants the soul some time between conception and birth. Persons holding to creationism and believing the soul is imparted sometime after conception generally would have no moral problems with an abortion occurring before the soul is implanted.

While being aware of the arguments in favor of each position and recognizing the problems of each, I am more comfortable with the traducianist position. However, even if one does accept the creationist position, one cannot be certain *when* God imparts the soul. Therefore, to be safe, it seems to me the wisest assumption would be to say that it is at conception (which is, in fact, the view of many who hold the creationist position). If one assumes a later point in prenatal development, and if this assumption is wrong, great damage has been done. It is my conviction that Christians ought to be opposed to abortion at any time from conception onward.

However, Christians need to take responsibility for a pro-life position. If we believe that a pregnant teenager should bear her child, we need to support her, counsel her, and minister to her, perhaps directing her to a Christian agency that will help her through her time of pregnancy. If we expect the mother who already has five children to bear her sixth, we need to be there with aid to make life worth living. We have no right to be only pro-prenatal life, we must also be pro-postnatal life. We cannot insist that women bear children because of our moral convictions and then walk away. We have to back up our moral convictions with support and action.

ADOPTION

It is estimated that between 10 and 15 percent of married couples cannot conceive because of sterility or low fertility. Many of these couples would like to have children and so turn to adoption. In the United States adoptions reached a peak of 175,000 in 1970, but by 1995 only about 50,000 children a year were being adopted. There are two primary reasons for the drop in the number of adoptions. First, births among those single women who would normally give up their children for adoption are down because of birth control and abortions. Records show that 75 percent of abortions involve single women. The second reason is that more single women who do bear children are keeping them rather than putting them up for adoption. In 1972, 8.7 percent of children born to single women were placed in adoption; by 1981, it was 4.1 percent; and by 1988, it was 2.0 percent (Lamanna and Riedmann 1997:337).

Currently, the waiting period for a healthy, white infant is five to ten years, the time varying from one state to another. The waiting time is much shorter, usually only a year or two, for children over six years of age, handicapped children, or other hard-to-place children. A number of Americans are looking overseas for foreign children because of the lack of American babies available for adoption. In 1994 about 8,000 children from other countries were adopted by American couples (Strong, DeVault, and Sayad 1998:354).

Life Cycle of the Family

D I S C U S S I O N   Q U E S T I O N S

1. Do you believe a Christian couple should choose to remain child-free? Give reasons for your answer.

2. What role do you feel social research findings should play in a couple's decisions concerning timing and number of children? Why?

3. To what extent are humans responsible for the reproductive capacity God has given them?

4. How would you rate, in order of importance, the advantages and disadvantages of the various birth control methods described? Why?

5. Do you think Christians should use sterilization as a birth control method? Why or why not?

6. How do you understand and reconcile God's command to "be fruitful and multiply" with the teaching that people are to subdue nature?

S U G G E S T E D   R E A D I N G

Elizabeth Bartholet, *Adoption and Politics of Parenting* (Boston: Houghton Mifflin, 1993). Written by a Harvard law professor who is both a biological mother and an adoptive mother. She presents data on adoption and discusses the current political climate around adoption and the changes she would like to see.

Glade B. Curtis, *Your Pregnancy,* 3d ed. (Tucson, Ariz.: Fisher, 1997). Written by an OB/GYN physician, this book describes pregnancy week by week, covering both fetal development and medical advice for the mother. The author deals with emotional and marital issues during pregnancy as well as the physical aspects.

Arlene Eisenberg et al., *What to Expect When You're Expecting,* 2d ed. (New York: Workman, 1994). A thorough guide for expectant parents. This comprehensive handbook is very readable and helpful.

Mike Samuels and Nancy Samuels, *The New Well Pregnancy Book* (New York: Fireside, 1996). A comprehensive guide to pregnancy and childbirth. This book is user-friendly and helpful.

Child Rearing

Children, obey your parents in the Lord, for this is right. "Honor your father and mother"—which is the first commandment with a promise—"that it may go well with you and that you may enjoy long life on the earth." Fathers, do not exasperate your children; instead, bring them up in the training and instruction of the Lord.

EPHESIANS 6:1–4

You know, before I had children, I used to think how much fun it would be to have some of my own. I really enjoyed other people's kids. I didn't realize, but probably I enjoyed them so much because I was only around them for short periods of time. I really love my kids, but sometimes I wish I could get away from them for just a little while. The responsibility for raising children is so much greater than I had ever thought.

QUOTED IN BILL R. WAGONSELLER AND
RICHARD L. MCDOWELL, *YOU AND YOUR CHILD*

I can identify with the second quote above. My wife and I were married for five years before we had our first child. During those years we spent a great deal of time with children. We were houseparents in a children's home. We ran a day camp. We conducted children's church. We were sponsors for junior high and senior high youth groups. Yet, none of those children were our ultimate responsibility. We were more or less free to discontinue our association with them and our care for them at any time.

Then we became parents, and my lack of preparation for the role was a real surprise. I had never held a newborn infant—my motto being "look but don't touch"—much less changed a diaper before I became a parent. The first time I changed my newborn son I was literally baptized into the art of diaper changing. My experience confirmed for me that in the American culture there is little or no socialization for the role of parent for men and only haphazard socialization for women as they care for siblings and baby-sit.

ROLE OF PARENTHOOD

An elementary school teacher has to have at least a bachelor's degree, and in some states a master's degree, and be state certified in order to teach. In most states day-care workers have to be licensed. Child psychologists and pediatricians must be board certified and state licensed. In short, most people working with children must be trained and certified or licensed. However, any couple can have a child and become parents without regard to qualifications, training, or fitness. It is incredible how little socialization and training goes into preparing people for such a critical role. LeMasters, basing his conclusions on his research with parents, writes,

> It seemed to us that these couples had received very inadequate preparation for the parental role. Most of the husbands felt that they had had no preparation whatsoever for the father role, and even a majority of the wives felt that their preparation for the role of mother had been quite inadequate. (1970:11)

LeMasters suggests that there are three factors missing in parenthood preparation. The first factor is the lack of formal training for parenthood in secondary schools and colleges. Generally, courses in this area are either absent or they are electives. One college where I taught offers a course entitled "Parent-Child Relations," but only teacher-education majors are required to take it. The second factor is that most Americans grow up in small families with children closely spaced and thus have little or no opportunity to care for siblings. The third factor suggested by LeMasters is what is called the "romantic complex" about babies and parenthood. Parents whose children have grown tend to look back at the infant years and remember only the good times. They therefore pass on a romanticized view of that stage of life to young couples. The media also encourage this view—examine the advertising for baby products as an example.

Continuing his analysis of parenthood, LeMasters lists thirteen characteristics of this role:

1. The role of parent in modern America is not well defined. It is often ambiguous and hard to pin down.
2. The role is not adequately delimited. Parents are expected to succeed where even the professionals fail.
3. Modern parents are not well prepared for their role as fathers and mothers.

Child Rearing

4. There is a romantic complex about parenthood.... In some ways the romantic complex surrounding parenthood is even deeper and more unrealistic than that relating to marriage.

5. Modern parents are in the unenviable position of having complete responsibility for their offspring but only partial authority over them. Our thesis on this point is that parental authority has been eroded gradually over the past several decades without an equivalent reduction of parental responsibility.

6. The standards of role performance imposed on modern parents are too high. This arises from the fact that modern fathers and mothers are judged largely by professional practitioners such as psychiatrists and social workers rather than by their peers—other parents who are "amateurs" and not professionals.

7. Parents are the victims of inadequate behavioral science.... They have been told repeatedly by psychiatrists, social workers, sociologists, ministers, and others that nothing determines what the child will be like but the influence of the parents.... This is obviously not true.

8. Parents do not choose their children, unless they are adoptive parents. Thus they have the responsibility for children whether they find them congenial or not. This, of course, is nothing new in parenthood the world over, but the expectations of role performance for modern American parents are such that the nature of the child can impose severe strain.

9. There is no traditional model for modern parents to follow in rearing their children. The old model has been riddled by critical studies, yet a new model that is adequate has not developed. Instead we have had a series of fads and fashions in child rearing based on the research of the moment.... This has not been much help to the parents who probably need the most help—parents from low-income groups.

10. Contrary to what some may think, parenthood as a role does not enjoy the priority one would expect in modern America. The needs of the economic system in particular come first, as can be seen in the frequency with which large firms transfer young managers and their families around the country.

11. Other new roles have been assumed by modern parents ... that are not always completely compatible with the role of parent.

12. The parental role is one of the few important roles in contemporary America that one cannot honorably withdraw from. Most of us can escape from our jobs if they are too frustrating; many of us escape from our parents when we marry; and a considerable number of husbands and wives manage to withdraw with some honor from marriages that they no longer find enchanting. But it is harder to pull out of parenthood, especially for mothers, even when the parent knows he or she is failing.

13. And last but not least, it is not enough for modern parents to produce children in their own image: The children have to be reared to be not only different from their fathers and mothers but also *better.* (LeMasters 1970:51–54)

This list of characteristics was written almost thirty years ago, yet much of what LeMasters says is still true. However, modern life has changed since then to make parenting even more difficult: increased employment, both in terms of the number of parents in the workforce and the number of hours worked; the average person works 163 hours a year more than they did twenty years ago; more parents are working second jobs. Lamanna and Riedmann (1997:349–50) present seven factors that impact modern parenting:

1. There is a greater emphasis today on using positive communication techniques and avoiding corporal punishment. Expectations for parents are higher than they have ever been.

2. Parents are raising children in a pluralistic society with diverse and conflicting values. The values taught at school may not agree with the values taught at home. Neighbors may have different values. Parents' wishes are not supported in the school and community like they once were.

3. The emphasis on the role and responsibility of parents for how their children turn out puts pressure on parents.

4. Experts on child-rearing present differing theories and techniques. Parents often receive conflicting counsel.

5. While parents have full responsibility for raising their children, they don't have full authority, and their decisions are often questioned by school counselors and teachers, medical providers, social workers, and other authorities.

6. With longer life expectancy, middle-aged parents may find themselves caring for both children and aging parents. They are often referred to as the *sandwich generation*.
7. There are more single-parent families, divorced parents, stepfamilies, and blended families. These situations often involve conflicting rules and values.

CRISIS OF PARENTHOOD

Several social scientists view the process of becoming a parent as a crisis (e.g., Bigner 1979; Duvall 1977; Eshleman 1981; LeMasters 1970). The addition of a child, a newborn, helpless infant that is in need of constant care, places a strain on a marriage. Two people who had each other all to themselves now find themselves involved with a third person who demands much of their time and attention. Duvall reports, "Hundreds of couples studied over the years concur that parenthood is a critical experience, and that marital satisfaction drops sharply with the coming of the first baby." She continues, "Research finds that having a baby is hard on

FIGURE 11.1

Level of Marital Satisfaction at Various Stages of the Family Life Cycle

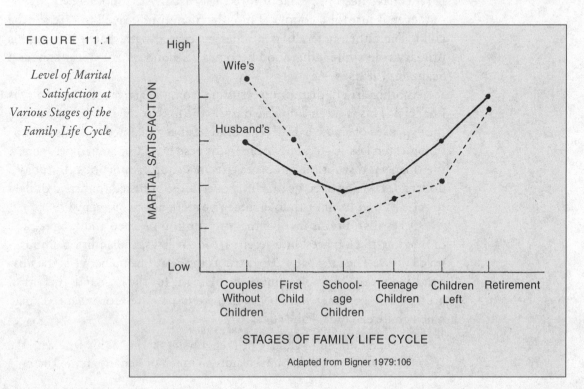

Adapted from Bigner 1979:106

223

a marriage in the sense that more sex difficulties arise—problems in which the wife is more concerned and the husband more dissatisfied" (Duvall 1977:240). Bigner (1979:105) reports on a large-scale study of married couples that found that marital satisfaction dropped sharply with the birth of the first child and did not return to preparental levels until the last child had left home (see figure 11.1). Studies since then have confirmed his findings (Lamanna and Riedmann 1997:314).

While the studies cited above show that marital satisfaction falls during the child-rearing years, we should remember that the results are reported in terms of averages. For many couples the child-rearing years are times of joy, and they see these years as some of their happiest. We also need to keep in mind that these are self-reports and that individuals' perceptions of their level of marital satisfaction are relative.

The birth of a child brings many disruptions to the marital relationship. The first, at which we have already looked, is the acquisition of a new role, that of parent. Becoming a mother is usually more of a transition for a woman than becoming a father is for a man. This is because the woman generally ends up with more responsibility for the baby. If both parents have been in the labor force, it is usually the mother who drops out, even if just for a couple of months (maternity leave), to care for the child. The father generally continues his career, with that remaining his primary role while fatherhood becomes a secondary role (Scanzoni and Scanzoni 1981:564–65).

Another area of disruption resulting from the arrival of a new baby is financial. This is often a double blow—the loss of the wife's income and the expenses of a new baby. If the child has been planned for, this disruption is often less severe. However, in the case of an unplanned pregnancy, the financial disruption can be a crisis of major proportions. In today's dollars, it takes an average of a little over three hundred thousand dollars to raise a child from birth to eighteen years of age (Longman 1998:57).

Other disruptions involve the interruption of sleep and fatigue, loss of freedom to go places, interference from in-laws, and additional household chores. The new baby also disrupts the relationship between the husband and wife. This is often more problematic for the husband. As Duvall points out, "Few men have been adequately prepared for what to expect when children come." She adds:

> Most difficult of all may be the intimate sharing of his wife with the intrusive little rival that now claims so much of her attention. The hus-

band has had his wife all to himself during their courting and honeymoon days and has learned to take her for granted as his partner and companion during the establishment phase of marriage. He must now see her time, energy, and love directed to the demanding baby in ways that may fill him with intense feelings of being left out and neglected.... One of the hazards to be expected ... is that the mother may devote herself disproportionately to the new baby, and that the young father may retreat emotionally to a doghouse of his own making. Until he can share his wife maturely and participate with her in the experiences of parenthood, he may feel like little more than a fifth wheel around the place. (1977:230)

STAGES OF PARENTHOOD

Several schemes for dividing the period of parenthood into various stages have been developed (Duvall 1977; Lamanna and Riedmann 1981; Scanzoni and Scanzoni 1981). Drawing on these schemes, I would like to suggest five stages of parenthood: (1) New Parent Stage, (2) Preschool Children Stage, (3) School-age Children Stage, (4) Teenage Stage, and (5) Disengagement Stage.

New Parent Stage

This stage, obviously, begins with the birth of the first child. As we have already seen, this stage is a crisis. Actually, the birth of the first child, especially if the baby is healthy, is a moment of elation and rejoicing. The beaming mother has the assistance of nurses and aids at the hospital as well as a steady stream of well-wishers. The proud father is busy calling grandparents, relatives, and friends. The first few days are quite exciting. It is when the mother and baby come home from the hospital that reality sets in. The nursing staff is no longer there to help with the baby. The full responsibility for around-the-clock care for the baby falls on the couple.

This stage is a period of adjustment. The couple must adjust to a third member of the family and to the baby's schedule. Adjustment to new roles is necessary. The couple must develop new ways of relating and must work out interpersonal conflicts. Duvall suggests five major issues a couple needs to work through at this stage:

1. Seeing beyond the drudgeries to the fundamental satisfaction of parenthood
2. Valuing persons above things

3. Resolving the conflicts inherent in the contradictory developmental tasks of parents and young children, and of fathers and mothers
4. Establishing healthy independence as a married couple
5. Accepting help in a spirit of appreciation and growth (1977:245)

Preschool Children Stage

By the time the first child reaches the preschool stage, about three to five years of age, there may be one or two younger siblings. The parents have generally adjusted to their roles as mother and father and are more confident and experienced in dealing with additional children. At this stage the child is able to talk, and patterns of interaction between the child and parents are beginning to develop. Also, by this stage the parents have begun to develop a style of parenting. We will examine various styles of parenting later in this chapter.

The demands and pressures of parenthood at this stage often result in little time for the couple to enjoy each other's company. Research reveals that couples with preschool children have fewer arguments and experience less resentment than earlier in their marriage. On the other hand, they also have less positive support from each other. What has usually happened is that they have settled into a routine of family living that, while producing fewer negative reactions, results in less enjoyment and companionship (Duvall 1977:260–61).

An important task for couples at this stage is to strengthen their relationship. There needs to be creativity and affection in the partnership. Duvall suggests some of the major tasks of this stage:

1. Supplying adequate space, facilities, and equipment for the expanding family
2. Meeting predictable and unexpected costs of family life with small children
3. Assuming more mature roles within the expanding family
4. Maintaining mutually satisfying intimate communication in the family
5. Rearing and planning for children
6. Relating to relatives
7. Tapping resources outside the family
8. Motivating family members (1977:261–62)

Child Rearing

School-age Children Stage

By this stage most children are fairly self-sufficient. They can dress themselves and care for their basic hygiene. The children need less direct parental care and supervision. In fact, they are gone from the home six to seven hours a day at school. However, the child's life and therefore also the parents' lives become more complex. There are after-school activities—Brownies, Cub Scouts, church activities, and little-league sports. Frequently there are also music lessons, dance classes, or other extracurricular activities.

In fact, Lamanna and Riedmann (1981:409–10) warn that children today face demands from school, church, and recreational organizations that may overextend them. The child is shuffled from one activity to the next. This may produce what they call the "hurried child." They suggest that parents need to take responsibility for seeing that the demands on their children at this stage do not become overwhelming.

This is also a stage when children are starting to make friends outside the home and are becoming more peer conscious. This is another area where parental supervision and guidance are important. Because parents cannot be with their children all the time, it is important for them to help their children find friends who have the same values and standards as they do.

By this stage the parents have been married for at least seven years and have been parents for at least six years. Family routines are probably well established. Duvall sees six major tasks associated with this stage of parenthood:

1. Providing for children's activity and parents' privacy
2. Keeping financially solvent
3. Furthering socialization of family members
4. Upgrading communication in the family
5. Establishing ties with life outside the family
6. Developing morally and building family morale (1977:281)

Teenage Stage

This stage often involves turmoil between parent and child. In fact, both parent and child may be experiencing personal crises at this time. One or both parents may be experiencing the onset of midlife crises (see Chapter 12). The teenager is experiencing puberty with its hormonal and physical changes, for the child is beginning the process of becoming an adult. The teenager is also beginning the process of cutting the ties with the parents, preparing for the time when he or she will leave home.

Another problem particular to our society is that social change is so rapid that teenagers today are growing up in a culture that is radically different from that which their parents experienced. I grew up in a world where only the United States had nuclear weapons. My teenage son is growing up in a world where a dozen nations have the potential to set off a nuclear holocaust. I grew up in a society where drugs were a ghetto problem; my son's middle-class school has a drug program. I grew up in a society that would not let Elvis Presley on television because of the suggestive way he shook his hips, and *Playboy* magazine was sold under the counter. My son lives in a day when R-rated movies are shown on prime-time television and pornography is displayed in the local corner store. These and many other major differences in the social milieus that parents and teenagers were raised in adds to the potential for misunderstanding. The widespread drug usage, the permissive sexual attitudes, the epidemic of venereal disease, and the rise of premarital pregnancy make the parenting of teenagers more difficult than ever.

Some of the tasks parents face at this stage, according to Duvall, include:

1. Providing facilities for widely different needs within the family
2. Working out ever-changing financial problems
3. Sharing the responsibilities of family living
4. Keeping the marriage relationship in focus
5. Bridging the communication gap between the generations
6. Maintaining the ethical and moral stance that is meaningful to them (1977:307)

Disengagement Stage

This can often be a difficult stage for parents. They have functioned in the role of father or mother for twenty or more years, in many instances for over half their lives. When the last child leaves, the role of parent, at least as practiced when the children were at home, abruptly comes to an end. Some of the problems associated with this stage will be discussed in the next chapter.

The tasks facing parents at this stage include:

1. Rearranging physical facilities and resources

2. Meeting the expenses of a launching-center family
3. Reallocating responsibilities among grown and growing children
4. Coming to terms with themselves as husband and wife
5. Maintaining open systems of communication within the family and between the family and others
6. Widening the family circle through release of young adult children and recruitment of new members by marriage
7. Reconciling conflicting loyalties and philosophies of life (Duvall 1977:342)

HUMAN DEVELOPMENT

Before we can go much further in our discussion of parenthood and child rearing, we need to look at human development. An understanding of human development provides a foundation for child rearing. In Luke 2:52 we read, "Jesus grew in wisdom and stature, and in favor with God and men." This verse gives us the four basic aspects of human nature. "Wisdom" refers to the *psychological*, "stature" to the *biological*, "in favor with God" to the *spiritual*, and "men" to the *social development* aspect. We need to understand how children develop in each of these areas (see tables 11.1 and 11.2). It is also useful to have an overall model of human development. Perhaps one of the most influential and helpful models is that of Jean Piaget (Pulaski 1980; Singer and Revenson 1978; Wadsworth 1971).

Before we look at Piaget's stages of development, we need to understand some of the presuppositions of his model. One of the foundational premises of Piaget's work is that children are not miniature adults. Their ways of thinking are not merely simplified adult ways. The cognitive processes of children are qualitatively different from those of adults. Much of Piaget's research has centered on the cognitive development of children; that is, how they grow from a child's cognitive processes to adult cognitive processes. Piaget also argues that this development is systematic. Piaget has divided this systematic development into a series of periods. He says that the periods are *sequential* and *necessary*. By necessary, he means that a child cannot skip a period; each period must precede the next. The ages attached to the periods are statistical averages; some children will enter a period earlier, and some later. Each child proceeds at his or her own pace. This leads to another point: Piaget postulates that humans have a *readiness factor*; that is, there are critical periods of development. By readiness factor

TABLE 11.1

Child Development

AGE	PHYSICAL	PSYCHOLOGICAL	SOCIAL	SPIRITUAL
0–1 Year Infant	Rapid growth—the baby triples its birth weight. Becomes mobile, sits and stands.	Mentally it is a time of discovery. Emotionally the baby is sensitive—capable of anger and joy.	Socially limited. Begins to recognize familiar faces. Coos and babbles at people.	Spiritually dependent on parents.
2–3 years Toddler	Able to walk, beginning to run. Very active. By 2 years, half of adult height is attained.	Mentally—language acquisition, use of symbols. Limited cognitive ability. Emotionally fearful, separation anxiety.	Socially egocentric. Tends to engage in parallel play rather than with peers; i.e., *by them* rather than *with* them.	Imitates—folds hands, prays, can enjoy Sunday school.
3–5 years Preschool Kindergarten	Growth rate slowing. Large-muscle coordination. Active—playing.	Mentally—explorer and curious. Able to memorize brief items. Emotionally—responds to others, still fearful.	Conforming, still egocentric but able to play simple games. Follows older siblings.	Willing to accept whatever taught. Can sing and participate in Sunday school.
6–8 years Primary Grades 1–3	Slow but steady growth. Adult teeth. Small-muscle coordination.	Mentally entering concrete-operations stage. Able to manipulate symbols. Learning to read and do math. Emotionally insecure, needs love and security.	Friendly, able to make friends and play organized games. Beginning to see others' point of view.	Able to respond to the gospel. Open to accepting Christ. Eager to please.
9–11 years Junior Grades 4–6	Plateau in growth. Energetic. Able to engage in complex physical activities.	Mentally approaching adult intelligence. Observant and investigative. Emotionally expressive. Able to give and receive	Strong identification with own sex. Socially active, involved in organized sports, clubs, church activities, scouting, etc.	Concerned with relating truth to life. Grasping implications of biblical teachings.

TABLE 11.2

Adolescent Development

AGE	PHYSICAL	PSYCHOLOGICAL	SOCIAL	SPIRITUAL
12–14 years Early Adolescence Junior High	Puberty, major hormonal and physical changes. Growth spurt. Sexual development.	Mentally critical and testing. Trying out new mental capabilities. Emotionally a period of fluctuations, many ups and downs.	Peer oriented. Need for companionship. Beginning to break from parents.	Open to spiritual challenge. Idealistic. Looking for purpose.
15–17 years Middle Adolescence Senior High	Strengthening. Girls reach full adult height and build. Boys grow slowly, and coordination catches up.	Mentally alert. Able to engage in inductive and deductive reasoning. Emotionally experiencing new feelings—love, rejection, loyalty, etc.	Dating—period when boys and girls are interested in each other. Organized sports and clubs.	Looking for reality. Critical period—not interested in pat answers. Time for lifetime commitments.
18–22 years Late Adolescence College and Career	Boys reach full adult height and build. Both sexes at the peak of physical ability.	Mentally involved in synthesizing learned data. Preparation for life career. Emotionally stabilizing. Maturity.	Mate selection. Dating becomes more serious and moves into courtship.	Spiritual growth and commitment. Looking to put faith in action.

is meant that at a certain point in his or her development, a child is ready to master a specific task. Attempts to teach that behavior to the child before he or she is ready will result in frustration. However, when the critical period of development is reached, the child can readily master the task.

Piaget's Periods of Development

Piaget's model divides the process of cognitive development into four periods: (1) sensorimotor, (2) preoperational, (3) concrete operations, and (4) formal operations. We will look at each of these periods and discuss some of their basic characteristics.

Sensorimotor Period

This period covers the first two years of life. Piaget (1952) has divided this period into six stages. *Stage one,* birth to one month, is characterized by innate reflexes, such as sucking and grasping. Some of these reflexes combine to form primitive schemes, such as the sucking and swallowing reflexes to allow nursing. The infant is totally egocentric and is unable to distinguish between self and the environment. *Stage two,* one to four months, is characterized by the infant's ability to distinguish the limits of his or her own body and engage in repetitious movements. *Stage three,* four to eight months, is characterized by the baby's ability to adapt familiar and simple learned behaviors to new situations. The baby's interest begins to shift from his or her own body to the environment. The baby will grasp for objects within sight, but if the object is put out of sight, under a blanket for example, the baby will act as if it does not exist. *Stage four,* eight to twelve months, is characterized by intentional behavior. At this stage the baby will reach under the blanket for the object. The baby is quite mobile, engages in a great deal of imitative behavior, and enjoys imitating sounds. *Stage five,* twelve to eighteen months, finds the child walking, responding to simple verbal directions, and recognizing familiar persons and objects. *Stage six,* eighteen to twenty-four months, is marked by the beginning of the acquisition of language. It is a transition to the next period.

Preoperational Period

This period covers from two years to seven years of age. Piaget has divided this period into *two stages.* The *first stage* is the *preconceptual stage,* two to four years. The main characteristics of this stage are language acquisition and the use of symbols. The child begins the process of conceptualization, such as associating height and age or adding *ed* to verbs for past tense, but tends to over-generalize. The child is egocentric and assumes that everyone sees the world as he or she does.[1] The child cannot mentally understand another person's point of view. For example, a child at this stage can be taught the behavior of sharing but cannot comprehend the concept of sharing. The child must be taught to share in each specific situation.

The *second stage* of this period is the *prelogical or intuitive stage,* from four to seven years. One of the major characteristics of this stage is that the child cannot master the principle of conservation. This means that he or she cannot conceive of a thing being the same in different states. When my son was about four years old, he saw me put water in an ice-cube tray and put it in the freezer. Later he saw me take out ice cubes. Then he asked me, "Who took the water away and put the ice cubes in the tray?" Piaget uses a classic experiment to demonstrate this point. He takes a tall, thin drinking glass and a short, fat drinking glass, each of which holds the same amount of fluid, and, in front of the child, pours water from one to the other. To an adult this would be a clear demonstration that they hold the same amount of fluid. When both glasses are then filled, and a child in this stage is asked which glass has the most water in it, the child invariably replies that the tall glass has the most water.

Another characteristic of this stage is that the child judges naughtiness in terms of damage rather than intention. When a child in this stage is told a story about a boy who breaks a dozen cups accidentally and a boy who breaks one cup intentionally, and then is asked which boy deserves the greater punishment, the child usually replies that the boy who broke twelve cups deserves the greater punishment. When the child is asked why, the response is that he broke more cups.

The child continues to be egocentric at this stage. If you observe parents or other adults dealing with young children, you will frequently hear them ask the child, "How do you think that made Bobby feel?" or some other question that asks the child to see the situation from another person's point of view. They might as well have asked the child to solve an algebraic equation. The child is incapable of seeing another's point of view.

---

[1]There is a difference between being egocentric and selfish. The egocentric person cannot understand another's point of view and so naturally does what he or she wants. The selfish person can understand another's point of view, but disregards it and selfishly does what he or she wants. The egocentric person has no idea that the other will be upset. The selfish person does understand but still acts.

Concrete Operations Period

This period runs from the seventh to the twelfth year. This stage is a giant step toward adult thinking. At this point the child is able to master the principle of conservation, is able to judge naughtiness in terms of intention, and can master what Piaget calls *reversibility*. Reversibility is what makes possible deductions such as "If one plus one equals two, then two minus one must equal one."

From a Christian perspective, one of the interesting characteristics of this stage is that the child becomes less egocentric and is able to see things from another's point of view. This makes it possible for a child to comprehend the message of the gospel. Howard Newsom writes,

> Children in concrete operations are fully capable of understanding their need for a personal Savior. Most children will gladly respond to an invitation to commitment. Studies indicate that a larger percentage of people become Christians during this age span than at any other period of life. (1978:40)

Formal Operations Period

Extending from twelve years of age to adulthood, this period involves the ability to reason logically and think abstractly. The youngster is capable of inductive and deductive reasoning. In other words, in this stage there is full adult cognitive ability. While Piaget does not have stages within this period, he points out that not all adults reach the full development of this stage.

STYLES OF PARENTING

As we saw earlier in this chapter, there is not a basic model for parenting in our society. In fact, many different styles of parenting are practiced. LeMasters has classified styles of parenting into five basic models (LeMasters 1970; LeMasters and DeFrain 1989). While any classification scheme has its limitations and tends to oversimplify, LeMasters' approach is a useful means of organizing a discussion of parenting. His five models are the martyr, the buddy or pal, the policeman or drill sergeant, the teacher-counselor, and the athletic coach.

The Martyr Model

In this model parents have the attitude that nothing is too good for their children, and they claim that they would do anything or make any sacrifice for their children. According to LeMasters, there are several characteristics found with this model. One is parental guilt. The parent generally feels he or she is never doing a good enough job.

Another characteristic is overprotection, which may result from guilt. The parent is afraid that something may hurt the child and thus attempts to create a super-safe environment for the child. These parents spoil their children, fail to set realistic goals for them, and seldom hold them accountable.

LeMasters found that this model often was used by divorced parents, parents with poor marriages, and parents with handicapped children. The response of the child to this type of parenting is generally either open revolt or meek submission. Whichever outward behavior is exhibited, the child feels hostility and resentment toward the parent. The parent, as a martyr, continues to do "what is best" for the child in the face of this resentment and hostility.

The Buddy or Pal Model

A number of parents in American society have adopted this model. LeMasters suggests that parents who adopt this model are following the expression, "If you can't beat them, join them." The parents are trying to influence and direct their children as a peer. Another reason for the popularity of this model, suggested by LeMasters, is the emphasis on youth in the American culture. Parents may be attempting to recapture some of their own youth.

LeMasters says one of the major problems with the buddy or pal model of parenting is that it is very difficult for the parent to retain authority. If the parent attempts to exercise authority, the child feels betrayed and resentful. LeMasters says it is easier for the traditional authoritarian parent to slacken the rules occasionally than for the buddy or pal parent to pull in the reins when necessary.

The Policeman or Drill Sergeant Model

This model of parenting involves setting strict rules and limits and punishing any and all infractions. The parent is the final authority and expects compliance with his or her rules. LeMasters feels that this model generally will not work in American society for two reasons. First, the culture is antiauthoritarian. As he puts it, Americans are "allergic" to authority (1970:217). Second, adolescent peer influence is too powerful.

According to LeMasters, the only situation in which the policeman or drill sergeant model will work is one with abundant love. "Strict or even harsh discipline will be tolerated by many children," he says, "but warmth and love have to be so obvious and plentiful that the child can never doubt that the parent has the child's best interests at heart" (1970:217). LeMasters' conclusion about strictness and love is supported by susequent research (McClelland et al. 1978:42–53, 114). From this study the researchers concluded that strictness in parenting inhibited the level of maturity children would attain unless there was love in the home. They write, "Further analysis showed that the impact of strictness depended very much on whether there was love in the home. If the mother really loved the child, how strict the parents were didn't seem to make much difference later on" (McClelland et al. 1978:46). They add, "Father's affection for the child is also important for thinking maturity.... It is important to realize that children of affectionate fathers ... are, in fact, more apt to think and reason in ways that show tolerance and understanding" (McClelland et al. 1978:49).

The Teacher-Counselor Model

LeMasters calls this the developmental model. He says the child is seen as a moldable organism with its potential limited only by its opportunities. While parents practicing this model may be firm in their discipline, they are never harsh. These parents tend to use psychological punishment rather than physical punishment. The parent is viewed as having the right answers and guides the child. A good teacher-counselor puts the needs of the child first.

This model reflects the philosophy of John Dewey. LeMasters says this model has been the dominant one of many middle-class parents, and he believes that this model tends to be too permissive. Also, since the parent is expected to be the expert, it tends to produce anxiety and guilt. LeMasters also feels this model caters too much to the needs of the child, and that this is unhealthy because in society there must be a balance between the needs of the individual and the good of society.

The Athletic Coach Model

In this model, the parent functions much as an athletic coach. As a coach prepares his or her players for the game, so a parent prepares his or her child for the game of life. The coach cannot play the game for the players, but only prepares and trains the players for the game. The coach uses discipline, support, training, and example to prepare the players. Again, LeMasters feels that love is an important ingredient for this model.

CHILD ABUSE

Whichever model of parenting they use, parents are supposed to care for and protect their children. While most parents do take care of their children in a reasonable manner, a growing number of parents engage in behavior that is harmful to their child's physical and/or emotional health and welfare. There are more than a million cases of confirmed child abuse each year. Authorities estimate that the true number of children who are abused each year approaches three million. Close to thirteen hundred children each year are killed by their parents or other relatives (Strong, DeVault, and Sayad 1998:467–68).

Types of Child Abuse

Although there is not an agreed-upon definition or set of categories of child abuse, one commonly used typology looks at four areas of child abuse: (1) physical abuse, (2) sexual abuse, (3) psychological abuse, and (4) neglect (Dworetzky 1981:401).

Physical Abuse

One study found that 3.5 percent of the parents surveyed admitted they had reacted with physical violence sufficient to cause injury toward at least one of their children in the past year (Dworetzky 1981:401). Of those cases of child abuse reported by physicians, approximately 67 percent had bruises and/or welts; 32 percent had abrasions, contusions, or lacerations; 10 percent had been burned or scalded; 8 percent had wounds or punctures; and 5 percent had skull fractures (Dworetzky 1981:401).

Sexual Abuse

In the early 1980s in Minnesota, in a well-publicized case involving several sensational trials, two brothers, their wives, and the brothers' parents were all sentenced to jail for having sexual relations with their children and grandchildren. It was alleged that the children were forced to engage in sexual acts with their parents, aunts and uncles, and grandparents in a group setting. I know a therapist who counseled with a young father who had been the victim of sexual abuse by his father and had just discovered that his father was abusing his son. He also counseled with two girls who had been sexually abused by their fathers. In one case the girl was a pastor's daughter who feared her father was now abusing her younger sister. Are these isolated instances? Unfortunately, they are not. In a national survey among adults, researchers found that 27 percent of women and 16 percent of men had experienced sexual abuse as a child (Finkelhor et al. 1990).

In researching the case histories of sexual abuse, which usually involves fathers or stepfathers and daughters, researchers have found a familiar pattern. The victims are generally the eldest or only daughters. They were first approached sexually between the ages of six and nine. Sexual contact was usually continuous, lasting an average of three years. Psychological rather than physical force was generally used, and the relationship was kept secret. In more than half the cases the mothers were incapacitated by illness or mental problems or absent from the home due to work. The daughters had taken over many of the mothers' household tasks. The relationship between the mothers and daughters frequently was strained.

Sexual abuse is often difficult to uncover for two reasons. First, the victim must describe to strangers intimate and embarrassing incidents. Second, the victim must betray his or her parent and risk destroying the family. As this problem is brought out into the open and the victims are able to realize they are not the only ones in this type of situation, victims may be more willing to confide in others who can help them.

Psychological Abuse

Parents who would never think of physically harming their children may engage in behavior that results in emotional damage. Dr. Shirley O'Brien, a human development specialist, writes:

> Emotional abuse comes in many forms and disguises, such as the following: teasing, yelling, desertion, disinterest, name calling, downgrading, continual criticism, scary threats, and any other behavior that destroys or damages a child's self-esteem or self-image.
>
> The type of emotional abuse that is especially detrimental is verbal abuse that bombards the child until he not only has lost his self-esteem but develops a negative self-image because of constant negative reinforcement. (1980:20)

In psychological abuse the distinction between normal and abnormal behavior is often difficult to define. Most parents tease, yell at their children, are disinterested, criticize, and use threats from time to time. If this type of behavior is continual and not offset by positive behaviors, and if it results in psychological harm to the child, it may be diagnosed as psychological abuse.

Neglect

Some authorities treat neglect as a separate topic; others include it under child abuse. Wherever it is considered, the effect is the same on its victims. O'Brien defines neglect as "withholding necessary food, clothing, shelter, and education opportunities, or other forms of inadequate care and supervision that might lead to endangering the child's well-being." She adds, "Neglect also means withholding love, socialization, and proper stimulation" (1980:9). It is estimated that as many as one third of abused children also suffer from some form of neglect (Justice and Justice 1976:19). For example, in the United States, it is estimated that 40 percent of all children have not been properly immunized against disease (Dworetzky 1981:401). Due to neglect many children have never been seen by a dentist, and almost a third of the children in the United States have an iron-deficient diet (Bee 1981:125).

Abusive Parents

What type of person would abuse his or her own child? Child abusers come from all social classes, races, ages, and both sexes. There is no typical child abuser. However, there are some social factors that are associated with child abuse. Abuse is highest among young parents, the unemployed, those in lower socioeconomic levels, and those who were abused themselves as children (Scanzoni and Scanzoni 1981:586–87).

Abused Children

Again, children of all races, ages, and social classes are the victims of abuse. However, there are certain social factors that are often associated with child abuse. Young children between the ages of three months to three years are the most susceptible to physical abuse (Scanzoni and Scanzoni 1981:587). Children in large families (four or more siblings) are more frequently subject to abuse. The children of unwed mothers and those resulting from an unwanted pregnancy have a greater chance of being victims of abuse (Scanzoni and Scanzoni 1981:587).

According to one researcher, there are three reasons why children under four years of age are more frequently the victims of physical abuse.

First, a small child is more susceptible to injury from physical punishment because of his or her frailty. Infants are particularly prone to head injuries. Second, parents easily become frustrated with very young children because they cannot reason or communicate with them. Third, the young child, by its very presence, may be creating economic hardship, disrupting the marital relationship, or in other ways creating stress for the parents (Scanzoni and Scanzoni 1981:581–88).

CHRISTIAN CHILD REARING

We have looked at the role of parenthood, various models of parenting, and some malfunctions of parenting. Parenting is a topic that the Bible also addresses. Parents are instructed to teach their children the Word of God (Deut. 6:6–9; 11:18–21; Prov. 22:6; Eph. 6:4). Parents are also told to discipline their children (Prov. 13:24; 23:13–14; 29:15, 17). In addition, parents are commanded to instruct and discipline their children in a way that does not provoke them (Eph. 6:4; Col. 3:21).

Several Christian authors have written on the application of these principles. Paul Meier (1977), a psychiatrist, drawing on his psychiatric training and his study of the Word of God, has come up with five principles for Christian child rearing: (1) love, (2) discipline, (3) consistency, (4) example, and (5) the father.

Love

Meier says that two types of love are necessary for effective parenting. First, the mother and father must love each other; and second, the parents must love the child. He argues that love is the basis of Christianity. God demonstrated his love by sending his Son to die for our sins (John 3:16). As God loves his children, so parents should love their children. The essence of love is found in 1 Corinthians 13:4–7. We saw earlier that social research on parenting recognized the importance of love in child rearing.

Love also helps a child develop a good self-image and self-confidence. We love what we value. As parents show their children that they love them, they are showing them that they value them. As parents value their children, the children will come to value themselves. When we love someone, we want to do what is best for that person. One of the best ways to build self-worth and self-confidence in a youngster is by the use of sincere praise. Flattery will backfire, but sincere praise will build up the child.

Child Rearing

Every child has characteristics and behaviors that are praiseworthy. If parents would be just half as quick with praise as they are with criticism, they would see tremendous change. Actually, a good rule might be to use twice as much praise as criticism. Where flattery builds false pride, praise will build a positive self-image.

Discipline

Meier agrees with Dobson (1970) that a quick spanking is an effective means of disciplining young children. Dobson expands on this. He feels that spankings should be restricted to incidents of rebellion. However, Dobson believes that parents should use positive reinforcement where possible. That is, parents should reinforce desired behaviors.

Discipline involves teaching correct behavior as much as it involves correcting wrong behavior. Many times it is more profitable to concentrate on good behavior rather than on bad behavior. For example, a parent asks a child to straighten up her bedroom. The parent comes to check on the bedroom and finds the job well-done—except for some items left on the dresser. What is the parent most likely to say to the child? You are right. The parent will probably comment on the dresser, pointing out what was not done. It would be more effective in this case to praise the child for the work that was done correctly. That is reinforcing the behavior the parent wants to see continued. Psychological research clearly indicates that in most situations rewards are more effective behavior modifiers than punishment.

Discipline also involves setting guidelines and limitations. Guidelines and limitations not only function to keep the child in line but also to keep problems out. Boundaries provide security and protection. No matter how hard young people fight against the boundaries parents set for them, they need them and want them. It is a paradox, but there can be freedom only within boundaries. Without boundaries you do not have freedom but anarchy. Parents need to provide their children with guidelines and limitations in order for them to develop healthy and happy lives.

Consistency

Parents need to be consistent in their discipline as well as consistent with each other. They should agree on rules and punishment. If one is lenient and the other is strict, the child learns that discipline is arbitrary. If parents have a disagreement about discipline, they should deal with it privately.

Parents also need to be consistent with discipline from situation to situation and from time to time. Children are smart. My children will ask my wife for something when she is on the phone or busy with something because they believe she will say yes to get rid of them. It is important for parents to be consistent and fair.

Example

It really does not matter what we *say;* children learn from what we *do.* Most values are caught—not taught. We are all familiar with the expression, "Do as I say, not as I do." Unfortunately, it does not work that way. Modeling is one of the most powerful teaching methods. It can be used for good or harm.

Father

Not only does the Bible put a great deal of emphasis on the father, but social research confirms the importance of the father in child rearing. In one study involving 994 couples with children, researchers found that children who spent more time with their fathers had fewer behavior problems. In another study involving 14,700 teenage girls, researchers found that the closer a relationship a girl had with her father, the more likely she was to delay sex and the less likely she was to use drugs and alcohol (Elias 1998).

In our society many fathers have abdicated their responsibilities. They may still be feeding and clothing their children, but they are not involved with child rearing. It is important for the father to be involved in his children's lives. He should be involved in discipline, spiritual development, education, and recreation.

Dan Kiley, a child psychologist, has written a book entitled *Nobody Said It Would Be Easy* (1978). There is a lot of truth in that title. Parenting is hard work and requires responsibility and dedication. It is also a rewarding experience.

Child Rearing

1. Why do you think American society provides so little preparation for the role of parent?

2. What, in your opinion, is the reason that the role of parent is not well-defined in the North American culture?

3. Do you believe that fathers should be entitled to maternity leaves from work, the same as mothers, to help care for the new baby? Why?

4. Which of LeMasters' five models of parenting do you believe would be most effective? Why?

5. In your opinion, why is there so much child abuse in the American society, and what can be done about it?

6. What principles for parenting do you find in Deuteronomy 6:6–9; Proverbs 2:1; 3:1; 13:24; 22:6; and Ephesians 6:4?

James Dobson, *On Parenting* (New York: Inspiration Press, 1997). This book brings together *The Strong-willed Child* (1985) and *Parenting Isn't for Cowards* (1987) under one cover. Combining these two works provides parents with practical insights from a Christian child psychologist. His counsel is practical and helpful for those facing many of the common parenting problems.

Greg Johnson and Mike Yorkey, *Faithful Parents, Faithful Kids* (Wheaton, Ill.: Tyndale, 1993). This book deals with discipline, developing a healthy relationship with your children, communication, transferring values, and contemporary issues facing parents. A Christian perspective combined with wise counsel makes this a helpful and practical book.

John Maxwell, *Breakthrough Parenting* (Colorado Springs: Focus on the Family, 1996). Maxwell's thesis is that every child has tremendous potential and that parents can help develop and release that potential. He shares priorities and motivational techniques and emphasizes rewarding those behaviors you want to develop. This book contains some fresh and creative ideas.

Bruce Narramore, *Help! I'm a Parent*, 2d ed. (Grand Rapids: Zondervan, 1995). Written by a psychologist and researcher, this book offers practical advice from a Christian perspective for parents.

The Middle Years

The middle of the thirties is literally the mid point of life. The halfway mark. No gongs ring, of course. But twinges begin. Deep down a change begins to register in those gut-level perceptions of safety and danger, time and no time, aliveness and stagnation, self and others.

GAIL SHEEHY, *PASSAGES*

Middle age, what is it? Some people speak of midlife, middlescence, and middle age as interchangeable concepts; others see them as being distinct. We will treat them as synonymous concepts. But to what do they refer? One writer sees this period as beginning when we have completed our preparation for life, and ending at retirement (Howe 1959). Other writers see this period covering the years from 30 to 70 (Maas and Kuypers 1974; Hulme 1962). Still others see it as the forties (Fried 1967; Peterson 1967; Goolrick 1975), while yet another writer puts it at 45 to 64 (Vander Zanden 1996). A friend of mine suggests that people should multiply their age by two at every birthday, and when the result is more years than they expect to live, they have arrived at middle age. A survey of the literature indicates that there is no general agreement on the beginning or ending of middle age. For our purposes, we will consider middle age as the years from 35 to 55.[1]

Who are the people that make up this age group? According to the U.S. Bureau of the Census, it comprises about one in four Americans. They are generally economically well-off and have the lowest unemployment rate of all age groups. Their income is at or near their lifetime peak. Chief executives and members of corporate boards have generally reached

---

[1]It should be noted that the U.S. Census Bureau uses forty-five to sixty-four as middle age, and many sociologists follow this because that is the way data is collected by the Census Bureau. However, these ages do not cover the years when many crises occur—the late thirties and early forties. Psychologists generally prefer to use thirty-five to fifty-five or other years in this range.

those positions by age 55; their average annual compensation is about three hundred thousand dollars a year. While that kind of income is not typical of most middle-aged people, the average income of middle-aged people is well above the national average. People between 45 and 54 years of age head about 15 percent of all households, but account for almost 21 percent of all household income. Middle-aged couples are more likely to own their own home. More than three out of four families headed by a person age 55 live in their own home. Middle-aged persons are less likely to be victims of crime than the general population. They also have a higher voter turnout rate—almost 70 percent compared with a national average of under 55 percent.

More than eight out of ten persons in their middle years live in a family. The divorce rate for this age group is well below the national average, but it has doubled since 1950. Almost two out of three couples have no children under 18 living at home by the time the couple reaches age 55. It is during this period of life that many individuals face a series of crises. In this chapter we will examine some of these crises and see how they affect marriage and the family.

Before we look at these crises, it should be pointed out that we will be dealing with generalizations, statistical norms, averages, and case studies. The reader should be careful not to stereotype persons in this age range or assume that everyone will go through each of these crises with equal intensity. For some persons middle age is a smooth transition with few problems. However, for many others it is a turbulent time with significant crises and problems. Because many readers of this book are college students whose parents are in this age bracket, and because individuals and couples in this age range make up a significant part of most of our churches and hold many of the offices and positions of responsibility, it is important for us to understand this age group. We will explore some of the unique crises of this stage of life and offer some suggestions for dealing with them.

PHYSICAL-PSYCHOLOGICAL DIMENSION

As one considers the human life cycle, there are two periods or stages that involve major physiological changes with accompanying emotional crises: puberty and middle age. While the physiological changes that take place during puberty are fairly rapid and obvious, the changes that take place during the second stage that involves major physiological changes—middle age—are more gradual and not always obvious. Some physiological changes that take place during this stage are common to both men and women, and some are unique to each sex.

First we will look at those changes that are common to both sexes. For most persons the peak of physical strength and stamina comes in the late twenties and early thirties. By age 35 most adults begin to notice a slight decline in both strength and stamina. For example, very few professional athletes are still competing after age 35, and those few who do continue to play, usually play "skill" positions where their experience can make up for loss of speed and strength. Fran Tarkenton, a quarterback for the Minnesota Vikings, played injury-free football until his mid-thirties, but was injured his last two seasons, was unable to throw long passes, and finally retired at the old age of 39.

Discussing Tarkenton's injuries raises another characteristic of middle age: people become more prone to major illness. As Rouch points out,

> Our first major illness is likely to occur in middlescence. Whether it does or not, we will be confronted with the deaths of relatives or close friends. Death thus becomes more immediate than before.... Combined with our natural bodily changes, [it] is a powerful force pulling us toward inwardness. (1974:122)

Sheehy sees facing one's death as the major issue or crisis of middle age. She says,

> Each of us stumbles upon the major issue of midlife somewhere in the decade between 35 and 45. Though this can also be an ordinary passage with no outer event to mark it, eventually we all confront the reality of our own death. And somehow we must learn to live with it. The first time that message comes through is probably the worst. (1976:8)

Not only do individuals face declining physical strength and well-being in themselves, but for the married, also in their partners. In addition, married people are confronted not only with their own deaths but also with the death or loss of their partners.

Other physical changes that are common to both men and women are changes in appearance. The body metabolism in both sexes changes during this period, and there is a tendency to put on weight. This tendency is so common that it has come to be called "middle-aged spread." Women's breasts and buttocks, which were firm and well-shaped, begin to sag. Women experience menopause during this period, and this can result in both physical and emotional changes. Both men and women begin to get double and triple chins, wrinkles, facial sags, and graying hair.

Many men will begin to bald during this period. These physical changes are related to those aspects of appearance that are associated with "sex appeal" or attractiveness to the opposite sex. Frequently during this stage both men and woman feel that they are losing their attractiveness to the opposite sex, and there is a tendency to want to "prove they still have it." While it is more common for a man to have an affair during this stage, women are also prone to extramarital affairs.

On the other hand, the failing attractiveness of a marriage partner, along with declining physical stamina, can often cause the sexual dimension to become a growing problem for the married couple. With the lessening of sexual drive comes an added need for closeness, stability, acceptance, and companionship. All of these changes subtly put an additional burden on a marriage and the relationship between marriage partners.

As Belkin and Goodman point out, middle age is a period of adjustments. They believe that middle-aged couples are often caught between two conflicting expectations. They write:

> For many years the sexual expectations of married couples in middlescence were consistent with the myth of less sexual activity. Therefore, they were not, at least superficially, troubled by the decline in their marital sex life. But things have changed, middle-aged couples now have greater sexual expectations, but they may find themselves confused about their new roles and the "new norms" of middle-age sexuality.... To some extent these new norms may be just as unrealistic as the old ones, and they may place just as many social pressures upon couples to conform to values they do not feel comfortable with. (1980:357)

It is a myth that couples become asexual in their middle years. Clinebell reports on a study that found that couples between 45 and 54 had a median frequency of sexual intercourse of once a week (1977:50). Clinebell argues that sex in middle age can be rich and rewarding. He suggests eight guidelines for sexual enrichment in the middle years:

1. Liberate your attitudes about sex.
2. Keep your total relationship growing, and sex will tend to improve.
3. Discover and enjoy the special romance and new meanings that are possible in mid-years sex.
4. Create new ways to let your inner "child" sides play.
5. Discover what you enjoy most and coach each other on how to give maximum mutual enjoyment.

6. Enjoy leisurely nondemanding pleasuring.
7. Avoid the triple traps of hurry, fatigue, and too much alcohol.
8. If do-it-yourself methods such as those described above do not enhance your sex life sufficiently, get the help of a trained sex therapist who is also trained in marriage counseling. (1977:51–58)

CAREER DIMENSION

Some time between the ages of 35 and 55, both men and women will face a crisis period in their careers. Thirty or 35 is usually felt to be a turning-point age when a person is no longer "young" or "just starting out" or "preparing for a career" but has reached a climactic point of readjustment. The woman, if married, may feel a little desperate about soon becoming too old to return to her career. The working wife realizes that if she doesn't quit work and have a family soon, it will be too late. The single woman in her early thirties can no longer "mark time" waiting for the "right man" to come along. She suddenly realizes that she may never be married, and she must make a life for herself alone.

The married man in his early thirties now tries to refine and narrow his goals. He feels the pressure to put everything into his goal of reaching the top. The early thirties are usually not as great a crisis time for a man as they are for a woman. He will hit the midlife career crisis in his early forties. He suddenly realizes that he may never reach the top, or that the goal he set has been reached (or is within reach) and it brings no satisfaction, or he feels bored and in a dead-end, locked-in position. He knows that the early goals and values have to be adjusted.

Age becomes the enemy for both men and women as they realize that half of their lives are over, and there is a desperate "now or never" feeling about life. The family budget is under heavy strain as the children go to college. The "nest is empty," or almost, and the woman's all-consuming mothering role comes to an end. Now is the switch time, a time of readjustment for the couple and their family. The woman, after years of nurturing, now starts to build her self-identity. The man, after years of building his self-identity, now reexamines his values and often seeks deeper meaning in life through relationships and causes.

During middlescence the person has usually finished raising his or her children and probably has reached a plateau in occupation. At this point in life most people have a good picture of what they can accomplish occupationally. This insight, along with the empty-nest syndrome with all the role reversals that go with it, is very traumatic. The family has to be reorganized, and new roles and expectations must be accepted.

"It is not through more caregiving that a woman looks for a replenishment of purpose in the second half of her life," says Gail Sheehy. "It is through cultivating talents left half-finished, permitting ambition once piggybacked, becoming aggressive in the service of her own convictions rather than a passive-aggressive party to someone else's" (1976:294). When the period of procreation ends for the woman, her creative energies can be poured into new pursuits. "If the struggle for men in mid-life comes down to having to defeat stagnation through generativity," Sheehy states, "I submit that the comparable task for women is to transcend dependency through self-declaration" (1976:294).

Marriages can be shaken by the midlife crisis. The husband can become envious of the time his wife now spends on herself and her new career. He is used to being the center of her life and can't help thinking rather selfishly, "She should be here when I need her." The wife in her anxiety as she goes "back to work" becomes self-absorbed and a little frantic as she tries to fit into the academic or working world. The husband, instead of being supportive as she was when he was starting out, often sees her excitement and self-awareness as a threat. After the crisis period and adjustments are made, the husband and grown children experience pride in the wife and mother's accomplishments. They are pleased that she is not dependent on them for her identity and happiness and that she is becoming an ever more interesting person.

Emotional stability during this period is threatened. Life often centers around the children of the home; so when they go out on their own, it brings on a need for reordering expectations and roles. Many people have so much emotional involvement invested in their children that letting loose of their hold on them and reordering their expectations and roles is difficult. This situation threatens the very personhood of many parents. These problems of emotional instability can creep into a marriage relationship and have the potential to be devastating. Children usually leave home at the time when occupational concerns and business are at a peak. This concern occupies the attention of one or both spouses, while at the same time as marriage partners they are in deep need for renewed companionship. This need for companionship is multiplied by the fact that the children have left the home.

The Middle Years

The man in his midlife crisis often cries out from boredom and frustration, "I need a change!" This is the same cry of the woman who has spent her married life in one occupation—that of homemaker. Each needs to see his or her work as having purpose. Attitudes have a great deal to do with dissatisfaction and boredom. Reuel Howe in *The Creative Years* describes some ways that attitudes must change:

1. Our attitude toward ourselves as persons in a world of things. Rather than resent this person-thing dilemma, we should expect it. Much of our time is devoted to the business of living in which our relation to one another is relatively impersonal and functional.
2. We need to change our attitude toward work to one of acceptance because it is socially necessary and meets some aspect of human need.
3. We need to see our work as a part of God's work. A job, any job that serves a constructive purpose, even a menial job, has the meaning of a ministry; and by our faithfulness to it, we serve both God and man. (1959:176–80)

Understanding is necessary on the part of husband and wife as each goes through the midlife crisis:

The intensity of the middle-age crisis depends on the need-satisfyingness of the relationship and particularly on the success achieved in the previous stages of intimacy. If the basic art of loving mutually was learned during the young adult years, most couples take the middle-years crisis in stride. They reexamine their relationship and shift some patterns, but they know how to relate and how to go about changing and deepening their marriage to meet the needs of the second half of life....

The middle years can be highly productive and creative in which each partner finds new stimulation in developing interests and activities. Some of the energy that was formerly invested in the children is available for reinvestment in a second career for the wife, new hobbies for the husband, and joint projects in which the couple finds new meanings by giving themselves to meet some need in society. (Clinebell and Clinebell 1970:127–30)

FAMILY DIMENSION

Married couples do not live in isolation. Each partner is a member of two families: the family of orientation, the one they are born into; and the family of procreation, the one they form by marriage. Changes take place in both of these families during the middle years.

As we have previously pointed out, during the parents' middle years children have usually grown and are in the process of leaving home. Ideally, parents are to give their children room to become autonomous throughout their childhood development. This is not an easy task because our nature is to cling to those we love rather than giving them opportunity to become independent. But no matter how good a job the parents have done at making this transition more bearable, it still hurts. As James Peterson has so vividly expressed it, "Often both parents wander about the home and look at mementos from an exhilarating past—and try to remember how these rooms, now so still, used to echo with rock and roll, loud laughter, or singing" (1968:42).

This transition is much more difficult when the husband and wife have for the past eighteen or twenty years made their relationship revolve around the children instead of the enhancement of their own lives together. We often see that divorce occurs during this time of life because when the children leave, the parents are left facing each other, asking the question, "Who are you?" It is most important that the husband and wife regularly evaluate their relationship with one another. They need to keep the lines of communication open so they can grow together, rather than apart.

This crisis we have been discussing is commonly referred to as the "empty-nest syndrome." It is a phenomenon of the last half of the twentieth century. In previous generations women continued to bear children throughout their fertile years, often having their last child in their late thirties or early forties. By the time the last child left home, the couple were at or near the end of their lives. Today, however, most couples have had their last child before they are 35 and have life expectancies in the mid-seventies. That means the last child will leave home by the time they are 55, leaving them with twenty or more years of life remaining.

If the couple have built their lives around their children, there may be little left to their relationship. In fact, couples who have stayed together "for the sake of the children" may have little or no incentive to maintain the relationship after the nest is empty. At this time a couple can easily lose touch with each other. They may either divorce or live together as roommates, but not as husband and wife.

On the other hand, research indicates that marital satisfaction often increases during this period (Green 1978:326). The couple is usually reasonably well-off financially, still in relatively good health, and with productive years left. These years can be a time of growth for them both as individuals and as a couple. This can be a period when the couple can spend time and resources on themselves that had previously been spent on the children. This can be an exciting time for couples that are committed to each other and to their relationship.

While children are leaving home, changes are also taking place in their families of orientation. About the time a couple become free from the responsibilities of child rearing, they may find that they have to pick up responsibilities related to aging parents. Again, this is an area where recent changes in life expectancy and family size will have profound implications. In 1900 only about 42 percent of the population lived to be 65, and life expectancy was 47 years. By 1973 over 70 percent of the population lived to be 65. In 1973 that meant that out of four parents, a couple could expect three or four of their parents to live to age 65. That means a couple may end up with double the number of aged parents to care for. The average middle-aged couple has more living parents than children (Hess, Markson, and Stein 1993:160). Also, because family size has been reduced since 1900, there are fewer brothers and sisters to share the responsibility for aged parents. Couples are frequently faced with the agonizing decision of placing aged parents in a nursing home or bringing them into their home. These couples also face the deaths of their parents.

HUSBAND AND WIFE RELATIONSHIP

We have examined some of the crises and problems faced by couples during their middle years and discussed some ways these changes may impact the husband-wife relationship. The various crises of middle age may act as a wedge to drive a couple apart, or as an opportunity to pull them together. Actually, a couple will most likely respond to the crisis of midlife in the same ways that they have learned to respond to crises earlier in their relationship. However, couples can develop strategies for dealing with the crises of middle age. Nelson Foote, a sociologist who has pioneered the developmental approach to the study of marriage and the family, says:

> To expect a marriage to last indefinitely under modern conditions is to expect a lot. Certainly marriage counselors report many cases of mates who disclose no specific cause of dissatisfaction, yet complain that they have lost interest in their marriage. Successful marriage may thus come to be defined, both by married people and students of marriage, in terms of its potential for continued development, rather than in terms of momentary assessments of adjustment. (Quoted in Kephart 1981:377)

Reuel Howe, in his book *The Creative Years* (1959:119–25), suggests five strategies for developing a creative marriage in the middle years. These strategies consist of five affirmations. We will discuss each of them and see how they apply.

1. *Since we are made in the image of God, there is more to each of us than the other sees.* After having lived with another person for twenty or more years, it is easy to believe we know all about our spouse and to take him or her for granted, forgetting that he or she was created in God's image. Even as we can never fully understand or know God, so we can never fully understand or know another person. However, in the marriage relationship that understanding and knowledge should be growing. The more we seek to know and understand our partner, the deeper the relationship will grow.

This is especially true because people are always changing. My wife and I have been married for thirty-five years. I am not the same person I was thirty-five years ago. There have been many changes in my personality. The same is true for my wife. In essence, we have to keep rediscovering each other. We are both growing people and need to keep up with each other's growth.

2. *You will find life by giving yourself and cherishing the other person.* As we saw in Chapter 3 on dating, authentic love is not primarily an emotion but an act of the will. Love is behavior, thoughts, and actions. Emotions are the by-products of thoughts and actions. Authentic love is a commitment that carries married partners through crises so that they come out closer for the experience.

As we saw above, people are constantly changing, growing, and developing. The girl I "fell in love" with and married is now a mature woman and mother. She is not the same person that I first met. It is my opinion that in a good marriage a couple continually "refall in love." The commitment made at marriage needs to be constantly reconfirmed.

3. *The differences between man and woman can be good.* While I believe men and women are equal, I also recognize differences. The mistake of radical feminism has been to see *equal* and *same* as equivalent. Things and people can be different and of equal value and worth. Without getting into the debate concerning whether the differences are genetic or cultural, there *are* differences between men and women. These differences can bring added dimensions to a relationship. The husband has the additional benefit of a female perspective on issues, and the wife has the

The Middle Years

benefit of a male perspective. I have four eyes to see the world with, my own and my wife's. She sees things I do not see, and that is my gain. For a creative marriage, each partner needs to accept his or her own uniqueness and the uniqueness of the partner.

4. *Compatibility is the achievement of marriage, not a condition necessary to its beginning.* In many states incompatibility is grounds for divorce. But rather than being the basis for the destruction of a marriage, incompatibility should become the dynamic for the growth of a marriage. Two normal, healthy human beings are not going to be able to live together in the intimacy of marriage and not have differences. These differences should not become obstacles that divide, but building blocks for growth.

5. *It takes time to be married.* We have an expression in the American culture that says, "Time is money." If that is so, then marriage requires a large investment. It may be said that one will get out of marriage what one puts into it. Some will argue that it is the quality of the time and not the amount of time that counts. They are only half correct. The quality of the time is what counts, but it is not possible to have quality without sufficient quantity.

I once heard a chapel speaker say that he was glad to be married and past the dating stage of his life. I am married but have not passed the dating stage—and I hope I never do. My wife and I go out on a date at least once a week. We make time for each other. Time is necessary for a good relationship.

Harold Myra, publisher of *Christianity Today* and a middle-aged married man, has written a poem, "An Ode to Marriage," about marriage in the middle years. This poem catches the problems and potentials of midlife marriage and reflects Howe's five affirmations:

"You know, it could happen to us,"
    you said to me,
    sitting in your favorite chair as we sipped coffee,
    digesting the news of the latest couples splitting up.
"No matter how great we think we have it,
    if all *those* people can break up
    it could happen to us.
We're humans like them.
It is possible."
I didn't answer for a while.

We were both incredulous at the news.
Men and women of maturity
    decades-long marriages
    so many have exploded, one after another.
Almost every week, another set of names.
Not him! Not her!
They're too sensible, too solid.
"You're right," I finally admit.
We've never joked about divorce,
    never brought it up as an option.
We declared total commitment to each other
    and must reaffirm that always.
But maybe realizing it could happen to us
    helps us make sure it won't.
How terrible to think of an argument
    someday when one of us feels
    the need for the ultimate weapon,
"Well, obviously there's no sense staying together.
    We're just hurting each other,
    just keeping each other trapped."
Those are words mouthed in kitchens
    and bedrooms of "mature" Christian homes.
Remember how our love began?
Years ago, I offered you my arm
    that September night we first went out.
You reached for it
    as we leaped a puddle together.
Then you walked just close enough
    to show you liked it.
I glimpsed your face under the streetlight,
    excitement splashing gently on it. . . .
No commitment—just beginnings.
My arm pulled you that January eve
    tight beside me in that car.
Midnight. Time to leave.
"Good night" wasn't quite enough,
    and our lips touched gently
    in a kiss as light as angel cake.

The Middle Years

"I like you," it said,
    but nothing more.
November air had rough-scrubbed our faces.
As we wrestled playfully
    in your parent's farmhouse.
That moment I knew
    and breathed into your hair,
"I LOVE YOU."
The words exploded around us.
They meant far more than "you're nice."
They meant commitment.
Your words came back to me
    in firm, sure sounds:
"I love you too."
And our kiss of celebration
    was the beginning of a new creation.
Yes, I chose you.
Out of all the lovely girls I knew.
I chose you.
How marvelous are the women of planet Earth,
    hair flaring in the wind
    rich browns and golds
    a thousand delicious shapes
    girls who laugh saucily
    girls who read Browning
    girls who play sitars
    girls who fix carburetors.
Of all those fascinating possibilities,
I chose you.
Decisively. Permanently.
Is that self-entrapment?
Was a commitment made in youth
    to bind me a lifetime?
Ah, but it was as strong as birth,
    a fresh creation,
    soon to be a new flesh,
    you and I as one.
We chose each other.

Life Cycle of the Family

We created something new under the sun.
You to shape me
　　and I you,
　　like a Luther Burbank original.
We, our own new creation,
　　to produce fruit wholly unique,
UNIQUE IN THE UNIVERSE!
Then the wedding
　　flying rice and honeymoon
　　days and nights together.
Two persons
　　as unalike as birch and cypress
　　had chosen each other.
The heavens laughed
　　and the sands of the earth
　　lay ready for the tender feet
　　of our newborn self.
Does time change all that?
Were we naïve? Now, after we have
　　loved, argued, laughed, given birth,
what does it mean
　　when I hold you and say,
　　"I love you"?
Without the young-love ecstasy,
　　is it required rote
　　or reaffirmation of our new creation?
"I love you."
My temples don't pulse as I say it.
My body does not ache for coupling,
　　not as it did.
Yet the words carry more fact
　　than ever they did in courtship.
They embrace a million moments shared....
Standing together
　　atop Cadillac Mountain
　　and aching to absorb the blue-white-green beauty ...
Or angrily expounding to each other in the kitchen
　　about our particular stupidities,

The Middle Years

then sharing a kiss ten hours later ...
Bonding moments, holding us together.
How easily those bonds could be tyrannical.
"You always forget ..." "You never think ..."
And bitter moments bite into their flesh
    with binding ropes that tie them to the
    time and place instead of to each other.
Yet bonds can be a
    thousand multicolored strands
    of sorrow, joy, embarrassment,
    of anger, laughter shared
    as we watch God maturing us,
    as we gently tell each other
    of our joys, our fears,
    even of our fantasies.
Rope is rope.
Experiences are much the same:
    crabby days,
    laughing days,
    boring days.
We'll go through them "in love,"
    by commitment to each other,
    sharing, forgiving,
    not blaming, not hurting.
Yet when we do hurt,
    we ask forgiveness,
    so the ropes will bind us together.
For if they don't
    they'll wrap around our throats,
    so that each struggle will tighten the noose,
    and we'll have to reach for the knife to cut the bonds.
"I love you."
It sounds trite—
    but not if it's remembering
    the thousands of strands
    of loving each other when we don't feel lovely,
    of holding each other,
    of winking across a room,

of eating peanut butter sandwiches beside the surf.
And of getting up in the morning
thousands of times, together,
and remembering what we created,
the day we first said "I love you,"
Something permanent
and growing
and alive. (1979b:60–62)

DISCUSSION QUESTIONS

1. What do you think of when you think of a middle-aged person? Are your thoughts positive or negative? Why?

2. Male movie stars often retain their appeal to females into their fifties and sixties, while female stars rarely retain their appeal past their forties. Why do you think this happens?

3. A recent study found that a sample of college students considered their parents sexually inactive. When the parents of these students were surveyed, they were found to be, for the most part, sexually active. Why do you think the college students thought their parents were sexually inactive?

4. Do you believe the empty-nest syndrome affects men or women more? Career women or homemakers? Why?

5. What do you see as the implications of longer life expectancies coupled with women having fewer children?

6. What do you see as the biblical response to the aging process? How should Christians react to middle age?

SUGGESTED READING

Reuel L. Howe, *The Creative Years* (Greenwich, Conn.: Seabury, 1959). A well-written, captivating treatment of middle age. Writing from a Christian perspective, Howe deals with the crises of midlife marriage and offers biblical, practical counsel for dealing with them.

Daniel J. Levinson et al. *The Seasons of a Man's Life* (New York: Knopf, 1978). A classic work dealing with middle age. It contains interesting case studies illustrating the phases of aging.

Henry S. Maas and Joseph A. Kuypers, *From Thirty to Seventy* (San Francisco: Jossey-Bass, 1974). A forty-year longitudinal study of adult lifestyles and personality. It deals with major issues related to both men and women.

Gail Sheehy, *Passages* (New York: Dutton, 1976). A well-written and popular book that is fast becoming a classic. This work contains a number of case studies and deals with the major crises of midlife.

Aging and Death

Is not wisdom found among the aged? Does not long life bring understanding?

JOB 12:12

Rise in the presence of the aged, show respect for the elderly.

LEVITICUS 19:32

What is old age? When I was a teenager, I thought 30 was old. Now that I am in my fifties, I think 60 is still young. Obviously, old age is relative. However, we have to make an arbitrary determination in order to be able to discuss this stage of life. If we call the years from 35 to 55 the middle years, then we might view the years from 56 to 65 as the *mature years,* and after age 65, the *senior years.*

In one sense, we might say that people begin aging as soon as they are born. However, when we use the term *aging,* we are generally referring to a process of deterioration and movement toward death rather than just getting older. The first half of life is usually marked by growth and increasing strength, whereas the second half of life is marked by decline and increasing weakness. During the middle years this decline is generally gradual and often made up for by experience and knowledge. But as the person moves into the mature years, and especially the senior years, the rate of decline increases. Even experience and knowledge cannot always make up for diminished capacities.

As we discuss the characteristics of people in the mature and senior years, we need to be reminded again that we will be looking at generalizations, statistical averages, and norms. We need to be careful not to stereotype older persons. While one 70-year-old during the 1980s was infirm, senile, and in a nursing home, another 70-year-old served as president of the United States.

The senior years, or old age, begin at 65. Who are the people of this age group? They make up 13 percent of the population of the United

States, some twenty-five million strong. In 1900 only four out of ten people reached age 65. But it is estimated that persons 65 and older will make up 16 percent of the population by 2020 and 20 percent of the population by 2030 (Farley 1998:433).

While about 80 percent of the men over 65 are living with their spouses, just over a third of the women in this age bracket are living with a spouse. One of the reasons for this disparity is that men make up just over 40 percent of this age group, while women make up almost 60 percent. Another reason is that men often marry younger women.

Only about 6 percent of the population over 65 live in nursing homes, or about 1.5 million persons in 1980. Because of their longer life expectancy, there are more than two women for every man in nursing homes. Over 40 percent of nursing home residents are over 80 years of age. On the other hand, more than 11 percent of persons over 65 are active in the labor force—almost three million persons. However, roughly the same number of persons over 65 are living below the poverty level.

Perhaps the greatest effect on aging and population trends has been the dramatic increase in life expectancy (see figure 13.1). As this segment of the population increases, there will be major changes in America's culture and lifestyles. We are already seeing senior citizens becoming a powerful political force. Social Security is a major campaign issue in the 2000 presidential campaign in the United States. Those industries that serve the needs of the aging will be growth industries, and the job market for those serving the elderly will be expanding. The fields of *gerontology*, the study of aging and the problems of the aged, and *geriatrics*, the treatment of the aging, are rapidly expanding.

While in many cultures the aged are looked up to, honored, and revered, the American culture tends to disparage the old. It has generally been a youth-oriented culture, and aging is seen as a negative process. All one has to do is look at the commercials for hair dyes, wrinkle removers, and other products designed to remove the signs of aging to realize that aging is undesirable. These negative attitudes toward aging and the aged may be summed up in the term *ageism*. Ageism is the stereotyping of, and discrimination against, persons because they are old. As Orthner points out:

> Stereotypes of the elderly abound. Once people reach their sixties, they are supposed to graciously give up their jobs, their sex life, their sporty cars, their in-style clothing, and their time in favor of sitting, watching television, and rocking on their porch eagerly waiting for someone to visit them. The popular image of the elderly in the media, includ-

FIGURE 13.1

Growth in the United States of the Population 65 Years and Over, 1900–2030

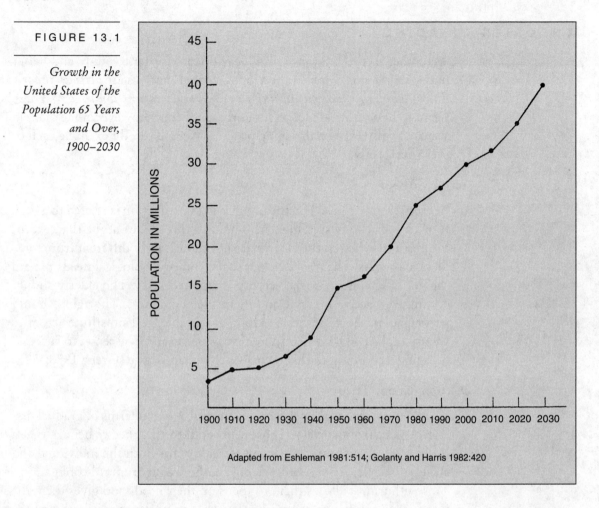

Adapted from Eshleman 1981:514; Golanty and Harris 1982:420

ing children's books and programs, portrays them as being sickly, passive, incompetent, and less self-reliant than other adults. (1981:427)

In spite of recent federal legislation forbidding discrimination in hiring and allowing persons to work past age 65, age discrimination is a continuing problem for the elderly. However, today more and more older people are advocating their rights and demanding the same respect and opportunities as other people. Examples of this movement are organizations such as the Gray Panthers, the National Council of Senior Citizens, and the American Association of Retired Persons—all formed to fight for the rights of the elderly. The Bible clearly teaches that we are to respect, honor, and care for the elderly (e.g., Lev. 19:32; 1 Tim. 5:1–3; James 1:27).

Life Cycle of the Family

THEORIES OF AGING

A number of theories have been developed in order to study and better understand aging. Four of the more accepted theories are *activity theory, disengagement theory, continuity theory,* and *maturation theory.* There seems to be some evidence to support each theory; however, none of them seems to fully explain the aging process. We will briefly examine each of these perspectives.

Activity Theory

Activity theory is based on the premise that satisfaction is related to a high level of social activity. Those who hold to this theory argue that, except for physical changes, the elderly are not significantly different from middle-aged adults. They believe that social and psychological needs remain the same. Therefore, social activity is still necessary. The elderly should continue an active lifestyle and main social contacts. The aging should participate in the labor force as long as possible, and substitute activities should replace work when retirement is necessary. The secret to successful aging, according to this theory, is to remain active (Green 1978:332).

Disengagement Theory

The *disengagement theory* views successful aging in terms of gradual disengagement from society. Those who hold to this theory believe that a process of gradual disengagement is healthy for both the individual and society. This theory sees older people withdrawing from role obligations. This withdrawal allows them to focus on their needs and gives them the freedom to pursue their desires. The theory postulates a double withdrawal—the society from the individual as well as the individual from society.

Continuity Theory

Continuity theory argues that people who, as they age, continue those roles and activities that they find satisfying have an easier time adjusting. The key is to continue those activities the person finds rewarding. For example, in academic circles to move ahead professors need to both teach and publish. Usually a professor prefers one activity over the other. In retirement a professor who enjoys research and writing can focus her full

Aging and Death

attention in that direction, while a professor who enjoys teaching might take up lecturing.

Maturation Theory

Maturation theory sees people becoming better-adjusted and more accepting of themselves as they age. As people age they are able to accept who they are and where they are in life. This theory sees aging as a maturing process rather than as a deteriorating process. With age comes experience and insight as well as perspective. This theory argues that, in general, older people are able to adjust to changes that come with aging.

Whichever theory of aging one accepts, there are many factors that characterize the mature and senior years. We will look at some of the major factors: grandparenthood, retirement, death, widowhood, and remarriage.

GRANDPARENTHOOD

Whereas grandparenthood was once reserved for the senior years, it has now moved into the mature years and even the middle years. We have seen that in 1970 the median age at first marriage for men was approximately 23 and for women approximately 21. If the first child was a daughter and was born two years after the marriage, she would be 24 in 1994. If the daughter married at that time (24 was about the median age for women in 1994) and had her first child two years later, her father would become a grandfather at age 49 and her mother would become a grandmother at age 47. In fact, many Americans are becoming grandparents in their forties.

With people becoming grandparents earlier, and with increased life expectancies, more and more youngsters will have all or most of their grandparents alive while they are growing up. Ironically, while children have more grandparents living than previous generations did, they are having less contact with their grandparents (Green 1978:326). In our highly mobile society, children frequently live hundreds or thousands of miles from their grandparents and see them only occasionally. Both of my grandmothers were frequently long-term residents in our home when I was growing up. My wife's grandparents lived across the street when she was growing up. Now my mother and my wife's parents live on the East Coast and we live on the West Coast.

Grandparenthood as a Status

While grandparenthood is a status with its associated role behavior, surprisingly little sociological research has been conducted on grandparenthood. One of the few studies to examine the role of grandparenthood was carried out by Bernice Neugarten and Karol Weinstein (1964). They discovered that approximately a third (36 percent of the grandmothers and 20 percent of the grandfathers) experienced some role strain or role conflict. Some of the grandparents found the role of grandparent alien to their self-image. Others were not sure of how involved they should be in the rearing of grandchildren. And some felt imposed upon with care-taking or responsibility for grandchildren.

In their research, Neugarten and Weinstein found that grandparents played one of five major roles. The first is the *Formal* role. Grandparents in this role carefully distinguish between parenting and grandparenting. They will provide special treats and indulge their grandchildren and provide babysitting. However, they are careful to leave parenting strictly to the parents. While they show an interest in their grandchildren, they avoid becoming involved in child rearing directly or by giving advice.

The second grandparent role is the *Fun Seeker.* This role is characterized by an informal and playful relationship with the grandchildren. The grandparent joins in the child's activities as a playmate. These grandparents tend to view their grandchildren as a source of leisure activity. The relationship is based on mutuality rather than authority. The goal of the relationship is for both parties to derive fun from it.

The *Surrogate Parent* is the third role grandparents may take. If this role is played, it is done so primarily by grandmothers. The grandmother assumes the actual child rearing responsibilities for the grandchild. This role often develops when the mother works outside the home and the grandmother provides child care. This role is also common when the mother is unwed. Green reports that one out of eight grandmothers have unwed daughters. He also writes that 52 percent of single teenage mothers receive help from their own mothers (1978:326).

The fourth role is the *Reservoir of Family Wisdom.* This tends to be an authoritarian matriarchal or patriarchal role. Grandparents who play this role are involved in the rearing of their grandchildren. When the parents do not want interference in child rearing, this role can result in resentment and conflict.

The last grandparent role suggested by Neugarten and Weinstein is the *Distant Figure.* In this role, the grandparent has only limited and brief contact with the grandchildren. The grandparent may see the grandchild only at Christmas or on his or her birthday. The grandparent is generally benevolent but distant and remote. The grandparent is not part of the grandchild's everyday life.

One of the interesting findings in Neugarten and Weinstein's study is the relationship between the age of the grandparents and the roles they played. They found that the majority of the Fun Seeking and Distant Figure grandparents were under 65 years of age, whereas the majority of the Formal grandparents were over 65. Apparently age did not affect the other two roles.

Another of the few sociological studies of grandparenthood deals specifically with grandmotherhood (Robertson 1977). This study concludes that the role of grandmother can be understood in terms of two dimensions, personal and social. The social dimension results from social and normative forces—society's expectations. The personal dimension stems from personal forces and needs. The study involved administering a scale to a sample of grandmothers. The answers to the items on the scale permitted the assigning of respondents to a high or low rating on each dimension. Combining the two dimensions resulted in four categories or grandmother roles (see figure 13.2).

The first role category is the *Apportioned* grandmother. These women scored high on both the social and personal dimensions and were equally concerned with doing what was morally right for their grandchildren and indulging them. Grandmothers in this category are the most involved with

FIGURE 13.2

Robertson's Four Grandmother Roles

		PERSONAL DIMENSION	
		High	Low
SOCIAL DIMENSION	High	Apportioned (29%)	Symbolic (26%)
	Low	Individualized (17%	Remote (28%)

Adapted from Robertson 1977

their grandchildren. They also tend to be widowed and not participating in the labor force. This apparently leaves them more time to be involved with their grandchildren.

The second type of grandmother role is the *Symbolic* type. These women scored high on the social dimension and low on the personal dimension. Grandmothers in this category were more concerned with what was morally good for their grandchildren. They wanted their grandchildren to have a good education, to develop good manners, to be polite, to have moral values and a good reputation. The grandmothers in this group were the youngest, and the majority were married and in the labor force.

The third role is the *Individualized* grandmother. These women scored low on the social dimension and high on the personal dimension. These grandmothers were not as concerned with norms but were more concerned with companionship. The grandmothers in this group were the oldest, with an average age of almost 70. There seems to be an indication that as grandparents become older their roles change.

The fourth role group is the *Remote* grandmother. These women scored low on both the social and the personal dimensions. These grandmothers were the least involved with their grandchildren. They carried out their grandmother role in a distant, impersonal, and ritualistic manner. This group obviously found little meaning or satisfaction in their grandmother role.

A more recent perspective, based on a national study, categorizes grandparent roles in three styles (Cherlin and Furstenberg 1986). One style is called *companionate.* In this style grandparents see their role as one of being a companion to their grandchildren. The relationship is based on companionship, affection, and fun. These grandparents generally live close enough to their grandchildren to have regular interaction with them, but they do not take on parental responsibilities. The research found 55 percent of grandparents surveyed fit this style.

The second style of grandparenting is called *remote.* These grandparents are not intimately involved with their grandchildren. This remoteness is not due to choice, but results from geographic distance. About 29 percent of grandparents fall into this category.

The third style is called *involved.* These are grandparents who take on parenting roles with their grandchildren. This role often emerges where the daughter is a single parent and the grandparents help with the parenting responsibilities. About 16 percent of grandparents make up this category.

From these studies (Neugarten and Weinstein 1964; Robertson 1977; Cherlin and Furstenberg 1986), it is clear that most grandparents are engaged with their grandchildren and most enjoy their roles. Lasswell and Lasswell conclude that "most middle-aged parents enjoy becoming grandparents even though they may not always like to think of themselves as old enough for this to happen" (1982:457). Commenting on these studies, Orthner writes, "The majority of grandparents . . . expressed only comfort, satisfaction, and pleasure with their grandparent role" (1981:420).

RETIREMENT

Retirement as an extended stage of life is a recent occurrence. In 1900 the average man lived only 2.8 years after retirement. Today, by age 65, 80 percent of all men and 90 percent of all women are retired and have fifteen or more years of life ahead of them (Farley 1998:442). While some people want to keep working after age 65, the majority of workers want to retire before then. On the one hand, recent federal legislation has made it possible for most workers to keep their jobs until at least age 70. On the other hand, some unions have negotiated a "thirty and out" pension program in their contracts that allows workers to retire even as soon as their early fifties. Many union contracts permit early retirement, and Social Security retirement benefits can be collected at age 62.

While both men and women are in the workforce and both retire, retirement affects a man more because his self-image is closely related to his occupation. Men have been socialized to see their identities in their careers and to judge their value in terms of their work (Green 1978:327).

Crises of Retirement

Reporting on studies related to retirement, Lasswell and Lasswell (1982:459–60) present the following five major crises faced in retirement.

Loss of Finances

Many retired persons have Social Security as their only source of income. Most private and corporate pension programs were not started until after World War II, so most workers eligible for these programs are just beginning to retire. For many workers retirement means a loss of income and a lowered standard of living. The vast majority of nursing home residents receive public assistance, and many of the elderly are on welfare.

For those who have adequate income, retirement is often welcomed. It is an opportunity to travel, pursue hobbies, or engage in other activities that had to be put off during the working years. The greater the resources older people have, the more likely they are to view retirement as a pleasant experience.

Loss of Self-Esteem

We have already seen that workers have their identities in their occupations. When people retire, to the extent their identity was related to the job, there is a loss of identity. Green (1978:328) points out that frequently blue-collar workers have a more difficult time than white-collar workers making the adjustment from worker to retiree.

Loss of Work-Oriented Social Contacts

For many workers, both male and female, most of their social relationships have centered around their work. They may have been part of a company or union bowling league or played golf with business associates. While both men and women develop social relationships through their work, research indicates that women who retire from the workforce have a harder time than men adjusting to the loss of social contacts (Lasswell and Lasswell 1982:460). This may be due to the nature of these relationships. In the American culture, relationships among men tend to be more instrumental, whereas among women they tend to be more emotional.

Loss of Meaningful Tasks

A person who has gone to work for forty or more years suddenly discovers that the meaning of life was related to a career. Even stable marriages may be shaken by the retirement of the husband. When a man retires, it changes not only his lifestyle but also that of his wife. If she has been a homemaker, her daily routine has more than likely centered around the husband's work schedule. If they are both in the workforce, they have most likely developed a division of labor in the home. Generally, the man is older than his wife and retires first. Tensions may result as the wife looks for a shift in the division of labor. A major task of retirement is to discover rewarding and meaningful interests to replace work. This may involve such activities as hobbies, volunteer work, or even starting a new career.

Aging and Death

Loss of Reference Group

Many workers, particularly those in professions, have identified with their peers. They have thought of themselves as doctors, lawyers, professors, bankers, or stockbrokers; now they are retired persons. Retired persons need to develop new reference groups. While they were in the workforce, their reference groups were occupational, but now new reference groups need to be formed. These may center around hobbies or other interests.

Types of Retired Families

Retired families may be studied in terms of the resources they have for their retirement years. One study (Streib 1972) classified older families in terms of four categories of resources: (1) physical health, (2) emotional well-being, (3) economic resources, and (4) social resources. On the basis of these four categories of resources, Lasswell and Lasswell discuss five types of retirement families. These types may be summarized as follows:

Type I: "The golden sunset family" has all four necessary resources: good physical health, good emotional health, adequate economic resources, and good social resources.

Type II: Those who are physically incapacitated but who are emotionally stable, have financial security, and who have family and friends for support.

Type III: These are older persons who are both physically and emotionally unhealthy, but who have enough money and family resources to take care of themselves.

Type IV: This type includes those who have only family to care for them. They are in poor physical and emotional health and have no money.

Type V: This type is "the totally deprived family," who end their years in misery. These are the families that present the most serious problems in old age because many of them lack any of the four important resources. (1982:461–62)

DEATH

In the Bible we read, "The days of our years are threescore years and ten; and if by reason of strength they be fourscore years" (Ps. 90:10 KJV). The Bible also says, "It is appointed unto men once to die" (Heb. 9:27 KJV). If it has not happened before old age, death certainly follows old age. While death can occur suddenly, for many it is an extended process. One researcher who has extensively studied the process of death and dying is Elisabeth Kubler-Ross (1969, 1974, 1981). She has discovered that the process of dying generally involves five stages: (1) denial and isolation, (2) anger, (3) bargaining, (4) depression, and (5) acceptance (1969). She points out that not all dying persons go through all five stages and not all go through them in the order given. However, enough people do go through all five stages in the order given to make her stages a valid generalization. We will examine each of the stages.

Stages of Dying

Denial and Isolation

Frequently a person's first reaction to a diagnosis of a terminal disease or medical problem is one of denial. The individual may respond with comments such as "The lab people made a mistake" or "The technician must have gotten my x-ray confused with someone else's" or "The doctor is overreacting." Some people will go from one physician to another seeking a different diagnosis. A more subtle type of denial involves carrying on business as usual while ignoring the diagnosis and its implications.

It is usually a shock to a person to learn of his or her impending death, even if it has been suspected. Denial is a psychological defense mechanism for handling shock. One therapist calls denial the shock absorber for human tragedy (Wright 1977b:134). Denial allows people to adjust gradually to the situation as they are able to cope. Joyce Landorf watched her mother pass through the five stages of dying. In her book *Mourning Song,* she shares with us valuable lessons about denial:

> I know that denial is needed in our emotions to act as a buffer or safety zone after we see the reality of someone else's (or our own) death. It gives a temporary measure of healing. It can also be used in our lives as a God-given diversion.
>
> Somewhere along the line we as Christians have been given the general feeling that if you are a Christian denial is not a problem, or in some cases, shouldn't even exist. What happens when a Christian does experience denial? And what if, in his denial, his actions do not appear to be too Christian?
>
> We need denial to help us through the most shocking moments of our painful knowledge.

We need denial—but we must not linger in it. We must recognize it as one of God's unique tools and use it.... However, after ... the initial danger has passed, we need not be dependent on it. (1974:47–53)

As Kubler-Ross points out, it is not only the dying person who passes through these stages but also close family and friends. One form denial can take with the close family and friends is isolation from the dying person. The more these people can avoid or isolate the dying person, the less they have to face the reality of their loved one's impending death. Writing about isolation, Wright indicates:

One of the problems that can occur is the Abandonment Syndrome. Dying people express the fear that their condition will make them so unacceptable to others around them that they will be abandoned, and in many cases studies have confirmed their fears.

Sometimes ... terminally ill patients are actually abandoned.... Often this is a reaction to the fears the person has of one's own death. Because of the implications of the loved one's death, we have to try to separate ourselves from him in some way. (1977b:136)

Norman Cousins, who was faced with a terminal diagnosis, has written:

Death is not the ultimate tragedy of life. The ultimate tragedy is depersonalization—dying in an alien and sterile area, separated from the spiritual nourishment that comes from being able to reach out to a loving hand, separated from a desire to experience the things that make life worth living, separated from hope. (1979:133)

Anger

When the reality of one's death breaks through the defense of denial, often the next reaction is anger. Anger is the usual response to frustration, and death may be the ultimate frustration. There may be many targets for the person's anger. The dying person may become angry with himself or herself, with loved ones, with physicians and nurses, or even with God himself. This anger may boil under the surface or it may explode in words and actions.

Bargaining

This stage generally follows the anger stage. The dying person begins to realize that anger, especially if it is directed at God, is not going to help him. Then he decides to attempt to bargain with God: "If you will let me live, God, I'll do such and such for you."

We find a classic case of bargaining in the Old Testament:

> In those days Hezekiah became ill and was at the point of death. The prophet Isaiah ... went to him and said, "This is what the Lord says: Put your house in order, because you are going to die; you will not recover."
>
> Hezekiah turned his face to the wall and prayed to the LORD, "Remember, O Lord, how I have walked before you faithfully and with wholehearted devotion and have done what is good in your eyes." And Hezekiah wept bitterly. (2 Kings 20:1–3)

We also find examples of bargaining in the New Testament, where close family and friends came to Jesus on behalf of dead or dying persons (e.g., the centurion, Matt. 8:8–13; Peter's mother-in-law, Matt. 8:14–15; Jairus's daughter, Mark 5:21–43; Lazarus, John 11:1–14). As with the case of Hezekiah, each was allowed to live longer.

As Christians, what should our response be to bargaining with God for our lives or the lives of our loved ones? The Bible teaches that God answers prayer and that he does heal. We also must realize that everyone eventually will die. As one pastor phrased it:

> God heals you of every sickness but your last. For the Bible says, "It is appointed unto man to die." In other words, should Jesus Christ tarry, every one of us here tonight at some time is going to die. Some bodily organ will cease functioning—it will break down and we will die. Think of the healing results during the ministry of Jesus. There were lepers cleansed of their diseases but they are not living today. Something else happened to them and they died. The woman with the issue of blood was healed of her disease but something else happened to her and eventually she died. They are not around today. God heals us of every disease, but "it is appointed unto man once to die." (Lyons 1973)

Depression

People generally reach this stage when they have exhausted their energy and resources on anger and bargaining. Kubler-Ross (1969:86) distinguishes between two types of depression. The first she calls *reactive depression.* This type results from the losses the person is experiencing in the process of dying. These losses include such things as self-esteem, self-reliance, job, physical strength, and physical appearance. The second types she labels *preparatory depression.* This results from anticipated losses and separation from all that is cherished.

Aging and Death

Acceptance

This is the final stage. This stage is reached when the person accepts his or her death. Joyce Landorf writes of her mother's acceptance of death:

> During the last week of my mother's life, we could distinctly feel her God-given confidence in dying. Even though she did not always understand the ways and workings of God, she spent the last week alive and in great beauty. The dignity of her inner confidence was apparent to all who saw her. (1974:113)

Christians are able to accept death because of their new life in Christ and their hope of resurrection. As the apostle Paul writes:

> I declare to you, brothers, that flesh and blood cannot inherit the kingdom of God, nor does the perishable inherit the imperishable.... For the perishable must clothe itself with the imperishable, and the mortal with immortality. When the perishable has been clothed with the imperishable, and the mortal with immortality, then the saying that is written will come true: "Death has been swallowed up in victory." "Where, O death, is your victory? Where, O death, is your sting?" The sting of death is sin, and the power of sin is the law. But thanks be to God! He gives us the victory through our Lord Jesus Christ. (1 Cor. 15:50, 53–57)

Death, Dying, and the Family

We have already seen that close family and friends, as well as the dying person, usually experience the stages of dying. However, the dying person and the family members may not all go through the stages at the same rate. Joyce Landorf recounts that when her mother was in the depression stage, she herself was already at the acceptance stage. However, her father was still back at the denial stage, and her sister was at the bargaining stage. Joyce Landorf shares some of the tensions and conflicts that arose because different family members were at different stages.

It is probably easier for most people to accept their parents' deaths than to accept a spouse's death. We all recognize that if life follows its normal course we will bury our parents. We are prepared and socialized to experience the death of parents. But most people are not prepared to experience the death of a spouse. We are not socialized to bury our mates.

When a parent dies in old age, the child is usually married and has a family of his or her own. The demands and responsibilities of that family, as well as the support and nurture of that family, usually limit grief and hasten acceptance. However, when a mate dies, there is a major void for the surviving spouse. Widowhood is a major crisis and a stage of adjustment for most people.

WIDOWHOOD

According to the 1990 U.S. Census, while less than one out of ten men between 65 and 75 were widowed, almost four out of ten women were widowed. Among men 75 to 85, less than one in five is widowed, while over six out of ten women are widowed. These differences result from two factors. The first is that on the average, women live seven years longer than men. The second is that on the average, men marry women about two years younger than themselves.

Becoming a widow or widower in the American culture can be a difficult transition because families rarely discuss or prepare for the death of any of their members unless there is a terminal illness. Usually there is no preparation for death. As Eshleman writes:

> Society compounds the difficulty of adjusting to the widowed status by placing an unstated taboo on the discussion of death between husband and wife or parents and children while they are alive. As a result, the widow or widower is often unprepared for the decisions that need to be made. Even if discussion preceded the death, the likelihood is great that loneliness, social isolation, and a need for major readjustments in living patterns will result. There is probably no other period in one's life where there is a greater effort at self-awareness. Feelings of inadequacy and guilt, which lead to depression, are frequent occurrences after the death of a spouse. (1981:530)

Widowers

Because women generally marry men who are older than they are and because women have a longer life expectancy than men do, the probability of a woman's becoming a widow is five times as great as that of a man's becoming a widower. While many more women than men lose their spouses, research indicates that men have a more difficult time adjusting to their mate's loss than women do (Nye and Berardo 1973:602; Kephart 1981:392). One of the reasons is that in many ways the role of a wife does not change in widowhood. A woman continues to cook, keep the house, and perform other household tasks, much as she did before her husband's death. In fact, the maintenance of routine can be a source of security and comfort in dealing with grief. On the other hand, a widower has lost his cook and housekeeper as well as his partner. It is generally easier for a widow than a widower to maintain separate living quarters. Also, married children are generally more open to having a widow than a widower come to live with them. In addition, widowers are more likely to be socially isolated. They are less likely to be living with children, to maintain relationships with the extended family, to have friends in the community, to attend church, or to belong to formal organizations or groups (Nye and Berardo 1973:605). One of the consequences of this isolation is that widowers have high suicide rates.

Widows

To say that widowers have a more difficult time than widows in adjusting to losing a mate is not to suggest that widows have an easy time. They also experience their particular problems. Traditionally, in North American society, women have placed greater value in their role as a wife than men have in their role as a husband. While women have often been identified as the wife of such and such a man, men have generally been identified by their profession or occupation. When a woman becomes a widow, she may, therefore, suffer more of a loss of status than a man who becomes a widower.

Another problem that widows have is the responsibility for the business and financial affairs of the family. While women are moving into the labor force in greater numbers and are learning to handle business and financial affairs, in many homes these matters are still cared for by the husband, with the wife having little or no knowledge in these areas. This is particularly true for couples who were married in the 1940s and 1950s and have more traditional marriages. It is these couples who now make up the segment of our population entering the retirement years. Most retired people today grew up in traditional homes where the husband handled business and financial matters.

Because of the imbalance in the sex ratio (about seventy men for every one hundred women), widows over age 65 have much less opportunity for remarriage than widowers. Also, as we have already seen, over 70 percent of the men over 65 are married. It is also interesting to note that the children and friends of a widow do not give her as much encouragement to remarry as they do a widower (Nye and Berardo 1973:605).

REMARRIAGE OF THE WIDOWED

Over thirty-five thousand marriages a year involve at least one partner over the age of 65 (Kephart 1981:393). However, the percentage of men remarrying is much greater than the percentage of women. Almost 50 percent of all widowed men under age 70 remarry (Golanty and Harris 1982:438), whereas only about 5 percent of the widowed women over 55 will remarry (Lamanna and Riedmann 1981:528). Golanty and Harris (1982:438–39) suggest that there are at least three factors that account for this imbalance in remarriage rates between widowers and widows. First, as we have already seen, widows greatly outnumber widowers, and this means that there are fewer potential mates for widows than widowers. Second, it is more socially acceptable for older men to marry younger women than for older women to marry younger men. This provides widowers with a larger pool of potential mates than widows have. Third, widowed men may be more motivated than widowed women to remarry. Because older men generally have a weaker social network than women, they may have greater desire for the companionship of marriage. Also, men have a greater need for cooking and housekeeping help than women do. Another reason may be that widows, recognizing the odds against remarriage, adjust better to widowhood and are not as interested in remarriage.

One study of remarriages in the senior years found five factors that were related to marital success:

1. The bride and groom had known each other for a long time.
2. The marriage was approved by their children and friends.
3. Both partners had adjusted well to other facets of retirement and aging.
4. The couple disposed of previously owned property and bought or rented a home for themselves.
5. There was sufficient income to live without economic hardship. (McKain 1969 in Lasswell and Lasswell 1982:471)

This study rated 74 percent of these remarriages successful on this five-factor scale: (1) showing respect and affection for each other, (2) enjoying each other's company, (3) having no serious complaints about each other, (4) being proud of each other, and (5) being considerate of each other (Lasswell and Lasswell 1982:471). It appears that the widowed may find remarriage is a viable option for them and that they can find happiness the second time around.

D I S C U S S I O N   Q U E S T I O N S

1.   Why do you think the aged tend to be disparaged in the American culture, whereas other cultures honor them?

2.   Which theory of aging do you believe best explains the process? Why?

3.   In your opinion, why is there so little social research conducted on grandparenthood?

4.   Why do you believe the children of the widowed are less likely to take in a widower? Why are they more likely to encourage a widower than a widow to remarry?

5.   Why do you think some family members may work through the stages of dying sooner than others when a loved one is terminally ill?

6.   What do Psalm 23 and 1 Corinthians 15 have to say about the process of death and dying?

S U G G E S T E D   R E A D I N G

Donald C. Cushenberry and Rita C. Cushenberry, *Coping with Life After Your Mate Dies,* 2d ed. (Grand Rapids: Baker, 1997). Written for those who have lost a mate. The authors deal with the grieving process and offer practical suggestions for moving ahead with life.

Elisabeth Kubler-Ross, *On Death and Dying* (New York: Macmillan, 1969). A classic treatment of death and dying. The author deals with the five stages of dying, fear of death, the dying person's family, and therapy for the dying. This book is basic to an understanding of this topic.

Joyce Landorf, *Mourning Song* (Old Tappan, N.J.: Revell, 1974).

Joyce Landorf Heatherly, *Mourning Song,* 2d ed. (Grand Rapids: Revell, 1994). A well-written and sensitive account of the death of the author's mother. This is an excellent illustration of Kubler-Ross's five stages. Landorf traces her mother's and the rest of the family's working through the stages.

Maximiliane Szinovacz et al., *Families and Retirement* (Newbury Park, Calif.: Sage, 1992). This study deals with retirement and the impact of retirement on family life. It looks at the timing of retirement and its impact on roles. It also looks at gender differences and retirement.

Divorce and Remarriage

When Jesus had finished saying these things . . . Some Pharisees . . . asked, "Is it lawful for a man to divorce his wife for any and every reason?"

"Haven't you read," he replied, "that at the beginning the Creator 'made them male and female,' and said, 'For this reason a man will leave his father and mother and be united to his wife, and the two will become one flesh'? So they are no longer two, but one. Therefore what God has joined together, let man not separate."

"Why then," they asked, "did Moses command that a man give his wife a certificate of divorce and send her away?"

Jesus replied, "Moses permitted you to divorce your wives because your hearts were hard. But it was not this way from the beginning. I tell you that anyone who divorces his wife, except for marital unfaithfulness, and marries another woman commits adultery."

MATTHEW 19:1–9

W hat God has joined together, let man not separate." Unfortunately we are seeing more and more marriages break up. There are a number of types of marital dissolution. In *annulment* a marriage is ruled invalid and for legal purposes never took place. Some of the grounds for annulment include bigamy (one of the parties being still legally married to someone else), incompetency on the part of one or both parties, deception, coercion, or one or both parties being minors. *Desertion* is a separation that is not legally sanctioned and is against the will of one spouse. Since desertion is not a legal process, there are no statistics on the extent of this type of separation. It is thought to be quite widespread, especially among the lower classes. In fact, it is often referred to as the "poor man's divorce" (Orthner 1981:373). By contrast, a *legal separation* involves the agreement of both parties, a separation agreement spelling out the conditions of the

Life Cycle of the Family

separation. A legal separation is a dissolution of the marital relationship, either temporarily or permanently, but not the dissolution of the legal marriage. *Divorce* is the legal termination of a marriage.

DIVORCE RATES

What is the extent of divorce in the United States? What percentage of marriages end in divorce? The answer depends on which statistics one uses. There are at least four types of divorce statistics. The first is the *number of divorces per year* (see table 14.1). This statistic does not really tell us much because it does not take into account increases or decreases in either the general population or the married population. The second is the *ratio of marriages to divorces per year* (see table 14.1). This statistic is also unreliable because it compares marriages taking place in one year with divorces from marriages that took place over many years. Therefore, if the number of marriages in a given year decreases, the divorce rate will appear to rise, even if the number of divorces decreases at a slower rate or remains stable.

A more accurate measure is the *crude divorce rate* (see table 14.2). This is the number of divorces per one thousand persons in the population that year. While this rate does take into account increases and decreases in the general population, it does not take into account age changes in a population.

TABLE 14.1			

Year	Number of Marriages	Number of Divorces	Marriage/ Divorce Ratio
1900	709,000	55,751	12.7/1
1910	948,166	83,045	11.4/1
1920	1,274,476	170,505	7.5/1
1930	1,126,856	195,961	5.8/1
1940	1,595,879	264,000	6.0/1
1950	1,667,231	385,144	4.3/1
1960	1,153,000	393,000	3.9/1
1970	2,158,802	708,000	3.0/1
1980	2,413,000	1,182,000	2.0/1
1996	2,344,000	1,150,000	2.0/1

Marriages, Divorces, and the Ratio Between Them in the United States

Source: National Center for Health Statistics, U.S. Department of Health and Human Services

TABLE 14.2

*Crude and Refined
Divorce Rates in the
United States*

Year	Crude Divorce Rate	Refined Divorce Rate
1920	1.6	7.0
1930	1.6	7.5
1940	2.0	8.5
1950	2.6	9.8
1960	2.2	9.2
1970	3.5	15.0
1980	5.3	23.5
1996	4.6	22.2

Sources: (Crude Rates) National Center for Health Statistics,
U.S. Department of Health and Human Services
(Refined Rates) Lamanna and Riedman (1981:460)
1980 and 1996 rates are projected from 1977 rates

For example, an aging population, such as in America, will have a greater percentage of its population married each year. Therefore, even if the percentage of marriages ending in divorce remained constant, the crude divorce rate would rise.

The most accurate and useful measure of divorce is the *refined divorce rate* (see table 14.2). This is the number of divorces a year per one thousand married women over age 15. This is the most valid statistic on divorce because it measures divorces by the number of women eligible for divorce. This measure allows an accurate comparison of divorce rates from one year to another without having to be concerned about age, size of population, or marital changes in the population.

One problem with all of these divorce rates is that they do not distinguish between first, second, and more divorces. That is, a few people having several divorces would produce the same rate as many people having one divorce. For example, in 1980, of every one hundred women who married for the first time, thirty-eight will have their marriages end in divorce. Of these thirty-eight women, twenty-nine will remarry. Of those twenty-nine remarriages, thirteen will end in divorce. Therefore, out of one hundred women who marry, sixty-two will never experience a divorce, and yet those one hundred women between them will account for fifty-one divorces (thirty-eight plus thirteen). Actually, sixty-two married women had no divorces, while thirty-eight married women had fifty-one divorces (Belkin and Goodman 1980:427).

People who divorce give various reasons for their divorces. Legitimate grounds for divorce vary from state to state, because each state enacts its own divorce laws.

THE DIVORCE EXPERIENCE

Paul Bohannan, a social scientist who has conducted a good deal of research on marriage and the family, has argued that divorce is a process. He also says, "Divorce is a complex social phenomenon as well as a complex personal experience" (1970:30). He sees the complexity of divorce arising from the number of things happening at once. To better understand divorce, Bohannan has divided the process into six overlapping experiences: (1) the emotional divorce, (2) the legal divorce, (3) the economic divorce, (4) the coparental divorce, (5) the community divorce, and (6) the psychic divorce. This approach to understanding divorce has proven useful and is widely accepted (Strong, DeVault, and Sayad 1998; Lamanna and Riedmann 1997). We will look at each of these experiences individually, but in doing so, we must remember that they are overlapping experiences often occurring simultaneously.

The Emotional Divorce

When someone is courting, becomes engaged, and is married, it is an exciting time. The other person is treating him or her as someone special. The person realizes that someone has chosen and wants to make a commitment to him or her. When someone is going through a divorce, they are being rejected and treated as a problem. It is easy to see why divorce is an emotional experience.

The emotional divorce generally is the initial experience in the divorce process. It consists of a chain of events that lead up to divorce in the same way that a chain of events led to marriage. Even as neither party realized on the first date that their relationship would lead to marriage, so neither party may realize that a given event in their marriage is the first link in a chain leading to divorce.

Almost every married person, even after only a few months of marriage, knows what to say or do to hurt his or her partner. Each knows where to hit the other to "draw blood." As a couple learns each other's weaknesses and sensitivities, each gains in the ability to hurt the other.

Disagreements and fights occur in every marriage. Even healthy marriages have their times of conflict. However, in a healthy marriage the conflict tends to clarify issues, increase understanding, and lead to a developing relationship. But if the conflict results in hurting the other and undermining the relationship, then the process of emotional divorce has begun. Often when this happens, the couple fights over issues that are cover-ups for the real problem, which may be power, self-esteem, status, or some other such issue. Two issues over which couples frequently fight that often are cover-ups for deeper concerns are finances and sex.

As we saw in Chapter 8, money represents a number of things, including power, love, and status. Because money represents more than dollars and cents, it can easily become a cover-up for other issues. In one study of couples seeking divorce, reported by Belkin and Goodman, over a third claimed that finances were the source of their conflict (1980:433). While money management and budgeting are the source of endless discussion in most homes, it is when this area is used as a means for one party to attack the other that problems begin.

Sex is often used as a weapon in a conflict between a couple. Frequently sexual symptoms are the first indication to a couple that there is a problem. On the other hand, there are some couples for whom their sexual relationship is the only part of their marriage that seems to work. However, those types of relationships are the exception. Generally, when a couple's communication becomes strained, their sexual relationship is the first to suffer. Because sexual intercourse is one of the most intimate social relationships, emotional problems and misgivings generally show up here.

Sexual problems may take many forms. A sexual problem may manifest itself as general sexual dysfunction in women and impotence in men. On the other hand, it may result in adultery, which may be an attempt to hurt or humiliate the other.

The emotional divorce usually involves the couple's growing apart. One or both partners feel a lessening of commitment. Partners may feel cramped by the marriage or cheated by the other. Eventually one or both parties feel the need to dissolve the relationship. Sometimes a couple may experience an emotional divorce, yet never get a legal divorce. They live under the same roof and remain husband and wife in name, but emotionally they are divorced.

Another aspect of emotional divorce is loss and grief. Emotional divorce results in the loss of a loved one that is just as real as a loss by death. In some ways the loss from divorce may be worse, since in death the person is gone. Also, while friends, family, and church provide support for dealing with the bereavement of death, a person usually receives little or no support during the bereavement of divorce. In fact, the person going through the bereavement of divorce may in addition be the object of condemnation from family, friends, and the church.

The Legal Divorce

Judicial divorce is the legal dissolution of a relationship that often has already experienced its emotional dissolution. While California was the first state to adopt no-fault divorce in 1970, all fifty states have since, passed no-fault divorce laws. *No-fault divorce* allows for the dissolution of a marriage without the need to establish fault or guilt on the part of one party or the other. Four aspects of divorce have changed with the passage of these laws. One is that the need for fault-based grounds for divorce has been eliminated. Another is that it allows for a nonadversarial legal process. A third change is that divorce settlements are based on the basis of equity, equality, and circumstances rather than fault. The fourth change is gender equality in custody and support issues.

The Economic Divorce

Many states have what are called *community property laws.* This means that most items owned by either party are considered community property—that is, the property of the couple. In the case of a divorce, the community property and assets must be divided between the divorcing parties. Besides the division of current assets, most divorce settlements involve future assets. For example, if a wife worked to help her husband through medical school and then he divorces her, is she entitled to only half of their current financial assets, or is his education an asset and is she entitled to a portion of his future earnings?

There are two basic types of payments that involve future assets. One of these is *alimony.* This term is derived from the Latin word meaning sustenance or nourishment. Alimony is based on the idea that a husband, or a wife in some cases, has taken on the obligation of supporting a spouse and that obligation continues even after a divorce. The other type of payment is *child support.* This involves one spouse, generally the husband, paying for the support of the children who are living with the other spouse, usually the wife. Today more and more courts are awarding joint custody, whereby both parties have to share equally the cost of child support.

The Coparental Divorce

Children under 18 years of age are involved in 60 percent of all divorces (Strong, DeVault, and Sayad 1998:495). Bohannan uses the term *coparental divorce* to indicate that while parents divorce each other, they do not divorce their children. Even though a couple is no longer husband and wife after a divorce, they are still father and mother.

Divorce is every bit as much a trauma for the children as it is for the parents. In some cases it is more traumatic since the parents are divorcing by choice, but the children have no say in the matter. The children are often the center of long custody battles, used as pawns to seek revenge on a partner, and subject to dislocation and drastic changes in lifestyle. Some researchers in this area feel that the children of divorce go through a series of phases related to the loss of their family. These phases are similar to Kubler-Ross's five stages of dying, examined in the last chapter.

It is also quite common for children of divorced parents to experience guilt. They may believe that they are in some way responsible for the divorce. This problem is particularly true for younger children, who have trouble comprehending what is happening. The children of divorce are also subject to other psychological problems. One is the fear of desertion. "After all, if mom and dad could just leave each other, why couldn't they just leave me?" thinks the child. There is also resentment and a feeling of betrayal when one parent begins dating or remarries. Many children want mom and dad to get together again, and they realize that a new suitor interferes with that hope.

Custody

Until recently, mothers were generally given custody of the children in the case of a divorce. This was particularly true of young children under what came to be known as the *tender years doctrine.* Most courts held that children in their "tender years," preteens, were all but automatically placed in their mother's custody. Today, however, states have changed their divorce laws to eliminate the biases of the tender years doctrines. These laws now direct the courts to consider "the best interests of the child." That is, the parent best able to care for the child should receive custody (Orthner 1981:394).

The courts are also moving toward more liberal *visitation rights.* Visitation rights are the rights of the parents who do not receive custody of their children to visit their children and to have their children with them for holidays and vacation periods—that is, to spend time with their children.

The courts are also granting *joint custody* in more cases. In this situation, each parent has the children an equal share of the time, and the parents share equal responsibility for the children. Joint custody, when it is granted, is frequently associated with no-fault divorce, since neither party has accused the other with any type of violation.

Consequences for Children

In a major longitudinal study of a group of children of divorce, Wallerstein and Blakeslee (1990) found that the effects of divorce on children were long-lasting and affected their relationships into their adulthood. Other studies have found the following effects of divorce on children:

1. They have more psychological problems and are more likely to be in counseling.
2. They do not do as well in school, have higher drop-out rates, and are less likely to go to college.
3. Girls with divorced parents are more likely to start sexual activity at an earlier age, be sexually active, and cohabit.
4. Children with divorced parents are more likely to get divorced themselves.
5. As adults they experience more physical illness. (Yorburg 1993:340–42)

Research has found three basic factors associated with good adjustment to the divorce by the children. The first factor was psychologically healthy parents. The second was a lack of rancor and revenge between the divorced parents, and regular and dependable visitation by the parent who had not been given custody. The third was that the children had an emotionally nurturant relationship with the father. According to the researchers, this was critical for good adjustment for both sexes (Wallerstein and Kelly 1980:71).

The Community Divorce

Becoming divorced not only changes one's relationship to one's spouse, but it also changes one's status from married person to single person. In most of their social circles, the couple had related to others as couples. When a person is divorced, those relations are not the same. In fact, divorced persons move from the world of marrieds back to the world of singles. However, if they have children, they do not really fit in with the premarried singles.

Today many organizations have been formed to provide support and social outlets for single parents. Perhaps the best known of these is Parents Without Partners. These organizations provide information, discuss common problems, engage in civic projects, and sponsor social activities for their members. Whether they have children or not, the newly divorced face many adjustments in relating to the community.

The Psychic Divorce

The psychic divorce involves emotionally and psychologically separating oneself from the other person. Bohannan suggests that this may be the most difficult of the six aspects of divorce and continues after the legal divorce is final. If two people have shared life as intimately as a married couple does for an extended period of time, it is often difficult for the one person to get the other "out of his or her system." In marriage, people have become one; and in divorce, they must become autonomous again. Divorced persons must get over the positive feelings they have for each other; however, attachment often continues for some time following a divorce. One study found that 86 percent of divorcing people still had some attachment for their spouses (Kitson 1982:379). But perhaps even more important, divorced persons need to get over negative feelings resulting from the divorce. Those negative feelings are much more harmful and create more problems than any lingering feelings of affection can ever overcome.

REMARRIAGE

Divorce apparently does not sour most people on marriage. Two-thirds of all divorced people eventually remarry. In fact, one-third of them will remarry within a year, and half of them within three years. Almost half the marriages that take place in America are remarriages for at least one of the partners (see table 14.3).

How do remarriages compare with first marriages in satisfaction or happiness and in stability? When it comes to happiness, remarried couples report similar levels of happiness with their marriages as first-married couples report with theirs (Coleman and Ganong 1991). However, it is

Life Cycle of the Family

Previous Marital Status	Percent of marriages
First marriage both partners	54
Remarriage for groom	11
Remarriage for bride	11
Remarriage for both partners	20
Widowed or unknown	4

Source: Clarke 1995:4

difficult to compare these results because remarried persons are more likely to enter their second marriage with different expectations than people entering a first marriage. When we look at stability, we are looking at hard statistics rather than self-reports; so we can be on more certain ground. Remarriages have a 20 percent higher divorce rate than first marriages. Also remarriages do not last as long. The average length of marriage for first divorces is eight years, for second marriages it is six years, and it is only four years for third marriages. The strongest indicator of divorce in remarriages is the presence of children (Lamanna and Riedmann 1997:519–20). Remarriages are not as stable as first marriages.

RECONSTITUTED OR BLENDED FAMILIES

When Ralph and Sonja were divorced, Ralph received custody of their three-year-old daughter Judy because of Sonja's emotional instability. A few years later Ralph met Sue, who was also divorced and had custody of her two-year-old son Jason. A year later Ralph and Sue were married, and Sue became Judy's "mother," and Ralph became Jason's "father." Together they form what is called a *reconstituted* or *blended family.* Some thirty million adults and one out of every five children in America live in reconstituted families (Einstein 1983:67; Lamanna and Riedmann 1997:513).

Reconstituted families face some unique problems. One is that children end up with two "fathers" or two "mothers," their biological parent and their stepparent of the same sex. Children generally end up being members of two households with two distinct sets of rules. The role of a stepparent is poorly defined, and the stepparent has little or no authority. Children in reconstituted families also end up with extra grandparents. Some of the major problems parents encounter in reconstituted families are presented in table 14.4.

Divorce and Remarriage

TABLE 14.4

*Major Problems
Encountered by
Parents in
Reconstituted
Families*

Problem	Husbands	Wives
Child rearing	35%	35%
Financial	20%	16%
Sexual	11%	6%
Religion	10%	6%
Political	9%	11%
Outsiders	9%	14%
Recreation	6%	11%

Adapted from Lamanna and Riedmann 1981:497

DIVORCE, REMARRIAGE, AND THE BIBLE

While there is sincere disagreement among Christians on the issues of divorce and remarriage, most agree that God's ideal plan is for a couple united in marriage to remain so for life (Gen. 2:24; Matt. 19:5–6; Rom. 7:2; 1 Cor. 7:39). Most also agree that divorce is a consequence or a result of sin (Deut. 24:1; Matt. 19:8). Also, most agree that divorce is displeasing to God (Mal. 2:16).

However, after these points of agreement comes much controversy. There are two basic issues involved. The first relates to whether divorce is always a sin or is wrong only under certain circumstances. The second relates to whether remarriage is ever permitted, and if so, under what circumstances. For both the Old Testament and New Testament Hebrews, these two questions would generally run together, since divorce presupposed remarriage and was customary (Ellisen 1977:63; Martin 1974:18–19).

The accounts in all three Synoptic Gospels of the way Jesus dealt with the issue of divorce and remarriage are similar (Matt. 5:31–32; 19:3–9; Mark 10:2–11; Luke 16:18). Jesus presumes divorce will result in remarriage. He argues that remarriage results in adultery because divorce does not break the marriage bond. In the Matthew account he includes an exception, and that is the case of fornication.

To understand Jesus' teaching we need a little background information. In the Matthew 19 and Mark 10 passages, he is responding to a question from the Pharisees. Deuteronomy 24:1 reads, "If a man marries a woman who becomes displeasing to him because he finds something indecent about her, and he writes her a certificate of divorce, gives it to her and sends her from his house . . ." A major debate existed in Jesus' day as to what was meant by "something indecent." The conservative rabbinical school of

Shammai argued that it referred to sexual immorality, whereas the liberal rabbinical school of Hillel argued that it meant anything that displeased the husband, even burning the supper. Many scholars believe that this debate was the basis and context for the Pharisees' question to Jesus (Bustanoby 1978; Duty 1967; Ellisen 1977; Martin 1974; Woodson 1979).

It is interesting to note that Jesus, in his response to the Pharisees' question concerning the correct interpretation of the Law of Moses, did not appeal to Moses, but to the creation account. In essence, Jesus said, "Let's see what God's original intention was." Moses' teaching on divorce, according to Jesus, was an accommodation to human sinfulness, not part of God's original plan. As in so many other areas where the Pharisees questioned and challenged Jesus, he responded by referring to God's purposes and plans rather than to the law. Jesus appeared to be more concerned with the spirit of the law as a reflection of God's purposes than with the letter of the law.

Those who believe that divorce and remarriage are always wrong and that only death can break the marriage bond have to deal with the exception clauses in Matthew 5 and 19. This is generally done in one of two ways. The first is to claim that since the clauses are not recorded in Mark or Luke, they were probably never uttered by Jesus. They were either an explanatory note added by Matthew that eventually became part of the text or they were added by the early church to soften Jesus' teaching on divorce and remarriage. The fact is that there is not a shred of evidence that the exception was added later. The exception clauses have been accepted as genuine by the translation committees for the King James Version, the American Standard Version, the New American Standard Bible, and the New International Version. They have been accepted as genuine by the Roman Catholic Church.

Some may ask why the exception clause was recorded by Matthew but not by Mark and Luke. The basic explanation was that each of the gospel accounts was written with a different primary audience in mind. Matthew wrote for Jewish believers, Mark for Roman believers, and Luke for Greek believers. Each writer included or omitted material as it was relevant to the message he was attempting to communicate. The Gospels are not basically biographies but theologies. The Greeks and Romans, with no awareness of the rabbinical debate that was the context for Jesus' response, did not require those comments. The Jewish readers, who were aware of the debate, needed those comments.

Divorce and Remarriage

The other major New Testament passage dealing with divorce and remarriage is 1 Corinthians 7:12–16, verses 12 and 15 in particular: "If any brother has a wife who is not a believer and she is willing to live with him, he must not divorce her.... But if the unbeliever leaves, let him do so. A believing man or woman is not bound in such circumstances." While everyone agrees a believer cannot prevent a nonbelieving mate from leaving, the issue is whether or not the remaining believing mate is free to remarry. Again, scholars are divided on this question. The majority of the works I consulted felt the believer was free to remarry.

Divorce and remarriage is a difficult and controversial issue in many of our churches. There is no question that divorce is a major issue and a destructive force in our society. There is no question that Christians must be pro-family and do everything possible to prepare young people for marriage and to help couples maintain their marriages. Yet when divorce does occur, what should our response be? It is not my purpose to develop or defend a position on this question. That has been done quite thoroughly by others (see Suggested Reading at the end of the chapter). However, I would challenge each reader to study the Word of God, read the scholars, and come to his or her own convictions.

MARRIAGE AND THE FAMILY: A FINAL THOUGHT

In this book we have looked at many facts and figures, theories and models, as well as problems and opportunities related to marriage. However, behind the statistics and theories are real men and women, real boys and girls. There are joys and tears, hopes and fears, love and hate, happiness and misery. While God does not promise us a problem-free life, it is my conviction that if we faithfully and diligently apply God's Word in our personal lives and family lives, we can have marriages and homes that will be places of opportunity and challenge, love and wholeness. It is my prayer that all readers will make the Lord Jesus Christ a part of their life and family.

DISCUSSION QUESTIONS

1. Do you believe that no-fault divorce is helpful or harmful? Why?

2. Should parents who want a divorce but have young children stay together for the sake of the children? Why?

3. Should divorced couples with children be automatically given joint custody unless there is a compelling reason for one spouse or the other to have custody?

4. Why do you think so many divorced people remarry soon after their divorce?

5. Do you believe it is ever permissible for a believer to divorce his or her spouse? Is it ever permissible for a divorced Christian to remarry? On what do you base your views?

6. What, if any, do you see as biblical grounds for remarriage following divorce?

SUGGESTED READING

Jay E. Adams, *Marriage, Divorce and Remarriage in the Bible* (Grand Rapids: Zondervan, 1980). An in-depth study of the relevant passages dealing with divorce and remarriage. The author deals with divorce between two believers and between a believer and a nonbeliever. He also discusses what he understands to be the biblical grounds for remarriage.

Archibald D. Hart, *Helping Children Survive Divorce* (Waco, Tex.: Word, 1996). A clinical psychologist, the author discusses the problems faced by children whose parents get divorced. Written for parents, the book offers practical steps for helping children through the process.

Don Houck and LaDean Houck, *The Ex Factor: Dealing with Your Former Spouse* (Grand Rapids: Revell, 1997). Written by a couple who are in their second marriage and are dealing with ex-spouses, the book discusses ten personal, relational, and spiritual issues involved in dealing with a former mate.

H. Wayne House, ed., *Divorce and Remarriage* (Downers Grove, Ill.: Inter-Varsity, 1990). This book is a debate among various evangelical scholars on the different views of divorce and remarriage for Christians. It presents different perspectives.

Appendix: Sexually Transmitted Diseases

GONORRHEA

Gonorrhea is the disease that is largely responsible for the STD epidemic. Although it is curable by penicillin (and other drugs for those who must not use penicillin), recently strains of gonorrhea that are resistant to treatment have evolved. Persons who treat themselves with nonprescribed penicillin may use the wrong type of drug, or may stop taking the drug before all the organisms that cause the disease have been killed. The surviving organisms are the strongest of those that caused the infection. The disease progresses in infected individuals, who pass the hardy strain of gonorrhea on to others through sexual contact. Close to a million Americans are infected annually.

Transmission of Gonorrhea

The organism that causes gonorrhea can be transmitted only through sexual intercourse, including vaginal, anal, or oral-genital intercourse. Outside of the body, it dies almost immediately. A man has a 20 to 50 percent chance of contracting gonorrhea from one act of intercourse with an infected partner; a woman has a more than 50 percent chance after one act of vaginal intercourse with an infected man.

Symptoms of Gonorrhea

Although many men first notice symptoms of gonorrhea within three to five days after exposure to it, asymptomatic (lacking symptoms) gonorrhea is becoming more common among men. Symptoms may appear as soon as one day or as late as two weeks after exposure. When symptoms appear in the male, he first has a thin, clear discharge seeping from the opening of his penis. After a day or two the discharge becomes heavy and creamy. It is usually white but may be yellow or yellow-green. The tip of the penis becomes swollen, with the lips of the urethral opening standing out from the glans. Urination is painful or causes a burning sensation and may become difficult.

If treatment is delayed for more than a few days, the infection spreads up the urethra, and may eventually invade the prostate gland and the epididymis, or symptoms of gonorrhea may seem to go away. If untreated, however, the man can still spread the disease to his sexual partners. The untreated man may also become sterile.

Most women who contract gonorrhea experience no symptoms at all for the first weeks or months of their disease. Before the disease is discovered, permanent damage may be done to the Fallopian tubes, causing sterility. Some women, however, do notice a change in the vaginal secretions from the normal clear or white to a yellow-green or greenish color. The gonorrheal discharge is rarely noticeable unless another infection is present at the same time.

Complications of Gonorrhea

If left untreated, gonorrhea can cause severe pain and infection in both men and women. Damage to the reproductive system is not reversible, and sterility results. In women who have had such damage, the likeliness of an ectopic pregnancy (pregnancy that occurs outside of the uterus, in the Fallopian tube or abdominal cavity) is greatly increased. Fertilization occurs in the Fallopian tubes. If the tubes are partially blocked by scar tissue from the gonorrheal infection, the fertilized egg cannot pass to the uterus and develops elsewhere instead. Eventually, the area hemorrhages and the woman experiences severe pain and internal bleeding. If she does not receive immediate medical attention, she may die.

Treatment of Gonorrhea

The most effective treatment is penicillin given by injection. Tetracycline is often used with people who are allergic to penicillin.

Prevention of Gonorrhea

The condom is the best means of preventing transmission of the disease, but it is not 100 percent effective. Many birth control clinics include a test for gonorrhea as a part of a routine checkup. STD clinics test for gonorrhea and other venereal diseases, often without charge. Routine checks for gonorrhea and syphilis are important for sexually active persons, especially women. However, it should be emphasized that increasing numbers of men are contracting gonorrhea without the warning symptoms.

SYPHILIS

Although syphilis is not as widespread a disease as gonorrhea, it is more serious because of the excessive damage that it can do when untreated. It may affect any of the body's organs when in the late stage. The diagnosis of syphilis is difficult because symptoms at various stages resemble the symptoms of other diseases.

Transmission of Syphilis

Syphilis is highly contagious for about the first year of the disease, if untreated. It is most commonly passed from one person to another through vaginal, anal, or oral-genital intercourse. It can travel from one partner to the other through the intact skin of the sexual organs. A man wearing a condom can contact syphilis from his partner "since the organism can enter at the junction of the penis and rest of the body." The syphilitic rash is also highly contagious. Within a few hours after the organisms enter the body, they are carried by the bloodstream to all parts of the body.

Stages and Symptoms of Syphilis

Primary Syphilis

Around three or four weeks after exposure to syphilis (or as early as ten days or late as three months), a chancre or sore appears on the body at the point of entry of the organism. On a man it is usually on the glans of the penis, but it may be elsewhere. A woman who has had vaginal intercourse usually does not notice the chancre, since it usually develops on her cervix or vaginal walls. Many women, therefore, are not aware when they have primary syphilis unless informed by their sexual partners.

When the chancre first appears, it is a dull red bump about as large as a pea. The bump's surface becomes eroded, and the chancre becomes a dull red open sore that may be covered by a scab. The chancre does not hurt, and does not bleed easily. It may have a rubbery pink border. If left untreated, the chancre heals by itself within one to five weeks after its appearance.

Secondary Syphilis

The infected person continues to infect his or her sexual partners, even when symptoms do not exist. The disease usually progresses to its second stage about six months after exposure, when a skin rash develops. The rash is extremely contagious to other people. It may not be obvious or may not appear at all. Nevertheless, the syphilitic person is still able to infect others.

Latent Syphilis

If secondary syphilis is not treated, it may become dormant or hidden for many years. About a year after the initial infection, the individual is no longer infectious to others, with one exception. A pregnant woman passes the disease to her fetus.

Late Syphilis

A number of years after exposure, the untreated individual may develop a number of complications, including heart disease, blindness, paralysis, insanity, and other serious complications.

Treatment of Syphilis

A complete physical examination should be given to persons who believe that they may have syphilis. If sores or rash exist, fluid taken from them is examined under a microscope. For years, blood tests have been given routinely to persons applying for marriage licenses in most states.

As with gonorrhea, the first choice in antibiotics to treat syphilis is penicillin (though a different type than the type used to treat gonorrhea), and the second choice is tetracycline.

GENITAL HERPES

Genital Herpes is caused by a virus, herpes simplex type II. It is closely related to herpes simplex type I, a virus that causes fever blisters. Some 31 million Americans had genital herpes in 1995 and a half million people are newly infected each year.

Transmission of Genital Herpes

Genital herpes is transmitted through sexual contact, genital, anal, or oral. It can also be transmitted to the genitals by hand if one has ordinary cold sores. The virus attacks the skin and especially the mucous membranes.

Symptoms of Genital Herpes

The early symptoms consist of a tingling or itching sensation. Two to fifteen days later, fluid-filled blisters appear on the genitals or buttocks, sometimes accompanied by feverishness and headaches. The first outbreak generally lasts about three weeks, then the lesions harden, scab over, and heal. Unfortunately the infection has not been cleared up. Rather, the virus travels from the genitals along nerve pathways to the base of the spinal cord. It lies dormant there until it is ready to break out again on the genitals. Researchers are not sure what triggers the recurrence of breakouts.

Complications of Genital Herpes

In addition to the physical pain and discomfort of genital herpes, there are more serious consequences. Women with genital herpes have a cervical cancer rate four times greater than that of noninfected women. Also a pregnant woman with an active case of genital herpes may pass the virus to her baby during delivery. The virus can cause a severe and potentially fatal form of encephalitis. It can also cause brain damage and/or blindness.

Treatment of Genital Herpes

As of the writing of this material there is no known cure for herpes. As someone has said, "Herpes is forever." There are some medications that relieve the symptoms in some cases, but a permanent cure has yet to be discovered.

Prevention of Genital Herpes

The best way to prevent genital herpes is to avoid sexual intimacy with an infected partner during active outbreaks and using a condom at other times. Work is under way on a vaccine to prevent the spread of herpes, but at this writing none is available.

ACQUIRED IMMUNE DEFICIENCY SYNDROME

Acquired Immune Deficiency Syndrome (AIDS) is caused by the Human Immunodeficiency Virus (HIV). The virus attacks lymphocytes in the immune system. A person with damaged lymphocytes has a high risk of contracting certain types of pneumonia and cancer normally controlled by lymphocytes.

Transmission of HIV

HIV is transmitted by body fluids, semen in sexual contact—oral, anal, or vaginal—and contaminated blood, and by hypodermic needles. There is no evidence that the virus is airborne or can be transmitted by touch.

Symptoms of AIDS

The symptoms of AIDS are many and varied; two of the more common are pneumonia and Kaposi's sarcoma, a cancer of the skin. The AIDS virus does not cause death. It damages the immune system, and other diseases cause illness and death.

Complications of AIDS

The diseases that an AIDS infected person contracts are always fatal. A person with the virus, even if not experiencing any symptoms, is still a carrier and can infect others.

Treatment of AIDS

There is no known cure for AIDS. In recent years new drugs have been developed that can hold HIV in check for longer periods of time, delaying and possibly preventing the onset of AIDS. However, there is no cure for HIV and the person is still contagious and can transmit HIV to another person.

Prevention of HIV

HIV is transmitted by body fluids. The spread of HIV is prevented when one avoids contaminated body fluids. Although condoms are recommended, they are not completely safe. Sexual intercourse in a monogamous, uncontaminated relationship and the avoidance of intravenous drug use are the best protection.

CHLAMYDIA

As many as four million Americans a year are infected with chlamydia. The organism, *Chlamydia trachomatis,* has the properties of both bacteria and a virus. It affects the urinary tract and reproductive organs of both sexes.

Transmission of Chlamydia

Chlamydia is primarily transmitted through genital sex. It can also be transmitted through anal sex.

Symptoms of Chlamydia

Symptoms in women include vaginal discharge or pain when urinating. Symptoms in men include a whitish discharge from the penis and pain while urinating. Symptoms may also include pain and swelling in the testes. Both men and women can experience a low-grade fever. Since about half of all people infected with chlamydia show no symptoms until the disease has caused serious complications, sexually active persons with multiple partners should be regularly tested.

Complications of Chlamydia

If untreated, chlamydia may result in pelvic inflammatory disease, infection of the Fallopian tubes and ovaries. This can result in damage to the Fallopian tubes and ovaries and result in sterility. If a pregnant woman is infected she can infect her baby at birth resulting in serious eye, ear, and lung infections.

Treatment of Chlamydia

Chlamydia can be successfully treated with antibiotics. The most commonly used are doxycycline and tetracycline. Erythromycin is also used, especially with pregnant women.

OTHER SEXUALLY TRANSMITTED DISEASES

Both men and women may develop irritating genital diseases that may be spread through sexual contact or other means (such as a washcloth) as well. These diseases may be confused with gonorrhea and often develop in conjunction with it. In the male, the disease is known as *urethritis* (inflammation of the urethra), and in the female, *vaginitis* (inflammation of the vagina). The affected area burns or itches, and there may be an abnormal discharge from the male's urethra or female's vagina. Females may have itching or burning sores on the clitoris, inner lips, vestibule, cervix, or vagina. Urethritis and vaginitis are caused by a number of different organisms, and treatment for the different organisms varies. Therefore, medical examination and diagnosis are essential.

Another STD is genital warts. These are sometimes painful warts that appear in the genital or rectal areas. They are caused by a virus. The warts must be surgically or chemically removed. The virus is usually transmitted through sexual contact.

Bibliography

Adams, Jay E. 1980. *Marriage, Divorce and Remarriage in the Bible.* Grand Rapids: Zondervan.

Ambry, Margaret K. 1992. "Child Chances." *American Demographics* 14:55.

Bach, George R., and Peter Wyden. 1968. *The Intimate Enemy: How to Fight Fair in Love and Marriage.* New York: Avon.

Balswick, Jack, and Judith Balswick. 1991. *The Family.* Grand Rapids: Baker.

Bancroft, Emery H. 1976. *Christian Theology: Systematic and Biblical,* 2d rev. ed. Grand Rapids: Zondervan.

Baron, Robert A., and Donn Byrne. 1994. *Social Psychology.* Boston: Allyn and Bacon.

Bartholet, Elizabeth. 1993. *Adoption and the Politics of Parenting.* Boston: Houghton Mifflin.

Basso, Ellen B. 1973. *The Kalapalo Indians of Central Brazil.* New York: Holt, Rinehart and Winston.

Bee, Helen. 1981. *The Developing Child,* 3d ed. New York: Harper & Row.

Begley, Sharon, and John Carey. 1982. "How Life Begins." *Newsweek,* January 11, 38–43.

Belkin, Gary S., and Norman Goodman. 1980. *Marriage, Family, and Intimate Relationships.* Chicago: Rand McNally.

Bem, Sandra Lipstiz. 1977. "Beyond Androgyny: Some Presumptuous Prescriptions for a Liberated Sexual Identity." In *Family in Transition,* 2d ed., ed. Arlene Skolnick and Jerome Skolnick, 204–21. Boston: Little, Brown.

Bennet, Neil G., Ann Klimas Blanc, and David E. Bloom. 1988. "Commitment and the Modern Union: Assessing the Link Between Cohabitation and Subsequent Marital Stability." *American Sociological Review* 53:127–28.

Berelson, B., and G. A. Steiner. 1964. *Human Behavior.* New York: Harcourt.

Berkhof, Louis. 1949. *Systematic Theology.* Grand Rapids: Eerdmans.

Berscheid, Ellen, and Elaine Walster. 1969. *Interpersonal Attraction.* Reading, Mass.: Addison-Wesley.

Bigner, Jerry J. 1979. *Parent-Child Relations: An Introduction to Parenting.* New York: Macmillan.

Black, Eric. 1982. "Marriage Counselors Hear an Earful About Failure to Communicate." *Minneapolis Star and Tribune,* June 3, 1B–5B.

Black, Thom, and Paul Lewis. 1997. *Money Sense: Gaining Control of Your Family's Finances.* Grand Rapids: Zondervan.

Blue, Ron. 1991. *Master Your Money,* 2d ed. Nashville: Thomas Nelson.

Blumstein, Philip, and Pepper Schwartz. 1983. *American Couples*. New York: McGraw-Hill.

Bohannan, Paul. 1970. "The Six Stations of Divorce." In *Divorce and After*, ed. Paul Bohannan. Garden City, N.Y.: Doubleday.

Booth, Alan, and David Johnson. 1988. "Premarital Cohabitation and Marital Success." *Journal of Family Issues* 9:255–72.

Brandt, Henry, and Phil Landrum. 1976. *I Want My Marriage to Be Better*. Grand Rapids: Zondervan.

Broom, Leonard, Philip Selznick, and D. Darroch. 1981. *Sociology*, 7th ed. New York: Harper & Row.

Brunner, Emil. 1952. *The Christian Doctrine of Creation and Redemption*. Dogmatics: Vol. 2. Philadelphia: Westminster.

Bumpass, Larry L., James A. Sweet, and Andrew Cherlin. 1991. "The Role of Cohabitation in Declining Rates of Marriage." *Journal of Marriage and the Family* 53:913–27.

Burkett, Larry. 1989. *Debt-Free Living*. Chicago: Moody Press.

Burns, Ailsa, and Cath Scott. 1994. *Mother-Headed Families and Why They Have Increased*. Hillsdale, N.J.: Erlbaum.

Bustanoby, André. 1978. *But I Didn't Want a Divorce*. Grand Rapids: Zondervan.

Chapman, Gary. 1998. *Loving Solutions*. Chicago: Moody Press.

Cherlin, Andrew J. 1981. *Marriage, Divorce, Remarriage*. Cambridge, Mass.: Harvard University Press.

Cherlin, Andrew, and Frank Furstenberg Jr. 1986. *The New American Grandparent*. New York: Basic Books.

Christenson, Larry. 1970. *The Christian Family*. Minneapolis: Bethany.

Clarke, Sally C. 1995. "Advance Report of Final Divorce Statistics, 1989 and 1990." *Monthly Vital Statistics Report* 43:9.

Clayton, Richard R. 1979. *The Family, Marriage, and Social Change*. Lexington, Mass.: Heath.

Clinebell, Howard J. 1977. *Growth Counseling for Mid-Life Couples*. Philadelphia: Fortress.

Clinebell, Howard J., and Charlotte H. Clinebell. 1970. *The Intimate Marriage*. New York: Harper & Row.

Coleman, Marilyn, and Larry Ganong. 1991. "Remarriage and Stepfamily Research in the 1980s: Increased Interest in an Old Form." In *Contemporary Families: Looking Forward, Looking Back*, ed. Alan Booth. Minneapolis: National Council on Family Relations.

Collins, Gary R. 1972. *Effective Counseling*. Carol Stream, Ill.: Creation House.

_____. 1995. *Family Shock*. Wheaton, Ill.: Tyndale.

Cook, Kaye, and Lee Lance. 1996. *Man and Woman*. Grand Rapids: Baker.

Coombs, Robert H. 1966. "Value Consensus and Partner Satisfaction Among Dating Couples." *Journal of Marriage and the Family* 28:166–73.

_____. 1991. "Marital Status and Personal Well-being." *Family Relations* 40:97–102.

Cousins, Norman. 1979. *Anatomy of an Illness.* New York: Norton.

Cox, Frank D. 1981. *Human Intimacy: Marriage, the Family, and Its Meaning.* St. Paul: West.

Curtis, Glade B. 1997. *Your Pregnancy,* 3d ed. Tucson, Ariz.: Fisher.

Cushenberry, Donald C., and Rita C. Cushenberry. 1997. *Coping with Life After Your Mate Dies,* 2d ed. Grand Rapids: Baker.

Cynaumon, Greg. 1994. *Empowering Single Parents.* Chicago: Moody Press.

Dale, Robert D., and Carrie K. Dale. 1978. *Making Good Marriages Better.* Nashville: Broadman.

Dayton, Howard L. 1979. *Your Money: Frustration or Freedom.* Wheaton, Ill.: Tyndale.

DeGenova, Mary Kay. 1997. *Families in Cultural Context: Strengths and Challenges in Diversity.* Mountain View, Calif.: Mayfield.

DeJong, Peter, and Donald R. Wilson. 1979. *Husband and Wife: The Sexes in Scripture and Society.* Grand Rapids: Zondervan.

Delamater, J. D., and P. MacCorquodale. 1979. *Premarital Sexuality: Attitudes, Relationships, Behavior.* Madison: University of Wisconsin Press.

De Maris, A., and Gerald R. Leslie. 1984. "Cohabitation with the Future Spouse: Its Influence on Marital Satisfaction and Communication." *Journal of Marriage and the Family* 46:7–84.

Dobson, James. 1970. *Dare to Discipline.* Wheaton, Ill.: Tyndale.

_____. 1974. *Hide or Seek.* Old Tappan, N.J.: Revell.

_____. 1978. *Preparing for Adolescence.* Santa Ana, Calif.: Vision House.

_____. 1997. *On Parenting.* New York: Inspiration Press.

Downs, James F. 1977. "The Navajo." In *Cultures Around the World,* ed. G. Spindler and L. Spindler. New York: Holt, Rinehart and Winston.

Driscoll, R., K. E. Davis, and M. E. Lipetz. 1972. "Parental Interference and Romantic Love: The Romeo and Juliet Effect." *Journal of Personality and Social Psychology* 24:1–10.

Duty, Guy. 1967. *Divorce and Remarriage.* Minneapolis: Bethany.

Duvall, Evelyn Millis. 1977. *Marriage and Family Development,* 5th ed. Philadelphia: Lippincott.

Dworetzky, John P. 1981. *Introduction to Child Development.* St. Paul: West.

Einstein, Elizabeth. 1983. "Stepfamilies—Dealing with Anger and Disappointment." *U.S. News & World Report,* January 17, 67–68.

Eisenberg, Arlene, et al. 1994. *What to Expect When You're Expecting,* 2d ed. New York: Workman.

Elder, Carl A. 1976. *Values and Moral Development in Children.* Nashville: Broadman.

Elias, Marilyn. 1998. "Studies Find Dads Make Difference." *USA Today,* August 8, D1.

Ellisen, Stanley A. 1977. *Divorce and Remarriage in the Church.* Grand Rapids: Zondervan.

Eshleman, J. Ross. 1981. *The Family: An Introduction.* Boston: Allyn and Bacon.

Farley, John E. 1998. *Sociology,* 4th ed. Upper Saddle River, N.J.: Prentice Hall.

Feldman, Francis. 1976. *The Family in Today's Money World.* New York: Family Service Association.

Finkelhor, David, G. Hotaling, I. A. Lewes, and C. Smith. 1990. *Missing, Abducted, Runaway, and Throwaway Children in America.* Washington, D.C.: U.S. Department of Justice.

Fried, Barbara. 1967. *The Middle-Age Crisis.* New York: Harper & Row.

Fryling, Alice, and Robert Fryling 1996. *A Handbook for Engaged Couples,* 2d ed. Downers Grove, Ill.: InterVarsity Press.

Gangel, Kenneth. 1972. *The Family First.* Minneapolis: HIS International.

Getz, Gene. 1972. *The Christian Home in a Changing World.* Chicago: Moody Press.

Glass, Lillian. 1992. *He Says, She Says.* New York: Perigee Books.

Glenn, Norval. 1991. "The Recent Trend in Marital Success in the United States." *Journal of Marriage and the Family* 53:261–70.

Glenn, Norval, and Michael Supancic. 1984. "The Social and Demographic Correlates of Divorce and Separation in the United States: An Update and Reconsideration." *Journal of Marriage and the Family* 46:563–75.

Glick, Paul. 1984. "Marriage, Divorce, and Living Arrangements: Prospective Changes." *Journal of Family Issues* 4:7–26.

Golanty, Eric, and Barbara B. Harris. 1982. *Marriage and Family Life.* Boston: Houghton Mifflin.

Goolrick, William K., ed. 1975. *The Adult Years.* New York: Time-Life.

Gottman, John. 1994. *Why Marriages Succeed or Fail.* New York: Simon & Schuster.

Gough, E. Kathleen. 1959. "The Nayars and the Definition of Marriage." *Journal of Royal Anthropological Institute* 89:23–34.

Gray, John. 1992. *Men Are from Mars, Women Are from Venus.* New York: HarperCollins.

Green, Ernest J. 1978. *Personal Relationships: An Approach to Marriage and Family.* New York: McGraw-Hill.

Grunlan, Stephen A. 1972. "Terms of Address Among American College Students." Unpublished paper.

_____. 1982. "Sociology and the Christian." In *Christian Perspectives on Sociology,* ed. S. Grunlan and M. Reimer, 401–14. Grand Rapids: Zondervan.

Grunlan, Stephen A., and Daniel H. Lambrides. 1983. *Effective Lay Counseling.* Harrisburg, Pa.: Christian Publications.

Grunlan, Stephen A., and Marvin K. Mayers. 1979. *Cultural Anthropology: A Christian Perspective.* Grand Rapids: Zondervan.

_____. 1988. *Cultural Anthropology: A Christian Perspective,* 2d ed. Grand Rapids: Zondervan.

Grunlan, Stephen A., and Milton K. Reimer, eds. 1982. *Christian Perspectives on Sociology.* Grand Rapids: Zondervan.

Gundry, Patricia. 1977. *Woman, Be Free!* Grand Rapids: Zondervan.

_____. 1980. *Heirs Together.* Grand Rapids: Zondervan.

Harley, William F., Jr. 1996. *Give and Take.* Grand Rapids: Revell.

Hart, Archibald. D. 1996. *Helping Children Survive Divorce.* Waco, Tex.: Word Books.

Heatherly, Joyce Landorf. 1994. *Mourning Song,* 2d ed. Grand Rapids: Revell.

Hedges, Larry V., and Amy Nowell. 1995. "Sex Differences in Mental Test Scores, Variability, and Numbers of High-Scoring Individuals." *Science* 269:41–46.

Hendricks, Howard G. 1973. *Heaven Help the Home.* Wheaton, Ill.: Victor.

Henry, Tamara. 1995. "The Bigger the Family, the Lower the Kids' Grades." *USA Today,* August 7, D1.

Hess, Beth B., Elizabeth W. Markson, and Peter J. Stein. 1993. *Sociology,* 4th ed. Boston: Allyn and Bacon.

_____. 1996. *Sociology,* 5th ed. Boston: Allyn and Bacon.

Hite, Shere. 1976. *The Hite Report.* New York: Macmillan.

Hoebel, E. A. 1972. *The Study of Man.* New York: McGraw-Hill.

Holzman, John. 1990. *Dating with Integrity.* Waco, Tex.: Word Books.

Horton, Paul B., and Chester L. Hunt. 1980. *Sociology,* 5th ed. New York: McGraw-Hill.

Houck, Don, and LaDean Houck. 1997. *The Ex Factor: Dealing with Your Former Spouse.* Grand Rapids: Revell.

House, H. Wayne, ed. 1990. *Divorce and Remarriage.* Downers Grove, Ill.: InterVarsity Press.

Houseknecht, Sharon K. 1987. "Voluntary Childlessness." In *Handbook of Marriages and the Family,* ed. Marvin B. Sussman and Suzanne K. Steinmetz. New York: Plenum.

Howe, Reuel L. 1959. *The Creative Years.* Greenwich, Conn.: Seabury.

Howell, John C. 1979. *Equality and Submission in Marriage.* Nashville: Broadman.

Huggett, Joyce. 1985. *Dating, Sex and Friendship.* Downers Grove, Ill.: InterVarsity Press.

Hughes, Philip Edgcumbe. 1969. "Theological Principles in the Control of Human Life." In *Birth Control and the Christian,* ed. Walter O. Spitzer and Carlyle L. Saylor, 93–149. Wheaton, Ill.: Tyndale.

Hulme, William E. 1962. *The Pastoral Care of Families.* Nashville: Abingdon Press.

Ingrassia, Michele. 1994. "Virgin Cool." *Newsweek,* October 17, 59–69.

Jeeves, Malcolm. 1976. *Psychology and Christianity: The View Both Ways.* Downers Grove, Ill.: InterVarsity Press.

Johnson, Alan G. 1996. *Human Arrangements: An Introduction to Sociology.* Madison, Wis.: Brown & Benchmark.

Johnson, Greg, and Mike Yorkey. 1993. *Faithful Parents, Faithful Kids.* Wheaton, Ill.: Tyndale.

Johnson, Winston A. 1982. "Groups." In *Christian Perspectives on Sociology,* ed. S. Grunlan and M. Reimer. Grand Rapids: Zondervan.

Jones, W. H., R. O. Hansson, and A. L. Phillips. 1978. "Physical Attractiveness and Judgments of Psychopathology." *Journal of Social Psychology* 105:79–85.

June, Lee N., ed. 1991. *The Black Family.* Grand Rapids: Zondervan.

Jurich, Anthony, and Cheryl Polson. 1985. "Nonverbal Assessment of Anxiety as a Function of Intimacy of Sexual Attitude Questions." *Psychological Reports* 57:1247–53.

Justice, Blair, and Rita Justice. 1976. *The Abusing Family.* New York: Human Sciences.

Kaplan, Helen Singer. 1974. *The New Sex Therapy.* New York: Brunner/Mazel.

_____. 1979. *Disorders of Desire.* New York: Simon & Schuster.

Katz, Stan J., and Aimee E. Liu. 1988. *False Love and Other Romantic Illusions: Why Love Goes Wrong and How to Make It Right.* New York: Ticknor & Fields.

Kelley, Robert K. 1969. *Courtship, Marriage and the Family.* New York: Harcourt, Brace and World.

Kephart, William M. 1972. *The Family, Society and the Individual,* 3d ed. Boston: Houghton Mifflin.

_____. 1981. *The Family, Society and the Individual,* 5th ed. Boston: Houghton Mifflin.

Kiley, Dan. 1978. *Nobody Said It Would Be Easy.* New York: Harper & Row.

King, K., J. O. Balswick, and I. E. Robinson. 1977. "The Continuing Premarital Sexual Revolution Among College Females." *Journal of Marriage and the Family* 29:455–59.

Kinsey, A. C., W. B. Pomeroy, C. E. Martin, and P. H. Gebhard. 1953. *Sexual Behavior in the Human Female.* Philadelphia: Saunders.

Kitson, Gay C. 1982. "Attachment to the Spouse in Divorce." *Journal of Marriage and the Family* 44 (2):379–93.

Koons, Carolyn N., and Michael J. Anthony. 1994. *Single Adult Passages.* Grand Rapids: Baker.

Koteskey, Ronald L. 1980. *Psychology from a Christian Perspective.* Nashville: Abingdon Press.

_____. 1981. "Growing Up Too Late, Too Soon." *Christianity Today,* March 13.

Kubler-Ross, Elisabeth. 1969. *On Death and Dying.* New York: Macmillan.

_____. 1974. *Questions on Death and Dying.* New York: Macmillan.

_____. 1975. *Death: The Final Stage of Growth.* Englewood Cliffs, N.J.: Prentice Hall.

_____. 1981. *Living with Death and Dying.* New York: Macmillan.

Kurdek, L. A. 1993. "Predicting Marital Dissolution: A 5-Year Prospective Longitudinal Study of Newlywed Couples." *Journal of Personality and Social Psychology* 64:221–42.

LaHaye, Tim, and Beverly LaHaye. 1976. *The Act of Marriage.* Grand Rapids: Zondervan.

_____. 1998. *The Act of Marriage,* 2d ed. Grand Rapids: Zondervan.

Lamanna, Mary Ann, and Agnes Riedmann. 1981. *Marriages and Families.* Belmont, Calif.: Wadsworth.

_____. 1997. *Marriages and Families,* 6th ed. Belmont, Calif.: Wadsworth.

Lambrides, Daniel. 1982. Lecture given at St. Paul Bible College.

Landorf, Joyce. 1974. *Mourning Song.* Old Tappan, N.J.: Revell.

Lasswell, Marcia. 1974. "Is There a Best Time to Marry?" *The Family Coordinator* 23 (3):237–42.

Lasswell, Marcia, and Thomas E. Lasswell. 1982. *Marriage and the Family.* Lexington, Mass.: Heath.

Lee, Mark W. 1976. "Reasons Marriages Fail—Communication." In *Make More of Your Marriage,* ed. Gary Collins. Waco, Tex.: Word Books.

Leman, Kevin. 1981. *Sex Begins in the Kitchen.* Ventura, Calif.: Regal.

LeMasters, E. E. 1970. *Parents in Modern America: A Sociological Analysis.* Homewood, Ill.: Dorsey.

LeMasters, E. E., and John DeFrain. 1989. *Parents in Contemporary America: A Sympathetic View,* 5th ed. Belmont, Calif.: Wadsworth.

Levinson, Daniel J., et al. 1978. *The Seasons of a Man's Life.* New York: Knopf.

Levy, M. J. 1949. *Family Revolution in Modern China.* Cambridge, Mass.: Harvard.

Liberman, Gail, and Alan Lavine. 1998. *Love, Marriage and Money.* Chicago: Dearborn.

Linton, Ralph. 1936. *The Study of Man.* New York: Appleton.

London, Kathryn A. 1991. "Advance Data Number 194: Cohabitation, Marriage, Marital Dissolution, and Remarriage: United States 1988." U.S. Department of Health and Human Services: Vital and Health Statistics of the National Center (January 4).

Longman, Philip J. 1998. "The Cost of Children." *U.S. News & World Report,* March 30, 51–58.

Lyons, Christopher A. 1973. "The Healing Ministry of the Holy Spirit." Sermon delivered at the Wheaton Bible Church, Wheaton, Ill., September 23.

Maas, Henry S., and Joseph A. Kuypers. 1974. *From Thirty to Seventy.* San Francisco: Jossey-Bass.

MacKay, Donald M. 1979. *Human Science and Human Dignity.* Downers Grove, Ill.: InterVarsity Press.

McClelland, David, et al. 1978. "Making It to Maturity." *Psychology Today* (June): 42–53, 114.

McKain, W. 1969. *Retirement Marriages.* Storrs, Calif.: Storrs Agricultural Experiment Station, Monograph 3.

McLeod, Jane D. 1995. "Social and Psychological Bases of Homogamy for Common Psychiatric Disorders." *Journal of Marriage and Family* 57:201–14.

McMahon, Kathryn. 1989. "The Cosmopolitan Ideology and the Management of Desire." *Journal of Sex Research* 27:381-96.

Martin, John R. 1974. *Divorce and Remarriage*. Scottdale, Pa.: Herald.

Martin, Teresa C., and Larry Bumpass. 1989. "Trends in Marital Disruption." *Demography* 26:37-52.

Masters, William H., and Virginia E. Johnson. 1966. *Human Sexual Response*. Boston: Little, Brown.

Masters, William H., Virginia E. Johnson, and Robert C. Kolodny. 1995. *Human Sexuality*, 5th ed. New York: HarperCollins.

Maxwell, John. 1996. *Breakthrough Parenting*. Colorado Springs: Focus on the Family.

Mayers, Marvin K. 1976. *Christianity Confronts Culture*. Grand Rapids: Zondervan.

Meier, Paul D. 1977. *Christian Child-Rearing and Personality Development*. Grand Rapids: Baker.

Menchar, J. P. 1965. "The Nayars of South Malakar." In *Comparative Family Systems*. Boston: Houghton Mifflin.

Michael, Robert, et al. 1994. *Sex in America: The Definitive Survey*. Boston: Little, Brown.

Miles, Herbert J. 1971. *Sexual Understanding Before Marriage*. Grand Rapids: Zondervan.

Miles, Herbert J., and Fern H. Miles. 1978. *Husband-Wife Equality*. Old Tappan, N.J.: Revell.

Minirth, Frank B., and Paul D. Meier. 1978. *Happiness Is a Choice*. Grand Rapids: Baker.

Montgomery, John Warwick. 1981. *Slaughter of the Innocents*. Westchester, Ill.: Crossway.

Morgan, Marabel. 1973. *The Total Woman*. Old Tappan, N.J.: Revell.

Murdock, George Peter. 1949. *Social Structure*. New York: Macmillan.

Murstein, Bernard. 1976. *Who Will Marry Whom?* New York: Springer.

Myra, Harold. 1979a. *Love Notes to Jeanette*. Wheaton, Ill.: Victor.

———. 1979b. "An Ode to Marriage." *Moody Monthly* (May): 60–62.

Narramore, Bruce. 1995. *Help! I'm a Parent*, 2d ed. Grand Rapids: Zondervan.

Neugarten, Bernice L., and Karol K. Weinstein. 1964. "The Changing American Grandparent." *Journal of Marriage and the Family* 26:199–204.

Newcomer, Susan, and Richard Udry. 1985. "Oral Sex in an Adolescent Population." *Archives of Sexual Behavior* 14:41–46.

Newsom, Howard. 1978. "How Little Christians Grow." *Eternity* (September): 39–40, 45.

Norton, Arthur J., and Jeanne E. Moorman. 1987. "Current Trends in Marriage and Divorce Among American Women." *Journal of Marriage and the Family* 49:3–14.

Nye, F. Ivan, and Felix M. Berardo. 1973. *The Family: Its Structure and Interaction.* New York: Macmillan.

O'Brien, Shirley. 1980. *Child Abuse.* Provo, Utah: Brigham Young University Press.

Orthner, Dennis K. 1981. *Intimate Relationships: An Introduction to Marriage and the Family.* Reading, Mass.: Addison-Wesley.

Otterbein, Keith F. 1977. *Comparative Cultural Analysis.* New York: Holt, Rinehart and Winston.

Parrott, Les, and Leslie Parrott. 1995. *Saving Your Marriage Before It Starts.* Grand Rapids: Zondervan.

Parsons, Talcott, and Robert F. Bales. 1955. *Family, Socialization and Interaction Process.* Glencore, Ill.: *Free Press.*

Penner, Clifford, and Joyce Penner. 1981. *The Gift of Sex.* Waco, Tex.: Word Books.

Petersen, J. R., et al. 1983. "Playboy Readers' Sex Survey." *Playboy* (March: 178–84).

Peterson, James. 1968. *Married Love in the Middle Years.* New York: Association.

Peterson, Robert. 1967. *Life Begins at Forty.* New York: Trident.

Pfouts, Jane H. 1980. "Birth Order, Age-Spacing, IQ Differences, and Family Relations." *Journal of Marriage and the Family* 42:517–31.

Piaget, Jean. 1952. *The Origins of Intelligence in Children.* New York: Norton.

Piehl, J. 1977. "Integration of Information in the Courts: Influence of Physical Attractiveness on Amount of Punishment for Traffic Offenders." *Psychological Reports* 41:551–56.

Plog, Fred, and Daniel G. Bates. 1976. *Cultural Anthropology.* New York: Knopf.

Powell, Brian, and Lala Carr Steelman. 1993. "The Educational Benefits of Being Spaced Out: Sibship, Density, and Educational Progress." *American Sociological Review* 58:367–81.

Pulaski, Mary Ann. 1980. *Understanding Piaget.* New York: Harper & Row.

Queen, S. A., and R. W. Haberstein. 1971. *The Family in Various Cultures,* 4th ed. Philadelphia: Lippincott.

Raschke, Helen. 1987. "Divorce." In *Handbook of Marriage and the Family,* ed. Marvin B. Sussman and Suzanne Steinmetz. New York: Plenum Books.

Reimer, Milton K. 1982. "The Study of Sociology: An Introduction." In *Christian Perspectives on Sociology,* ed. S. Grunlan and M. Reimer, 1–27. Grand Rapids: Zondervan.

Reiss, Ira L. 1980. *Family Systems in America,* 3d ed. New York: Holt, Rinehart and Winston.

———. 1986. *Journey into Sexuality: An Exploratory Voyage.* Englewood Cliffs, N.J.: Prentice Hall.

Rinehart, Stacy, and Paula Rinehart. 1996. *Choices,* 2d ed. Colorado Springs: NavPress.

Robertson, Joan F. 1977. "Grandmotherhood: A Study of Role Conceptions." *Journal of Marriage and the Family* 39:165–74.

Robinson, Ira E., and Davor Jedlicka. 1982, "Change in Sexual Attitudes and Behavior of College Students from 1965 to 1980: A Research Note." *Journal of Marriage and the Family* 44 (1): 237–40.

Robinson, I., K. Ziss, B. Ganza, and S. Katz. 1991. "Twenty Years of Sexual Revolution, 1965 to 1985—An Update." *Journal of Marriage and the Family* 53:216–20.

Ross, Catherine, John Mirowsky, and Karen Goldsteen. 1991. "The Impact of the Family on Health." In *Contemporary Families: Looking Forward, Looking Back*, ed. Alan Booth. Minneapolis: National Council on Family Relations.

Rouch, Mark. 1974. *Competent Ministry*. Nashville: Abingdon Press.

Sala, Harold. 1998. *Joyfully Single in a Couples World*. Camp Hill, Pa.: Horizon Books.

Samuels, Mike, and Nancy H. Samuels. 1996. *The New Well Pregnancy Book*. New York: Fireside.

Sanders, Bill. 1991. *Life, Sex and Everything in Between*. Grand Rapids: Revell.

Sanford, John A. 1982. *Between People*. Ramsey, N.J.: Paulist.

Saxton, Lloyd. 1972. *The Individual, Marriage, and the Family*, 2d ed. Belmont, Calif.: Wadsworth.

_____. 1980. *The Individual, Marriage, and the Family*, 4th ed. Belmont, Calif.: Wadsworth.

Scanzoni, John. 1979. *Love and Negotiate: Creative Conflict in Marriage*. Waco, Tex.: Word Books.

Scanzoni, Letha D., and John Scanzoni. 1981. *Men, Women, and Change*, 2d ed. New York: McGraw-Hill.

Scanzoni, Letha, and Nancy Hardesty. 1975. *All We're Meant to Be*. Waco, Tex.: Word Books.

Schultz, Duane. 1981. *Theories of Personality*. Monterey, Calif.: Brooks Cole.

Scott, Stanley. 1998. *The Heart of Commitment*. Nashville: Thomas Nelson.

Seamands, David A. 1977. "Is Masturbation Sinful?" In *For Families Only*, ed. J. Allan Petersen. Wheaton, Ill.: Tyndale.

Shapiro, Howard I. 1977. *The Birth Control Book*. New York: St. Martin's Press.

Shedd, Charlie W. 1965. *Letters to Karen*. Nashville: Abingdon Press.

_____. 1968. *Letters to Philip*. New York: Doubleday.

_____. 1976. *The Stork Is Dead*. Waco, Tex.: Word Books.

Sheehy, Gail. 1976. *Passages*. New York: Dutton.

Shepard, Jon M. 1981. *Sociology*. St. Paul: West.

Shostak, Arthur. 1987. "Singlehood." In *Handbook of Marriage and the Family*, ed. Marvin B. Sussman and Suzanne K. Steinmetz. New York: Plenum.

Singer, Dorothy G., and Tracey A. Revenson. 1978. *A Piaget Primer: How a Child Thinks*. New York: International Universities Press.

Somers, Marsha D. 1993. "A Comparison of Voluntary Childfree Adults and Parents." *Journal of Marriage and the Family* 55:643–50.

Sperry, Len. 1978. *The Together Experience.* San Diego: Beta.

Spiro, Melford. 1968. "Is the Family Universal?—The Israeli Case." In *A Modern Introduction to the Family,* rev. ed., ed. N. W. Bell and E. F. Vogel. New York: Free Press.

Sprecher, S., P. C. Regan, K. McKinney, K. Maxwell, and R. Wazienski. 1997. "Preferred Level of Sexual Experience in a Date or Mate: The Merger of Two Methodologies." *Journal of Sex Research* 34:327–37.

Staples, Robert. 1981. "Black Singles in America." In *Single Life,* ed. Peter Stein. New York: St. Martin's Press.

Steelman, L. C., and J. A. Mercy. 1980. "Unconfounding the Confluence Model: A Test of Sibship Size and Birth Order Effects on Intelligence." *American Sociological Review* 45:571–82.

Stephan, C., and J. C. Tully. 1977. "The Influence of Physical Attractiveness of a Plaintiff on the Decision of Simulated Jurors." *Journal of Social Research* 101:149–50.

Stephens, William N. 1963. *The Family in Cross-cultural Perspectives.* New York: Holt, Rinehart and Winston.

———. 1970. "Predictors of Marital Adjustment." In *A Marriage Reader,* ed. L. Saxton. Belmont, Calif.: Wadsworth.

Sternberg, Robert, and Michael Barnes. 1988. *The Psychology of Love.* New Haven: Yale University Press.

Stewart, C. W. 1970. *The Minister as Marriage Counselor.* Nashville: Abingdon Press.

Streib, G. 1972. "Older Families and Their Troubles: Familial and Social Responses." *Family Coordinator* 21:5–19.

Strong, August H. 1907. *Systematic Theology.* Valley Forge, Pa.: Judson.

Strong, Bryan, and Christine DeVault. 1997. *Human Sexuality: Diversity in Contemporary America,* 2d ed. Mountain View, Calif.: Mayfield.

Strong, Bryan, Christine DeVault, and Barbara W. Sayad. 1998. *The Marriage and Family Experience.* Belmont, Calif.: Wadsworth.

Strong, Bryan, Sam Wilson, Mina Roberts, and Thomas Johns. 1981. *Human Sexuality: Essentials,* 2d ed. St. Paul: West.

Szinovacz, Maximiliane, et al. 1992. *Families and Retirement.* Newbury Park, Calif.: Sage.

Tally, Jim, and Bobbi Reed. 1990. *Too Close, Too Soon,* 2d ed. Nashville: Thomas Nelson.

Taylor, Jack. 1974. *One Home Under God.* Nashville: Broadman.

Teachman, Jay D. 1983. "Early Marriage, Premarital Fertility, and Marital Dissolution." *Journal of Family Issues* 4:105–26.

Teti, Douglas M., and Michael Lamb. 1989. "Socioeconomic and Marital Outcomes of Adolescent Marriage, Adolescent Childbirth, and Their Cooccurrence." *Journal of Marriage and the Family* 51:203–12.

Thiessen, Henry C. 1951. *Introductory Lectures in Systematic Theology.* Grand Rapids: Eerdmans.

Thomas, Elizabeth, and Ugo Colella. 1992. "Cohabitation and Marital Stability: Quality or Commitment?" *Journal of Marriage and the Family* 54:259–67.

Tucker, Raymond K., M. G. Marvin, and B. Vivian. 1991. "What Constitutes a Romantic Act." *Psychological Reports* 89:651–54.

U.S. Bureau of the Census. 1990. *Statistical Abstract of the United States,* 110th ed. Washington, D.C.: U.S. Government Printing Office.

_____. 1991. "Asian and Pacific Islander Population Doubled." *Census and You* 26:3.

_____. 1992. *Statistical Abstract of the United States,* 112th ed. Washington, D.C.: U.S. Government Printing Office.

_____. 1995. *Statistical Abstract of the United States,* 115th ed. Washington, D.C.: U.S. Government Printing Office.

_____. 1996a. *Statistical Abstract of the United States,* 116th ed. Washington, D.C.: U.S. Government Printing Office.

_____. 1996b. *Current Population Reports.* World Wide Web: http://www.census.gov.

_____. 1997. *Statistical Abstract of the United States,* 117th ed. Washington, D.C.: U.S. Government Printing Office.

Vander Zanden, James W. 1979. *Sociology,* 4th ed. New York: Wiley.

_____. 1987. *Social Psychology,* 4th ed. New York: Random House.

_____. 1996. *Sociology: The Core,* 4th ed. New York: McGraw-Hill.

Wade, Carole, and Sarah Cirese. 1991. *Human Sexuality,* 2d ed. San Diego: Harcourt Brace Jovanovich.

Wadsworth, Barry J. 1971. *Piaget's Theory of Cognitive Development.* New York: Longman.

Wagonseller, Bill R., and Richard L. McDowell. 1979. *You and Your Child.* Champaign, Ill.: Research.

Walker, Clarence. 1996. *Breaking Strongholds in the African-American Family.* Grand Rapids: Zondervan.

Walker, Graham. 1982. "The Christian Case for Military Service." *Moody Monthly* (July/August): 6–8.

Wallerstein, Judith S., and Sandra Blakeslee. 1990. *Second Chances: Men, Women, and Children a Decade After Divorce.* New York: Ticknor & Fields.

Wallerstein, Judith S., and Joan B. Kelly. 1980. "California's Children of Divorce." *Psychology Today* (January): 67–76.

Waltke, Bruce K. 1969. "Old Testament Texts Bearing on the Problem of the Control of Human Reproduction." In *Birth Control and the Christian,* ed. Walter O. Spitzer and Carlyle L. Saylor, 7–23. Wheaton, Ill.: Tyndale.

Wheat, Ed, and Gaye Wheat. 1977. *Intended for Pleasure.* Old Tappan, N.J.: Revell.

White, John. 1977. *Eros Defiled.* Downers Grove, Ill.: InterVarsity Press.

White, Lynn. 1990. "Determinants of Divorce: A Review of Research in the Eighties." *Journal of Marriage and the Family* 52:904-12.

Winch, Robert F. 1958. *Mate Selection.* New York: Harper and Brothers.

_____. 1963. *The Modern Family.* New York: Holt, Rinehart and Winston.

Winch, Robert F., Thomas Ktsanses, and Virginia Ktsanses. 1954. "The Theory of Complementary Needs in Mate Selection: An Analytic and Descriptive Study." *American Sociological Review* 19:242.

Wolf, Michelle, and Alfred Kielwasser 1991. "Introduction: The Body Electric: Human Sexuality and the Mass Media." *Journal of Homosexuality* 21:7-18.

Woodson, Les. 1979. *Divorce and the Gospel of Grace.* Waco, Tex.: Word Books.

Wright, H. Norman. 1974. *Communication: Key to Your Marriage.* Glendale, Calif.: Regal.

_____. 1977a. *Premarital Counseling.* Chicago: Moody Press.

_____. 1977b. *Training Christians to Counsel.* Denver: Christian Marriage Enrichment.

Wright, H. Norman, and Marvin Inmon. 1978. *Dating, Waiting, and Choosing a Mate.* Irvine, Calif.: Harvest House.

Wright, Rusty, and Linda Wright. 1979. *Dynamic Sex.* San Bernardino, Calif.: Here's Life.

Wu, Lawrence. 1996. "Effects of Family Instability, Income, and Income Stability on the Risk of a Premarital Birth." *American Sociological Review* 61:386–406.

Yang, Martin. 1971. "The Chinese Family Pattern." In *Exploring the Ways of Mankind,* 2d ed., ed. W. Goldschmidt. New York: Holt, Rinehart and Winston.

Yorburg, Betty. 1993. *Family Relationships.* New York: St. Martin's Press.

Zajonc, Robert B. 1975. "Dumber By the Dozen." *Psychology Today* (January).

Zajonc, R. B., and G. B. Markus. 1975. "Birth Order and Intellectual Development." *Psychological Review* 82:74–88.

Zelditch, Morris. 1964. "Cross-Cultural Analyses of Family Structure." In *Handbook of Marriage and the Family,* ed. H. T. Christensen. Chicago: Rand McNally.

Author Index

Subject Index